Everyday Hinduism

Everyday Hinduism

Joyce Burkhalter Flueckiger

WILEY Blackwell

This edition first published 2015
© 2015 Joyce Burkhalter Flueckiger

Registered Office
John Wiley & Sons, Ltd, The Atrium, Southern Gate, Chichester,
West Sussex, PO19 8SQ, UK

Editorial Offices
350 Main Street, Malden, MA 02148-5020, USA
9600 Garsington Road, Oxford, OX4 2DQ, UK
The Atrium, Southern Gate, Chichester, West Sussex, PO19 8SQ, UK

For details of our global editorial offices, for customer services, and for information
about how to apply for permission to reuse the copyright material in this book please
see our website at www.wiley.com/wiley-blackwell.

The right of Joyce Burkhalter Flueckiger to be identified as the author of this work has
been asserted in accordance with the UK Copyright, Designs and Patents Act 1988.

Library of Congress Cataloging-in-Publication Data is available for this title

Hardback ISBN: 9781405160117
Paperback ISBN: 9781405160216

A catalogue record for this book is available from the British Library.

Cover image: Jamini Roy (1887–1972), Three Pujarins, tempera on board, 36.5 × 70.5cm.
National Gallery of Modern Art, New Delhi

Set in 10.5/13.5pt Palatino by SPi Publisher Services, Pondicherry, India
Printed and bound in Malaysia by Vivar Printing Sdn Bhd

1   2015

Contents

Contents

Acknowledgements

My first thanks go to the many families and individuals I have worked with and learned from over my many years of ethnographic research in Chhattisgarh, Hyderabad, Tirupati, and Atlanta – many of whom have become close friends and family. This book would not have been possible without them.

The approach and topics of this book developed, in part, through teaching a course at Emory University titled "Introduction to Religion: Hinduism and Judaism," which I have co-taught many times with Michael Berger. I have learned from Michael new perspectives on Jewish traditions, many creative teaching methods, and ways to engage in comparison. This class has been one motivator in writing this book, and Michael's encouragement and collegiality have been invaluable.

In the first iterations of the class, some Hindu students objected to inclusion of some topics (such as caste or possession) that they had not heard about growing up, about which they had been taught differently, or that their families did not practice. I learned from them clearer ways to frame these topics and, more specifically, to make a distinction between Hindu practices in India and those their families may practice in the United States. I have also learned about a wide range of Hindu practices in the diaspora from these students and their families.

I also thank the Emory University graduate students on whose dissertation committees I have served and from whom I continue to learn (and some of whose ethnographic observations have entered this book). My gratitude extends to my colleagues Amy Allocco, Jenn Ortegren, Harshita Mruthinti Kamath, Kate Zubko, Paul Courtright, and Tara Doyle, who all read select chapters of this book and gave invaluable feedback. V. Narayana Rao read the entire manuscript, and we spent many hours talking about both the topics and the examples that found their way into the book, and many that did not.

Finally, I thank the engaged editors with whom I have worked at Wiley Blackwell – Rebecca Harkin and Georgina Coleby. Rebecca first approached me about writing this book for a Wiley series on "Everyday Religion," and encouraged me to persevere in the project when other demands threatened to derail it. Georgina's periodic encouraging emails also helped to keep the book on track, and she was diligent in following through with many publication details. Giles Flitney was a conscientious copy-editor. It was a joy to work with such enthusiastic and responsive editors.

A Note on Transliteration

To read roman transliterations of Indian-language words can be frustrating to those who don't know these languages, particularly given the varieties of transliteration systems that a reader may come across in different publications. I encourage readers to experience these variations as part of the "polytheistic imagination" of Indian traditions (see Introduction).

Many terms in this book are shared across Indian languages with slightly different pronunciations, and thus transliterations. For example, the name of the god Rama is pronounced with the final –a in Sanskrit and Telugu, but in Hindi it is pronounced without the final –a, thus Ram. Or the term for vow in Sanskrit is pronounced *vrata*, but in Hindi, *vrat*. Other terms have greater variations; for example, the festival of lights may be called Divali or Dipavali (lit., row of lights). I will use the Sanskrit transliteration for proper names (Rama, Ganesha) but will leave off the final 'a' for other nouns (such as *prasad* instead of *prasada*, *darshan* instead of *darshana*, *vrat* instead of *vrata*), since these are the pronunciations closer to the regional spoken languages in which I have worked.

Standard academic transliteration of Indian-language terms often uses diacritics, which I have chosen not to do – on the assumption that those who do not know Indian languages will not know the conventions of the diacritics and that those who do know Indian languages will not need diacritics to correctly pronounce the word. Rather, I render transliterations as close as possible to what will result in correct English pronunciation. Thus, I render both *ś* and *ṣ* as 'sh'; *shakti* (spiritual power) rather than *śakti*. Further, I have indicated aspirated consonants with an 'h': *chaturthi* (the fourth day) – such as Ganesha Chaturthi – rather than rendering the word according to standard academic transliteration of *caturthi*.

In direct quotations from authors who have used diacritics, the diacritics will not be indicated; so in these cases the reader will notice, for example, spellings of Shiva as Siva, or Vishnu as Visnu. I have indicated Indian-language terms (except for proper nouns) with italics and, for clarity, have chosen to italicize the 's' that indicates plural in English, although this 's' is not the way in which Indian languages indicate plural.

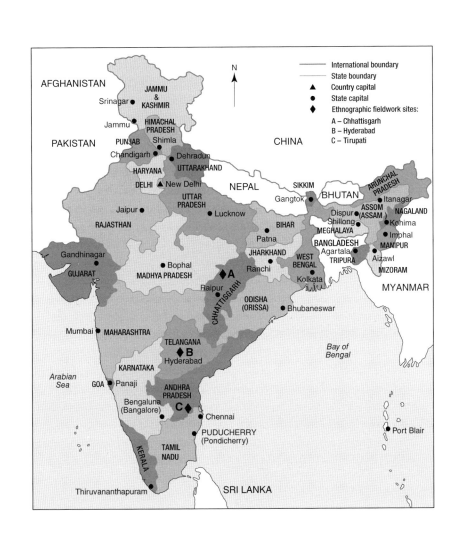

Introduction

Many introductory textbooks on Hinduism begin with the historical roots of Hindu traditions, starting with the sacred texts of the Vedas, then proceed through a primarily textual history of Hindu traditions, through the Upanishads, the Ramayana and Mahabharata epics, and *bhakti* (devotional) poetry of the medieval and premodern periods.[1] However, most Hindus do not experience or talk about their religious traditions along the trajectories of these kinds of textual histories. They may invoke the authority of what they consider to be "ancient texts" or "the old ways" and "custom," but they also – and primarily – experience these as contemporary practices.

The ethnographic focus of this book is these everyday ritual and narrative practices of specific people in specific places. Such a

[1] A notable exception is C. J. Fuller's *The Camphor Flame: Popular Hinduism and Society in India* (1992). For a critique of a textual, *brahminic*, "master narrative" approach, see Kumar 2010, in which he also critiques the lack of representation in these textbooks of regional and caste differences.

Everyday Hinduism, First Edition. Joyce Burkhalter Flueckiger.
© 2015 Joyce Burkhalter Flueckiger. Published 2015 by John Wiley & Sons, Ltd.

perspective reveals the fluidity, flexibility, and creativity of Hindu practices as well as some broad structures and parameters that may cross and be shared across space and time. For most Hindus, what they do – what rituals they practice, the festivals they celebrate, who they marry, what they eat – matters more on a day-to-day basis than the philosophical concepts of *karma*, *samsara*, and *moksha*. So while these concepts will come up in the practices described in this book, they will not be its focus. The ethnographic approach to Hindu practices in this book is not intended to be a comprehensive study of Hinduism; rather, it presents one starting point and framework for the study of Hindu traditions and is complementary to textual and historical approaches.

The Terms "Hindu," "Hinduism," and "Hindu Traditions"

The term "Hindu" (derived from the Persian word *sindhu*) was first used by "outsiders" (i.e., Persians and others) as a designation for those people who lived east of the Indus River. "Hindu" and "Hinduism" became terms used for a *religious* identity and "system" (an "ism") by British colonists in the 19th century to distinguish in their census materials those Indians who were not Christian or Muslim. Nevertheless, even if the terms were initially developed by "outsiders," they have become indigenous terms – used by Hindus in both India and the diaspora – that have come to identify traditions that share certain elements of a worldview, narrative repertoire, and ritual grammar. However, although contemporary Hindus may self-identify as Hindus on various government forms, school registrations,[2] and so on, when speaking among themselves, the term

---

[2] Telugu scholar V. Narayana Rao tells the story of when he first encountered and used the word "Hindu" to self-identify. Starting middle school in 1942, he was asked to fill out an admission form. There was a question about religious identity that gave him three choices: Muslim, Christian, and Hindu. He recounts that when he wondered what his identity would be, the teacher told him he was "Hindu," and so he put a check in that box (oral communication).

"Hindu" is much less commonly used than regional, sectarian, or caste identifications.

The parameters of Hindu traditions (a term I prefer over "Hinduism" in order to reflect the plurality of traditions) and the identifying features that "make someone a Hindu," are difficult to identify given the hundreds of sacred oral and written texts, the wide diversity of ritual practices, and the absence of a singular religious authority or class of authorities. Simply being born into a Hindu family is one means of identification, without requiring or implying any level of ritual practice or theology. On the other hand, we have an example of a Hindu man who asked an Orthodox Jewish anthropologist whether he was Hindu, further asking if he cracked coconuts when he worshipped god. When the anthropologist answered that he did not, the man determined the anthropologist was not a Hindu; for this man, ritual practice determined Hindu identity (Hiltebeitel 1991, 28).

Dharma: A Way of Life and Religious Tradition

The Indian language term most frequently used to translate "religion," *dharma*, implies correct action, practice, and ethics rather than a requisite set of beliefs (although it does not preclude beliefs). The term comes from the Sanskrit root *dhr*, which means to hold together, to support, or to order. *Dharma* can be interpreted, then, as that which holds the world together: ethics, ways of living, a "moral coherence" (Marriot 2004, 358); I use the term analytically to identify narratives and practices that help to structure or shape everyday Hindu lives.

I often ask my students in Hinduism classes how many have heard the now-common mantra, "Hinduism is not a religion, it's a way of life." Many Indian-American and non-Indian American students alike raise their hands. Then I ask, "How many of you have heard this saying in an Indian language?" No hands are raised. Most Hindus who speak this mantra have exposure to other religious traditions, such as Protestant Christianity, that tend to focus on

3

belief and textual and institutional authorities, rather than everyday practices, as being inherent to the religion. They have internalized this emphasis in their own definition of "religion" in English and know that Hinduism does not fit very well, and therefore exclude their own traditions from "religion."

The emphasis on texts and belief reflects a post-Enlightenment definition of what "counts" as religion. Religious studies scholar Vasudha Narayanan relates an interaction she had with one of her doctoral colleagues at Harvard University shortly after she had arrived in the United States in the 1970s; the student had given her several books to read on Hinduism and wanted to know what she thought of them. Her response, she writes, was,

> Food … my grandmother always made the right kind of lentils for our festivals. The auspicious kind. We make certain vegetables and lentils for happy and celebratory holy days and others for the inauspicious ceremonies like ancestral rites and death rituals. And none of the books mentioned auspicious and inauspicious times (Narayanan 2000, 761).

Given the centrality of everyday practices in Hindu traditions, over both time and space – including the foods one cooks at particular ritual occasions – I would prefer to expand the boundaries of what counts as "religion" to include "ways of life" rather than to exclude Hinduism. This inclusion may cause us to see practices in other religious traditions, such as cooking, in a new light – as *religious* practices. Some ritual traditions that are practiced by Hindus are also shared with Indian Muslim, Buddhist, and Christian communities (including rituals that divert the evil eye, some healing practices, and menstrual segregation); however, when a Hindu engages these practices, she/he frames them as something "we" (Hindus) do, or as *dharma* (appropriate conduct) as received from one's family, and so I include some of these shared practices in this book.

So how does a Hindu learn his/her *dharma*, given that there is no singular book, creed, or religious authority in Hindu traditions (compared, for example, to the Tanakh, Bible, and Quran for Jews, Christians, and Muslims – although these traditions, too, rely in many contexts on non-textual means of knowing or learning their traditions). While there is a class of *brahminic* Sanskrit texts called the Dharmashastras (ca. 500 BCE–400 CE), which provide intricate context-specific codes of social and ritual conduct, most Hindus do not learn their appropriate *dharma* from reading or hearing these texts, and many may not even know about or ever make reference to them. The primary way a Hindu learns his/her *dharma* is through observing and participating in family traditions and customs (Hindi *niyam*; Sanskrit *paddhati*), traditions passed from guru to disciples (who themselves become gurus or teachers), listening to performances of Hindu narratives, and simply by living in a Hindu-majority culture in which Hindu gods, temples, narratives, and rituals are "all around," and a child imbibes them almost through osmosis.

Leela Prasad, in her ethnography *Poetics of Conduct* (2007), analyzes the ways in which ethical (*dharmic*) practices are learned and known in the small South Indian town of Sringeri, which is the site of an important *matha* (monastery and site of *brahminic* learning and exposition, including of the Dharmashastras). Prasad is particularly interested in the ways in which the term *shastra* (authoritative tradition of ethical action, or *dharma*; teaching) is invoked in everyday conversations and narratives. Through analyses of conversational narration, she finds that there is wide scope for interpretation of *shastra* and its authority, going much beyond reference to the textual tradition of the Dharmashastras. She argues that "… narration itself is an ethical act …," and that stories are an important means through which Hindus learn *dharma*, that is, how to live in the world (Prasad 2007, 6). Prasad concludes that "'shastra' in lived Hinduism is truly elastic in its creative engagement of tradition, text, practice, and moral authority … as a moral concept, shastra coexists with other concepts of the normative" (12–13).[3] This book includes many of these coexisting ways in which Hindus learn and know *dharmic* ways of living.

---

[3] Many scholars have observed that the British colonists attempted to consolidate and singularize "Hindu law," by identifying the Dharmashastras as an Indian legal code, that resulted "in a decontextualized universal application of the Dharmashastras" in ways that they were not indigenously conceived (Prasad 2007, 227).

Context and Multiplicity

Although there is an Indian language term for universal *dharma* – *sanatana dharma* (lit., eternal, universal order) – there is not consensus as to what this universal might be. Put another way, it is not clear what the minimal practices or theologies might be that identify a person as a Hindu. In daily life, there is no assumption that there is a single *dharma* appropriate for all to follow. Rather, an individual's *dharma* is determined by region, caste, age, gender, class, and other specific contexts.

Varnashrama Dharma: One way through which to begin to understand context-specificity of *dharma* and Hindu practices is the *brahminic* textual model of *varnashrama dharma*, which articulates appropriate *dharma* according to one's *varna* (caste level) and *ashrama* (stage of life). This model identifies four *varnas*: Brahmin (teachers and priests), Kshatriya (warriors), Vaishya (producers), and Shudra (servants). In the model of *varnashrama dharma*, these caste levels intersect with the four stages of life for an upper-caste male: *brahmacharya* (student stage), *grihastha* (householder stage), *vanaprastha* (forest stage, withdrawing or retiring from householder responsibilities), and *sannyasa* (stage of renunciation of the world). We can imagine a grid, with the *varnas* on four horizontal rows and the *ashramas* on four intersecting vertical columns, creating context-specific squares that dictate the appropriate *dharma* for a person of a particular caste level at a particular stage of life. It is important to note that this conceptualization is based on a *brahminic* ideal for *upper-caste*, *male* participants; and Hindu traditions as lived were and are always more fluid than the model would indicate. That is, this model is prescriptive, not always descriptive. Nevertheless, *varnashrama dharma* serves as one analytic model through which to begin to think about the context-specificity of *dharma*. A woman's stages of life and associated *stri dharma* (women's *dharma*) are, roughly, pre-marriage/girlhood, marriage, and widowhood; and the *dharma* for each of these (gendered) life stages also vary considerably across caste levels.

The context-specific parameters of *varnashrama dharma* remain broadly relevant to contemporary Hindus as they negotiate transitions from one stage of life to another. For example, it is still common practice for a young adult to finish his/her education before getting married; and when there is pressure to get married, a student may protest that she/he is still in college, medical school, and so on, and that marriage should wait until his/her education is complete. Or, regarding the *vanaprastha* stage, many middle-class Hindus wait until after their children's education is completed and their marriages performed, and their own home mortgages are paid off, before taking extended periods of time to engage in volunteer work (such as ophthalmologists holding eye camps in needy communities), spending resources building temples, or going on lengthy pilgrimage circuits.

Context-specificity: A. K. Ramanujan has identified this principal of context-specificity as an "Indian way of thinking" (1989). He associates this context-specificity to the social organization of *jati* (lit., species or class; caste determined by birth):

> Such a pervasive emphasis on context is, I think, related to the Hindu concern with *jati* – the logic of classes, of genra and species, of which human *jatis* [classes] are only an instance. Various taxonomies of season, landscape, times, *gunas* or qualities (and their material bases), tastes, characters, emotions, essences (*rasa*), etc., are basic to the thought-work of Hindu medicine and poetry, cooking and religion, erotics and magic. Each *jati* or class defines a context, a structure of relevance, a rule of permissible combination, a frame of reference, a meta-communication of what is and can be done (1989, 53).

This framework of context-specificity expands beyond its relevance to *dharma*. Certain musical *ragas* have been composed to be performed at certain times of day, with the assumption that the context of time will affect the experience of the *ragas*; astrological contexts may affect the efficacy of rituals; and answers to almost any question may shift depending on the context in which it is asked. For example, if a Hindu student were to ask his/her parents what happens to a soul when a person dies, the answer she/he would receive would likely depend on the context in which it was asked. If a grandparent had just died, and the family was performing death rituals, the answer may be that the purpose of the rituals is to send the soul on to the world of the ancestors. If the question was being asked more generically, when no specific death had just occurred, the parents may give an answer to serve as a moral compass to their child, explaining the concept of *karma* (action and its consequences) and *samsara* (the cycle of birth and rebirth based on one's past actions). Or the child may have heard a story about or seen a lithograph picturing various heavens and hells that a soul may experience after death, depending on its actions in life.[4] None of these answers is "right" or "wrong"; rather, they coexist.

Polytheistic imagination: The Hindu acceptance of diverse, context-specific traditions, narratives, and rituals reflects what Diana Eck has called a "polytheistic imagination," one that includes but is not limited to the coexistence of multiple deities (1998, 22). That is, most broadly conceived, "truths" are multiple. While multiple truths may be theoretically or conceptually accepted, and a Hindu may not judge another person for the ways in which she/he practices particular Hindu traditions, however, this does not mean that every "truth" is accepted for any given family or individual; his/her "truth" is determined by the various, often changing contexts of his/her life, including region, caste, and family.

A revealing example of this polytheistic imagination, which illustrates the acceptance of different versions of the "same" narratives, can be seen in an interaction between two university students and a Brahmin priest at the celebration of the goddess

---

[4] These lithographs – which I have never seen in a home, but rather in sidewalk stalls selling lithographs – picture various sins and associated hells. For example, the man who has mistreated his oxen in life is pictured in a hell in which he becomes the mistreated oxen, or a thief is pictured with his hands cut off in the appropriate hell. In the system of heavens and hells, an individual's good or bad *karma* is "burned off" and then the soul re-enters *samsara*; however, the idea is more pedagogical than applied to individuals.

festival of Durga Puja in suburban Atlanta several years ago. The Bengali priest was an engineer for Atlanta's MARTA (Metropolitan Atlanta Rapid Transit Authority) public transportation system. However, he knew Sanskrit and he had agreed to serve as the priest at the Bengali Association of Greater Atlanta's Durga Puja celebration. As he and the students were cutting up fruit to be offered to the goddess, one of the students asked the priest a question: "Pandit-ji, I am Bengali and my roommate is Gujarati. My mother told me that Ganesha got his elephant head when Shiva cut it off and replaced it with the head of the first animal that his attendants found in the jungle. My roommate's mother gave her another explanation [since I didn't tape the conversation, I do not have the specifics of this explanation]. Which story is true?" The engineer-priest seemed baffled and there was an awkward silence before I suggested that this may not be a traditionally "Hindu" question. He responded enthusiastically, "Yes, they are both true!" The Indian-American students, however, seemed less than satisfied, as they had been raised in an American environment in which "truth" is more frequently imagined as singular, not multiple.

Ethnographic Selection and Chapter Topics

In writing an introduction to Hindu traditions, questions arise: "Which Hindus? Whose practices? What is the basis of selection?" An ethnographic perspective is necessarily selective and precludes an inclusive survey of traditions differentiated by region, caste, class, gender, and historical and social contexts. However, I have made an effort to use sufficient qualifiers so as to indicate that there may be many exceptions to what I describe. It may well be that a non-Hindu reader of this book may hear something quite different if she/he asks his/her Hindu friend, grocer, or neighbor about any of the practices described in this book. And some Hindu readers may read here about narrative variants or rituals that are not known in their own families and immediate communities. And this is why it is important to constantly remember the interpretive frameworks of context-specificity and polytheistic imagination presented above. I've chosen themes and topics for each chapter that most Hindus would recognize, if not the specifics of the ethnographic descriptions. And the specific case studies described will raise broader theoretical questions and issues relevant to other practitioners and contexts of rituals and narratives of everyday Hinduism.

Each chapter is framed with introductory and contextual material for the topic at hand, before an elaboration of that topic through my own fieldwork data, drawn from over 30 years of ethnographic research in Central India (Chhattisgarh), the Deccan Plateau (Hyderabad), South India (Tirupati), and the United States (Atlanta) (see map). I have also supplemented my own fieldwork with other published ethnographies about the Hindu practices I describe. Instead of writing a separate chapter on diasporic practices, I have integrated these into each chapter. It's important to note that the ritual practices of diasporic communities living, for example, in Singapore, Trinidad, London, New York, and Atlanta may vary widely, depending on when immigrants migrated, their caste and class, and the host cultures. The inclusion of Hindu practices in Atlanta is not meant to generalize for all diasporic communities but to suggest some of the ways in which particular ritual practices can and do adapt to new contexts.

Chapter 1 begins with a description of different kinds of "families of deities" with whom Hindus interact and whom readers will encounter in subsequent chapters. This is not to imply that all Hindus live in a theistic world, but the wide-ranging pantheon is an example of the polytheistic imagination characteristic of Hindu traditions, and the mythologies of the deities help to draw the reader into the rich imaginative worlds in which many Hindus live. Chapter 2 answers the question of how Hindus know the stories of gods and goddesses, in particular, with a description of modes of narrative transmission, both verbal and visual. Chapters 3 through 8 focus on different modes of Hindu ritual practice: devotional practices of *puja*, worship at temples and shrines, pilgrimage, celebration of festivals, vow-rituals (*vrats*), life-cycle rituals (*samskaras*), and finally, Hindu ritual practices that prevent, respond to, and interpret suffering (healing, possession, and astrology). The Afterword identifies some ways in which Hindu everyday practices and "ways of being in the world" are changing under contemporary shifting contexts.

References

Eck, Diana L. 1998. *Darsan: Seeing the Divine Image in India*. New York: Columbia University Press.

Fuller, C. J. 1992. *The Camphor Flame: Popular Hinduism and Society in India*. Princeton: Princeton University Press.

Hiltebeitel, Alf. 1991. Of Camphor and Coconuts. *The Wilson Quarterly* 15, 3: 26–28.

Kumar, P. Pratap. 2010. Introducing Hinduism: the Master Narrative – A Critical Review of Textbooks on Hinduism. *Religious Studies Review* 36, 2: 115–124.

Marriot, McKim. 2004. Varna and Jati. In *The Hindu World*, eds. Sushil Mittal and Gene Thursby, 357–382. New York: Routledge.

Narayanan, Vasudha. 2000. Diglossic Hinduism: Lentils and Liberation. *Journal of the American Academy of Religion* 68, 4: 761–779.

Prasad, Leela. 2007. *Poetics of Conduct: Oral Narrative and Moral Being in a South Indian Town*. New York: Columbia University Press.

Ramanujan, A. K. 1989. Is There an Indian Way of Thinking? An Informal Essay. In *India Through Hindu Categories*, ed. McKim Marriot, 34–51. New Delhi: Sage.

Recommended Readings

Davis, Richard H. 2002. Introduction: A Brief History of Religions in India. In *Religions of India in Practice*, ed. Donald Lopez. Princeton: Princeton University Press.

Flood, Gavin. *An Introduction to Hinduism*. 1996. Melbourne, Australia: Cambridge University Press.

Introduction

Jacobsen, Knut A. (editor-in-chief), and (associate editors) Helene Basu, Angelika Malinar, Vasudha Narayanan. 2012. *Brill's Encyclopedia of Hinduism.*

Keyes, Charles, and E. V. Daniel. 1983. *Karma: An Anthropological Inquiry.* Berkeley: University of California Press.

Mittal, Sushil, and Gene Thursby, eds. 2004. *The Hindu World.* New York: Routledge.

A Note on Caste

The caste system is one of the features of Indian religious and social traditions that many non-Indians associate with rigid social or religious hierarchy and discrimination, and about which they often have questions. Because caste implies much more than social hierarchy, I will take some time here to address some of its complexities. Anthropologist Diane Mines characterizes caste as: "one human mode of social differentiation: a mode of power, mode of action, mode of caring; sense of self in relations to others" (2009, 3). Caste is sometimes interpreted as reflecting and/or creating a division of labor; however, there are many more castes than there are occupations, and this association, always very fluid, is being lost in contemporary India.

There are two Indian-language words that have been translated as "caste" in English. The first is *varna*, which, along with its meaning of "color," indicates classification. The term appears in Rig Veda 10.90 to describe the classes of humans created from the sacrifice of

---

Everyday Hinduism, First Edition. Joyce Burkhalter Flueckiger.

the primordial man. From his head the Brahmins[1] were created; from his arms and torso, the Kshatriyas; from his thighs, the Vaishyas; and from his feet, the Shudras. The four categories are distinguished by the various human qualities (*gunas*) associated with each *varna*. While the concept of *varna* is known throughout India, it functions as an ideological model rather than one on the ground in everyday life.

The second and more commonly employed (in everyday conversation) Indian-language term translated as "caste" is *jati*, literally, species or birth; and this is the word I will be referring to throughout the book when I use the English "caste."[2] (Some Indians use the word *samaj* [lit., society] or *kulam* [lineage; also caste] when referring to this category of caste.) There are hundreds of regionally based, traditionally endogamous, distinct *jatis*. Traditionally, *jati* was not a hidden identity; it was visually displayed in body language, linguistic registers, women's hairstyles, styles and materials of ornaments, sari weaves, colors, and patterns, and unique festivals and rituals. Some, but not all, of these visual and aural indicators are slowly being lost, particularly in urban, middle-class contexts. Many Hindu surnames indicate *jati* identification and what region of India a Hindu or his or her ancestors are from. For example, most Indians would know that the surname Patel is a caste name from Gujarat, western India; Reddys are from Andhra Pradesh; Bhattacharyas are from Bengal.[3]

Over many years of ethnographic fieldwork in India, when people, speaking in Hindi, have tried to place me and figure out who I am – what my presence means in contexts in which they have rarely, if ever, seen a non-Indian – I have not been asked "what do

---

[1] The standard transliteration for Brahmin, according to the system I am using, would be Brahman. However, I have chosen the alternative spelling to avoid confusion with the term *brahman* (ultimate reality).

[2] *Jati* is the word, for example, used in Hindi translations of the Hebrew Bible for the species that went up two-by-two (*jati* by *jati*) into Noah's ark.

[3] In resistance to caste identification and inequalities, some Hindus, particularly post-independence, have dropped their caste-associated surnames and adopted names that cross caste levels.

you believe" or my "religion" (*dharma*); rather, I have most been frequently asked "what is your caste/*jati*?" (lit., "what were you born?") The question implies "where are you from, who is your family, how were you raised, what rituals do you practice" – ultimately, "who are you and why are you here?" This *jati* identity is assumed to permeate one's everyday action, from hygiene to food, from dress to ritual and festivals. In a discussion about caste with some university professors in Hyderabad a few years ago, several of them insisted that caste was no longer relevant on a day-to-day basis in their lives. However, when the discussion shifted to an upcoming dinner celebration, a comment was made about the delicious shrimp dish Mudaliars (a South Indian *jati*) made. Here, *jati* was an ethnic designation rather than one of hierarchical difference.

In many contexts of contemporary India and Indian diasporas – particularly the workplace and social contexts outside of the home – it has become politically incorrect to ask about or speak of a person's caste because of the traditionally hierarchical nature of networks of *jatis*. I was chastised by a New Delhi taxi driver several years ago, for example, when (after chatting for several minutes) I asked his *jati*; like my Indian friends above who were trying to place me, I was trying to place him in a regional, social context and wasn't thinking explicitly about hierarchy. He sternly told me, "We don't talk about caste here," implying "here in the city." Speaking Hindi, I apologized and explained that I was just coming from having lived in a village for several weeks where caste was openly visible and performed. He was amused and proceeded to tell me his personal life story of immigration to Delhi from the mountains of Himachal Pradesh – and his caste.

Although middle-class, modern-educated Hindus may not openly talk about caste and may not know the caste of some of their close friends and colleagues, if one knows how to "see" or "hear" expressions of *jati*, they can be observed in many contexts in contemporary India. Although some earlier expressions of caste are loosening (such as rules of commensality between *jatis* and unique clothing and jewelry styles among middle-class Indians), new ones are also emerging – such as caste-based regional political parties in India, formed to "promote social and political interests of respective castes as defined in the census" (Mines 2009, 42). Most alliances created through arranged marriages continue to be based on caste. Although many matrimonial advertisements state "caste no bar" and inter-caste, inter-religious marriages are increasing in number, most Hindu parents would still prefer that their children marry within their *jati*. The advantage of this is that their children would be marrying partners whose families speak the same regional language, cook the same cuisine, perform the same kinds of rituals, and celebrate the same festivals – all of which make them one of "us."

Historically, there has been discrimination based on caste, such that, for example, members of the "lowest" castes – which are outside the *brahminic varna* system altogether – were denied entry into some *brahminic* temples and other public spaces, and members of certain castes were (and some still are) forced by dominant castes to perform menial "untouchable" tasks. While the 1950 Constitution of India prohibits discrimination based on caste, more specifically practices of "untouchability," caste discrimination and caste violence continue to exist in many contexts. In an effort to mitigate the derogatory identification of castes as "untouchable," Gandhi introduced the term Harijans (lit., people or children of god) to make reference to those had been called "untouchables" by members of upper-castes. However, the term itself came to be considered condescending by many who were identified as Harijans. More recently, many members of these castes are self-identifying as Dalits (lit., broken or ground down; oppressed), while others continue to identify with their specific caste names (such as Dhobi, Chamar, Mala, Madiga, and so on).

To mitigate the effects of historical caste discrimination in representation in political and educational institutions and government employment, the Constitution of India – whose primary architect was a member of the then "untouchable" Mahar caste, Dr B. R. Ambedkar – instituted a system of reservations of seats in these institutions for members of specifically identified "low" castes and tribes (called in the Constitution, "scheduled" castes and tribes). This system of reservations has been periodically updated to reflect shifting demographics, and it continues to feed into complicated caste politics in contemporary India. This is one context in which caste is openly discussed, and the impact of reservations is felt both positively and negatively, depending on one's caste identity and status.

While all of the above-mentioned dimensions of caste are relevant to varying degrees in different contexts in contemporary India, for the purposes of the everyday Hindu ritual practices described in the chapters of this book, caste is most relevant in the ways in which its regional (and even more local) manifestations create a wide range of diversity, which I have made an effort to represent in the context-specificity of ethnographic descriptions.

Reference

Mines, Diane P. 2009. *Caste in India*. Ann Arbor, MI: Association for Asian Studies, Inc.

Recommended Readings

Bayly, Susan. 2005. *Caste, Society and Politics in India from the Eighteenth Century to the Modern Age*. New York: Cambridge University Press.

Omvedt, Gail. 1995. *Dalit Visions: The Anti-Caste Movement and the Construction of an Indian Identity*. New Delhi: Orient Longman.

Srinivas, M. N. 1995. *Social Change in Modern India*. New Delhi: Orient Longman.

Valmiki, Omprakash. 2008. *Joothan: An Untouchable's Life*. (trans.) Arun Prabha Mukherjee. New York: Columbia University Press.

Zelliot, Eleanor. 1992. *From Untouchable to Dalit: Essays on the Ambedkar Movement*. New Delhi: Manohar Publications.

1
Families of Deities

To enter the Hindu pantheon of gods, goddesses, and other powerful beings for the first time is much like an Indian bride marrying into a large extended family and being introduced to the relatives. Gradually, the bride learns which relatives she will encounter every day and whom she will see only once or twice a year at festivals or weddings, who her immediate neighbors are, and who will be her allies in her new home. While family networks are large and sometimes complicated, there is a core of relatives and neighbors whom the new bride gets to know rather quickly, followed by concentric circles of relatives who are significant, but not part of her daily life. Similarly, there is a family of deities with whom a Hindu interacts regularly in domestic worship, deities she/he may seek out in local temple visits, deities she/he may encounter only periodically (or maybe even a single time) – on pilgrimage, during festivals, and/or as a result of illness or a vow taken for a specific cause – and still others she/he may know narratively, but whom she/he does not

Everyday Hinduism, First Edition. Joyce Burkhalter Flueckiger.
© 2015 Joyce Burkhalter Flueckiger. Published 2015 by John Wiley & Sons, Ltd.

encounter ritually. This chapter will introduce some of these deities and some of the ways in which they relate one to the other to create "families"; and in the process, the chapter will display the polytheistic imagination and rich narrative worlds that characterize Hindu traditions.

The "families of deities" with whom Hindus interact may be created through literal or figurative kinship or they may be created ritually or narratively. Certain families of deities are identified with particular regions and/or are related through pilgrimage routes; other families are created through domestic or temple worship. To introduce the pantheon of deities that populates Hindu worlds, we start with conceptual and narrative families and then move to families of deities created through ritual practices. The deities described below may be found in the domestic shrines described at the end of this chapter and in temples, rituals, and festivals described in following chapters; many may also be encountered by readers of this book in museums and Hindu homes. However, given the expansive pantheon of deities in Hindu traditions, the families of deities described below are necessarily selective.

Most of the stories of gods and goddesses related in this chapter can be found in the *puranas*, a class of texts from which is derived most Hindu mythology known by contemporary Hindus. There are 18 "major" Sanskrit *puranas*, 18 "sub-major" ones, and a multitude of oral regional-language traditions also called *puranas*, including caste *puranas* that tell the story of how a particular caste came into existence and why that caste plays the occupational and/or ritual role that it does. The *puranas* tell the stories of gods and goddesses, demons, and human devotees, and the creation and dissolution of the world. For example, the acts of Krishna are narrated in the Bhagavata Purana; the creation of and acts of the goddess (Devi) in the Devi Mahatmya section of the Markandeya Purana; and many stories of Shiva in the Shiva Purana. *Sthala puranas* (lit., *puranas* about place) include narratives about the power of particular sacred places, the rituals that should be performed at those places, and the benefits the worshipper will derive from these rituals. I have not provided textual references for most of the narratives below since they circulate orally and are often not readily identified by either their narrators or audiences with a particular *purana*, and their oral performances may vary considerably from the textual, Sanskrit *puranas*.

The Trimurti

One conceptual family of deities is the Trimurti (lit., three forms): Brahma, Vishnu, and Shiva – identified in this configuration as the creator, preserver, and destroyer/transformer of the universe, respectively. The three deities are not traditionally worshipped together in this form; rather, the Trimurti is a concept within which the primary forces of life are identified: creation, sustenance, and death. I have heard many Hindus in the United States begin their explanations of the Hindu pantheon of deities, or even individual deities, to non-Hindus with the Trimurti, as a way to "make sense" for their audiences of the multiplicity characteristic of the pantheon. In contemporary Hindu practices, however, Brahma has lost his equal footing with Shiva and Vishnu; and the ritually significant triad is Shiva, Vishnu, and the goddess (Devi).

While Brahma images can be found on temple exteriors and he remains active in mythology as the deity from whose mouth the four Vedas emerge and as a bestower of boons, there are only a few temples in contemporary India dedicated to this god.[1] Several stories circulate about why Brahma is no longer popularly worshipped. One describes Brahma and Vishnu both trying to find the end of Shiva's *linga* (Shiva's aniconic form), the end of which no one could see. Brahma came back from his search saying he had found the end; Vishnu admitted that he had been unable to do so. However, Shiva knew Brahma was lying and declared a curse that Brahma would no longer be worshipped. Brahma's consort, on the other hand (who does not appear with him in the Trimurti configu-

---

[1] Two known Brahma temples are in the towns of Pushkar (Rajasthan) and Kumbhakonam (Tamil Nadu).

ration), Sarasvati – goddess of speech, language, and the arts – *is* actively worshipped by contemporary Hindus throughout India, particularly students. Shiva and Vishnu will appear in descriptions and narratives that follow below.

Mythological and Narrative Families

Shiva, Vishnu, and Devi (the goddess) all have multiple forms and narratives. The goddess appears both as consort of male deities and independently without a male consort. Their mythological families also include the deities' offspring and the animal mounts (*vahanas*) with which they are associated.

Vishnu

Vishnu appears narratively and iconographically in both cosmic form and as a series of incarnations (*avataras*, lit., descent) who come to earth to restore *dharma* by resolving very particular problems (often caused by demons with particular forms). In his cosmic form of Narayana, Vishnu rests between the cycles (*yugas*) of the universe upon an ocean of milk; he lies upon the serpent Sesha, whose multiple hoods shade him; his wife Lakshmi is depicted massaging his feet. This reclining Vishnu is sometimes portrayed with Brahma – who will actually *enact* the creation that Vishnu imagines – seated on a lotus that emerges from his navel. Vishnu is commonly experienced by Hindus in India and the Hindu diaspora – on an everyday basis, ritually – as the god who takes *avataras*, rather than in his cosmic form.

The Dasa Avataras, Manifestations of Vishnu: Vishnu has taken nine *avataras*, with the tenth still to come, to battle against those who threaten the *dharma* of the world; together these ten are known as the *dasa avataras*. (Note that *avatara* is also a more expansive category that includes manifestations of Vishnu outside of the *dasa avataras*; see Chapter 4 for a geographically local *avatara* of Vishnu.) Members of this *dasa avatara* conceptual family are not

Figure 1.1   Vishnu lying on the cosmic ocean, Northern Madhya Pradesh, 11th century CE (31.5 × 44 inches). Courtesy of the Michael C. Carlos Museum, Emory University. Photo by Bruce M. White, 2007.

traditionally worshipped together as a unit (that is, they are not a *ritual* family); however, they are frequently visualized together in artistic forms. The listings of the *dasa avataras* shift between different texts, particularly with the inclusion or not of Balarama and Buddha; but one common *puranic* and visually portrayed listing is as follows.

In the first of the four *yugas* – cycles of the universe that descend in length and quality of *dharma* observance by humans – the Satyayuga (lit., age of truth), Vishnu appeared as:

Matsya, the fish who saved the earth from a cataclysmic flood.
Kurma, the tortoise upon whose back the churning stick was placed in the narrative of the "churning of the ocean," in which the gods and anti-gods (*asuras*) churned up from the ocean bottom the elixir of immortality (*amrita*).
Varaha, the boar who defeated a demon who had rolled up the earth like a mat and carried it to the bottom of the cosmic ocean; Varaha brought up the earth on his tusks.

Narasimha, the half-man/half-lion, who defeated a demon who had been granted a boon that he would not be killed by man or god, could not be killed by any weapon, on earth or in space, at day or night, indoors or outdoors. Narasimha circumvented the boon by appearing as a man-lion, grabbing the demon at twilight, on a threshold, and tearing him open with his nails.

In the second *yuga*, Tretayuga, Vishnu appeared as:

Vamana, the dwarf who defeated the *asura* king Bali by asking for, and being granted, as much land as Vamana could cover in three steps. Much to Bali's surprise, the dwarf's first step covered the heavens, his second step covered the earth, and there was no room for the third step. At this point, Bali realized Vamana was Vishnu and offered his own head as the site of the third step.

Parusharama, Rama with the axe, the son of an ascetic who owned the gift-giving magical cow Kamadhenu. Parusharama defeated a king who sent his armies to the ascetic's *ashram* (hermitage) to steal Kamadhenu.

Rama, hero of the epic of the Ramayana, born into a royal family, who killed the ten-headed demon Ravana. (See Chapter 2 for a longer version of the story).

In the third *yuga,* Dwaparayuga, Vishnu appeared as:

Krishna, who came to destroy the evil king Kamsa (see below for further narratives).

Finally, in the Kaliyuga, the age in which we now live, Vishnu appeared as:

Buddha, who is sometimes included in the *dasa avatara* as a teacher who intentionally misguided the wicked by teaching them wrong religion, thus keeping them at distance from and unthreatening to the truth. But there are also instances in which he is described as

one who taught nonviolence and compassion and is thus interpreted positively.

Kalki is the tenth *avatara* who is yet to come, riding on a white horse;
he will destroy *adharma* (lit., that which is not in accordance with
dharma), and restore *dharma* to begin a new cycle of the four *yugas*,
starting again with the Satyayuga.

Of Vishnu's ten *avataras*, Rama and Krishna are the most commonly worshipped throughout India; Narasimha is also popular in
parts of South and Central India. In temples and home shrines,
Rama is worshipped with his wife Sita, brother Lakshmana, and the
monkey-form deity Hanuman, Rama's devotee and helpmate in the
Ramayana (see Chapter 2). Hanuman, on the other hand, often
appears alone in temples or roadside shrines, without a narrative
family; in this form he often appears covered with bright orange
vermilion (*sindhur*).

Krishna: Krishna is worshipped as a toddler (Bala Krishna), a
young boy, the cowherd lover Gopala with his beloved Radha,
and the prince/charioteer in the Mahabharata. As a toddler,
Krishna is loved for his "naughty" antics, including stealing
butter from the cowherd families among whom he lives. Another
favorite story narrates an incident when Bala Krishna put dirt
into his mouth, as toddlers are wont to do. When his mother
opens his mouth to take out the dirt, she sees the entire world and
(for a moment) realizes that her child is god. As a young man,
Krishna as cowherder draws the women of his village to a clear-
ing in the jungle with the beautiful call of his flute and engages in
erotic play with them.

Krishna is also the charioteer for the warrior Arjuna in the epic
narrative of the Mahabharata. As Arjuna prepares for battle against
his cousins (in a fight for inheritance of the throne) and gazes
across the battlefield, he loses courage – they are his brothers, after
all. And Krishna then gives the teaching that is known as the
Bhagavad Gita, in which he urges Arjuna to fulfill the *dharma* of a
warrior – that is, to engage in battle – but not to be attached to the
results of that action. Arjuna asks Krishna to show his full self,

realizing that he is more than a charioteer. Krishna's theophany reveals a cosmic deity encompassing the entire universe. As is common in many myths, the vision of the full power of the god in his cosmic form is too much to sustain, and Arjuna begs the god to return to his form of charioteer, with whom he can relate more easily. Through Krishna's various personae, we learn that human devotees may relate to and love god as a mother does her child, as a lover, and as a friend.

Shiva

Shiva appears in pan-Indian mythologies as well as in many very local stories where he appears with local names, in which he often takes disguise to test his devotees. In contemporary lithographs, he is often visualized as sitting in the Himalayas – a bare-chested ascetic with a tiger skin wrapped around him and a snake across his chest – with his wife Parvati (daughter of Himalaya). Or he may be shown to be seated in the Himalayas with River Ganga (sometimes identified as one of his two wives) flowing through his locks of hair, which break the impact of the river and keep the earth from being destroyed by the deluge. He is both an ascetic who retreats to the Himalayas for long periods of meditation, and a husband (albeit one whose father-in-law doesn't appreciate his ascetic dress and practices) who plays dice and engages in dance competitions with his wife Parvati. Shiva's *vahana* is Nandi the bull, who often appears with the god in lithograph and sculptural representations. In Shiva temples, Nandi sits outside the *garbagriha* (inner shrine room), facing the god.

Shiva as also known as the King of Dance, Nataraja, who has become the patron god of contemporary classical Indian dance. He dances in the cremation grounds, at the end of creation, and in the pine forest where he reveals his true self only when he begins to dance – both terrifying and enthralling his audience (see Chapter 4 for a fuller telling of this story).

In the inner shrine rooms of Shiva temples and roadside shrines, the god takes form as an aniconic black-stone *linga* (lit., the sign of

Shiva).[2] While the form is phallic (and there are several myths explicitly identifying it as such),[3] the *linga* is equated by its worshippers with the god himself, without any phallic connotations – and thus to speak explicitly of this association understandably offends some Hindus. The *linga* sits in a female womb shape, the *yoni*; together, they embody the generative, creative potentiality of the male and female. One of Shiva's remarkable forms is Ardhanarishvara, who is, quite literally, "the lord who is half man-half woman."

Ganesha: The most popular member of Shiva's family, found in a majority of *brahminic* temples and many domestic altars, is Ganesha, the elephant-headed deity who removes obstacles. (See Chapter 5 for photographs of his festival, Ganesha Chaturthi.) He is worshipped by Hindus before they set out on a new venture or journey, at housewarmings, before exams, or before worship of other deities – whenever the path ahead should be cleared of obstacles. Ganesha's *vahana* is the mouse. One widely told story about how Ganesha came to have an elephant head (and there are other variants) begins with his parents dwelling in the Himalayas.

Shiva has gone out to the mountains to meditate, leaving his wife Parvati behind. She's lonely and creates a son out of a paste of turmeric and ground lentils (a kind of body scrub) that she had rubbed on her body during her bath. One day, while she is taking her bath, Parvati tells her son to stand guard outside the door and not to let anyone in. Shiva returns from his ascetic retreat and is blocked from entering his home by a "stranger." He demands to be let in, but Ganesha refuses; and in anger, Shiva beheads him. Only when Parvati comes out of her bath, devastated by what she sees in front of her, does Shiva

---

[2] The only temple in which Shiva's central temple image is not a *linga* is in Cidambaram, Tamil Nadu, where the god is said to appear every evening to perform his *anandatandava* dance – and the central image in this temple is Nataraja; see Chapter 4 for a discussion of the *sthala purana* of this temple site.

[3] See Don Handelman and David Shulman, *Shiva and the Pine Forest* (2004).

learn whom he has beheaded. He sends his attendants out to the jungle to bring back the head of the first living thing they encounter, which happens to be an elephant.[4] Shiva attaches that head and Ganesha comes to life again and is worshipped in the form of an elephant-headed, human-bodied deity.

Kartikeya, Murugan: In Tamil Nadu and Tamilian diasporic communities, the brother of Ganesha – variously named Skanda, Murugan, Kartikeya, or Subrahmanya – is particularly popular; his *vahana* is the peacock. One narrative regarding the two brothers, Ganesha and Kartikeya, tells of a competition between the two to obtain the prize of knowledge from the sage Narada. The competition was a race around the world; Kartikeya was at a distinct advantage due to his peacock *vahana* and Ganesha's slower mouse *vahana* and considerable girth. Kartikeya raced off to his journey around the world, only to find upon his return Ganesha was already standing there. Ganesha had simply circumambulated his parents (Shiva and Parvati) three times, as parents are considered to be one's entire world; and Ganesha won the prize of knowledge.

[4]   Another variant of this narrative, told on Ganesha Chathurti in Telugu-speaking communities, expands on the reason for Ganesha's elephant head: a demon named Gajasura, who had traits of an elephant, once performed austerities to the god Shiva. Shiva appeared before him and promised to grant whatever wish the demon desired if Gajasura would suspend his powerful ascetic practice. Gajasura asked that Shiva reside in the demon's stomach. Shiva was obliged to grant the wish and entered Gajasura's stomach. Noticing Shiva's absence, the other gods went to Vishnu for help. Knowing what had happened, Vishnu took the guise of cowherd with Shiva's bull Nandi at his side. With the bull, Vishnu performed a traditional cowherd's song and dance in front of the demon. Captivated by the performance, Gajasura vowed to give the cowherd whatever he desired. Vishnu then revealed his true identity and asked that Shiva be released from Gajasura's stomach. Gajasura released Shiva, but made one final request, that his elephant head would always be remembered. So, when Shiva realized he had beheaded Parvati's son, as related above, he asked his attendants to bring back the head of the first animal they encountered in the jungle, which was an elephant. Attaching the elephant head to Ganesha's body fulfilled Shiva's promise to Gajasura that his (elephant) head would always be remembered.

Devi, the Goddess

The multiple manifestations of the goddess are a particularly good example of the Hindu idea of the plurality of singular identity; that is, while all gods are rarely referred to as manifestations of a singular god (*deva*), goddesses are frequently associated with a singular Devi. This concept is performed during the annual festival of Navaratri (Nine Nights of the Goddess), during which the goddess is celebrated with a different form and name each of the nine nights, and yet all are considered to be one, Devi. The goddess sometimes appears as a consort to Shiva, Vishnu, or Brahma (Parvati, Lakshmi, and Sarasvati, respectively), and at other times independently (even if she is narratively a consort, such as Sarasvati). Many other goddesses such as Durga and the *gramadevata* Seven Sisters have no consorts either narratively or in visual representations.

Durga: One of the most well-known narratives and images of the goddess is that of Durga and the demon Mahishasura. Like the demons Vishnu comes in *avatara* form to destroy, here, too, a demon has acquired powers through his meditation that ultimately threaten the *dharmic* order of the world. Mahishasura was granted the boon of not being able to be killed by any man or god; but he had not considered the possibility of being killed by a woman and had not, therefore, asked for this exemption. So the gods, including Vishnu and Shiva, create the goddess Durga out of their *tejas* (energy) and give her their weapons. After his generals have been destroyed by Durga, the demon tries to elude the goddess by turning himself into a buffalo. But Durga catches and beheads him; this scene is often portrayed in sculptures and paintings, usually depicting the demon in his original (human-bodied) form emerging from the buffalo at that moment of the latter's death.

The festival of Durga Puja – particularly popular in Bengal, but also widely celebrated in North India – celebrates Durga's battle and victory over Mahishasura.[5] During the ten days of this festival, temporary shrines (*pandals*) are erected to house clay or

[5] I was told by a village headman in the fall of 2014 on a return trip to Chhattisgarh that Durga Puja has become more and more popular in many villages in the region

Figure 1.2 Durga battling the buffalo demon, Rajasthan, ca. 900 CE (45 ×
25 inches) Courtesy of the Michael C. Carlos Museum, Emory University.
Photo by Bruce M. White, 2007.

plaster-of-paris images of the goddess, which are immersed in
bodies of water at the end of the festival.

Lakshmi: Lakshmi, the goddess of wealth and auspiciousness,
is the consort of Vishnu and is often shown by his side in temple
iconography; but she also appears independently (particularly

that traditionally did not celebrate the festival. He said with some regret that, with
the ubiquitous presence of television, village audiences were no longer interested in
sitting through 10 days of Ramayana dramatic performances during the Dashera
festival, and that Durga Puja had become more popular.

in lithographs), when she is seated on a lotus, flanked by two auspicious elephants, with gold coins flowing down from one of her hands. Lakshmi's qualities and the multiple forms of wealth she embodies and bestows are conceptualized through the configuration of the *ashta lakshmis* (eight Lakshmis), who are named:

Adi Lakshmi, she who has existed from the beginning of time;
Saubhagya Lakshmi, she who is and gives auspiciousness;
Dhana Lakshmi, she who is and gives wealth;
Dhairya Lakshmi, she who is and gives courage;
Vijaya Lakshmi, she who is and gives victory and success;
Vidya Lakshmi, she who is and gives knowledge;
Dhanya Lakshmi, she who brings fertility to the earth and takes the
    form of grain;
Santana Lakshmi, she who bestows children.

The *ashta lakshmis* appear in some goddess temples in a row of eight *murtis* along the side of a wall, but rarely in the inner *garbagriha* shrine room.

Gramadevatas, Village Deities

Shiva, Vishnu, and Devi appear throughout India and the Hindu diaspora, although they may take local names and have local narratives. In contrast, *gramadevatas* (lit., village deities) are tied to particular geographic places, the land itself, and rarely immigrate with diasporic communities.

Gramadevatas traditionally dwell on village boundaries in open-air shrines or under trees; however, urban neighborhoods have grown up around many of them, where their open-air shrines have become more fully established shrines or permanent temples. In South India the most common *gramadevatas* are the Seven Sisters, who guard village welfare, protect humans from disease (particularly poxes, rashes, and fevers associated with the hot season), and ensure the fertility and health of crops and animals. The Sisters are an expansive and shifting family, whose individual names may vary from village to village, town to town. Sometimes individual sisters are associated with specific illnesses (distinguishing between mumps, measles, chickenpox, and diarrhea, for example), and at other times they are conflated and associated more generally with the entire class of illnesses. Some of their common names are Yellamma, Mariamma, Gangamma, Mutyalamma, and Ankalamma. Whatever their names, they appear in their individual temples or shrines with their brother Potu Raju (in the form of an uncarved rock or cement pillar marked with turmeric and vermilion powder) facing them, standing guard.

The Seven Sisters are unmarried, but they often wear the gold pendant associated with marriage, and some – such as Gangamma in Tirupati, South India – have children.[6] When, in 1991, I asked the flower sellers at Gangamma's largest Tirupati temple who her husband was, given that she was wearing a wedding pendant (*tali*), they first answered she has no husband; however, ten years later – presumably under influence of a growing middle-class ideology of gender and sexuality that "requires" a husband if there are children – they responded that her husband must be Shiva. However, he is not visible iconographically in the temples nor does he appear as husband in Gangamma's oral narratives. The Sisters are rarely brought into domestic worship spaces because their needs (including, traditionally, animal sacrifice) are too many to be fulfilled by individual householders; rather, they are most often worshipped at their public shrines or temples.

Although individual Sisters may be found in multiple places, each place has a unique story of the goddess's presence and power at "this place." As an example of the ways in which *gramadevatas* are tied to a specific place, I give a synopsis of the story of Gangamma in the South Indian pilgrimage town of Tirupati and the nearby village of Avilala.

---

[6] Amy L. Allocco reports that, similarly, a (traditionally) unmarried snake goddess (*nagamman*) in Chennai is annually offered the pregnancy bangle ritual (*simantam*), although it is not clear that there is a husband or even a pregnancy.

As a little baby, Gangamma was found abandoned in a dry paddy field, from where she was taken in as a daughter by a Reddy-caste family, in the village of Avilala. There was a particularly powerful Palegadu (landowner) who used to demand sexual access to (sometimes marriage with) the beautiful virgins living in his domain. When his glance fell on a pubescent Gangamma as she was drying her hair on her rooftop, he desired her and approached her parents with his intention to marry her. Not knowing their daughter was the goddess, they were afraid and tried to resist his overtures. But Gangamma assured them they should assent; she would take care of herself. As the couple (Gangamma and the Palegadu) was circumambulating the sacred fire in the final marriage rite, Gangamma turned around to face the Palegadu and showed him her true self, stretching from earth to sky. Petrified, he ran away to Tirupati. She chased him for six days, taking a series of guises (those of milkmaid, ascetic, snake charmer, shepherd, sweeper, etc.) to disguise herself so that the Palegadu wouldn't see her before she saw him. Finally, hearing people praise Gangamma in her guise as a prince, the Palegadu came out of hiding to see who was competing with him for such praise; and Gangamma beheaded him. After killing the Palegadu, Gangamma wandered the village (*uru*), showing herself in her true form for the duration of what is now her annual festival. At the end of the festival (and its narrative), Gangamma departs from Tirupati, "over the seven seas." (See Flueckiger 2013 for other Gangamma narratives and their gendered variations.)

While narratively the goddess leaves Tirupati, *ritually* she stays and is served throughout the year and during her annual festival (see Chapter 5 for a fuller description of the festival). Gangamma is referred to as a daughter of *this* place, whom ancestors of the Avilala and Tirupati residents themselves knew, and who protects *this* village or neighborhood and its environs; she does not emigrate from the lands to which she is so closely tied, and does not accompany those of her worshippers who do so.

Shitala Mata (lit., the Cool Mother) is the North Indian goddess whose role as protector from illness approximates that of the Seven Sisters in the South; but like the Seven Sisters, Shitala, too, takes on much wider identities than that of "disease goddess." In Central India, a common village guardian is the male deity Thakur Dev, who has a protective ritual role, but no extensive narrative. He has traditionally appeared as a stone slab or a wooden post on village boundaries or guarding paddy fields; however, during a 2014 return trip to Chhattisgarh, I noticed something very new – an anthropomorphic form of Thakur Dev riding a horse (see Figure 1.3).

Figure 1.3   New image of Thakur Dev in village paddy fields, Chhattisgarh.

I was told that this form of Thakur Dev had begun to replace non-anthropomorphic forms only in the last two years. In Rajasthan, family and village guardians are often Sati Matas, women-become-goddesses who have committed *sati* (an act of self-immolation upon the death of their husbands), which signals their devotion, truthfulness, and resulting spiritual power.

Gramadevatas are often portrayed in academic writings as living in discrete narrative and ritual worlds from those of *puranic* deities such as Vishnu, Shiva, Lakshmi, and Durga. However, many Hindu devotees live with and serve both *gramadevatas* and *puranic* deities as *integrated* rather than discrete pantheons. Sometimes local *gramadevatas* are said to be in familial relationships with *puranic* deities. For example, the *puranic* deity Venkateshvara (whose temple is the destination of pilgrimage to Tirupati) is understood by Tirupati residents to be a brother of the *gramadevata* Gangamma; and he sends (atop a royal elephant) traditional bridal gifts of a sari and *pasupu-kumkum* (turmeric-vermilion) to his sister on the first day of her annual festival.

The association between the *puranic* god and *gramadevata* goddess is also performed on the domestic *puja* shelves – where both Venkateshvara and Gangamma have been installed and are worshipped daily – of the families who are key ritual actors in Gangamma's festival. One of these families, the Kaikalas, has the *mirasi* (right and responsibility) both to take the perambulating guises of Gangamma during her festival *and* to unlock the temple of Venkateshvara's brother, Govinda Raja Swamy, every morning. This family of ritual specialists performs its duties for both Gangamma and Venkateshvara's brother as integrated ritual responsibilities.

Temple Families

While various myths may bring different deities together in one story – such as Vishnu who watches Shiva dance, or the goddess Adi Para Shakti who creates the three gods (Brahma, Vishnu, and Shiva) in search of a husband – temples are generally dedicated to a single deity – for example, a form of Shiva, Vishnu, or the goddess – and his/her associated family members.[7] Each temple has a local name for the primary deity and a local story of how the deity came to take residence there (the *sthala purana*: the story of the place; see Chapter 4). Shiva is often named the lord (*ishvara* or *natha*) of a particular place. For example, in Kalahasti he is Kalahastishvara; in Varanasi, Vishvanatha; in Madurai, Shiva and Parvati are called Sundeshvara and Minakshi. Vishnu comes to Tirupati as Venkateshvara, whose wife is locally known as Padmavati or Alumelamanga; in Sri Rangam, Vishnu is Ranganatha. These local names identify the god/goddess with specific local landscapes, which makes them more accessible and locally meaningful to residents of "that place."

The first temples built in the United States often housed a wide array of deities, who appeared with equal importance (size and placement), given that there were not enough Hindus in a given American city from any single sectarian affiliation (Shaiva, Vaishnava, or Shakta [goddess]) or from a specific region in India to be able to support temples dedicated to a single deity. For example, one of the first temple spaces built in Atlanta was in the Indian American Cultural Association building (inaugurated in 1984).[8] An altar is located on one end of the carpeted, rectangular room on which a large ritual family of deities has been installed, including white-marble (characteristic of North Indian images), similarly sized, styled, and dressed images of Ganesha, Shiva, Durga, Parvati, Rama, Sita, Hanuman, Krishna, and Radha, as well as a smaller brass image of the Jain *tirthankara* (enlightened teacher) Mahavira, and a black-stone Shiva *linga* in front of them all. This rather unusual ritual-temple family of deities – while rarely found in India – has a democratic appeal here in the United States, with no single deity given precedence over another by size or style, except for perhaps the slightly larger Ganesha, who appears in the center. However, as more and more Hindus immigrated to the Atlanta metropolitan area, regionally styled and sectarian temples began to be

---

[7] There are important exceptions; for example, in Cidambaram, Shiva as Nataraja is the primary deity, but in a shrine close to the *garbagriha* is another shrine housing a large image of Vishnu lying on the ocean of milk.

[8] Each major Indian religious tradition (including Christianity and Islam) was offered a worship room, but only Hindus and Jains took up this offer.

built, including the South Indian Hindu Temple of Atlanta dedicated to Vishnu as Sri Venkateshvara and a newer temple on the same site to Shiva and Parvati as Ramalingeshwara and Parvathavardhani, respectively; the Gujarati Shakti Mandir to the goddess; the North Indian Shiv Mandir of Atlanta; the North America Shirdi Sai Baba Temple; the Gujarati Swaminarayan (BAPS)[9] temple; and the North Indian Hanuman Mandir.

Ritual Families in Domestic Shrines

Most Hindu domestic shrines display three-dimensional images (*murtis*) and/or lithograph representations of the deities whom family members worship on a daily basis. These sometimes crowded altars may be a single wooden shelf or small niche in the wall, a cabinet in the kitchen, a small moveable "temple" in the corner of a room, or (in wealthier homes) an entire little room set aside for the deities. To "read" these domestic altars of the gods and goddesses helps us to identify a variety of ways in which *devotional* families of deities are created. These ritually created families are more eclectic than are those represented in temples and shrines in India, and may include forms of Shiva, Vishnu, and the goddess, Ganesha, gurus such as Shirdi Sai Baba, and photographs of family ancestors.[10]

The basic deities on a domestic *puja* shrine usually include a family deity (*kuladevata,* inherited through patriline), a caste or village deity, and one or more personal deities (*ishtadevatas,* who may be the same as or different from the family deity). Other deities may be added when a family member performs a vow to a particular god or goddess or has gone on pilgrimage to a powerful dwelling of a deity. Domestic shrines can be interpreted as visual, non-linear life stories and reflections of networks of relationships of the families who create and maintain the shrines.

[9] BAPS is an acronym for Bochasanwasi Shri Akshar Purushottam Swaminarayan Sanstha.
[10] These photographs of ancestors are not usually kept on the same shelf as the deities, but may be on a different shelf of the *puja* shrine or outside of, but near, it.

We shift now to an examination of three specific domestic *puja* shrines that illustrate the ways in which families of deities are created in these shrines.

Domestic shrine of a Hyderabadi, Tamil Mudaliar-caste family: The Thangavelus are a Tamil family whose ancestors immigrated to Hyderabad three generations ago. The father, Thanganne, is a retired railway official and the mother, Revathi, is a retired university professor; their two adult children have both spent considerable time in the United States for higher education and employment, but have now both moved back to India. The family's domestic *puja* shrine is a wooden cabinet with four shelves whose glass-fronted doors are left open (see Figure 1.4). It is situated in the western corner (facing the auspicious eastern direction) of the front "hall," or public sitting room, of the home. Revathi told me that they had chosen this location, rather than the kitchen, because they cook non-vegetarian food in the kitchen. In most Hindu homes, one family member, often the matriarch, conducts daily morning worship to the deities of a domestic shrine. In the case of this family, however, Thanganne is now (post-retirement) responsible for daily morning worship (placing a small white flower atop each image, lighting incense and the brass oil lamp, saying some prayers), while Revathi maintains the shrine and its deities by washing them weekly; she also sets up temporary shrines in the home for festivals such as Ganesha Chathurthi and other periodic rituals.

The Thangavelu shrine is particularly eclectic. I asked both Thanganne and Revathi, individually, to explain how each deity had found his/her way to their *puja* shrine. A set of small black-stone deities was inherited from Thanganne's family, including a Ganesha, Shiva in the form of a *linga* and his bull *vahana* Nandi, Vishnu lying on the ocean of milk, and the Tamil poet-saint Andal. On their marriage, Revathi brought in another stone Ganesha and added hers to the patrilineal stone set; her daughter-in-law has added still another stone Ganesha to the set. Revathi explained that the black-stone set of the ritual family of deities will eventually find its place in the domestic shrine of the Thangavelus' son, and their daughter-in-law will carry the responsibility to maintain them.

Figure 1.4 Thangavelu domestic *puja* shrine, Hyderabad.

Joining this black-stone "family" on the same small yellow-painted wooden throne-shelf (*pitha*) are metal images of Gopala Krishna (Krishna as cowherd), Lakshmi, and the Ramayana "family" of Rama, Sita, and Hanuman (see Figure 1.5). A framed photograph of the image of the goddess Draupadi (wife of the five Pandava brothers/heroes of the great epic Mahabharata) as she appears in Thanganne's ancestral temple in Tamil Nadu also sits on the top shelf of the cabinet.[11] Joining Draupadi on the same shelf are brass images of Lakshmi and Sarasvati that Thanganne's sister added (Revathi elaborated, "Each person adds something"). Behind the

---

[11] Draupadi is worshipped primarily in South India.

Figure 1.5   Close-up of family-inherited ritual family of deities, Hyderabad.

black-stone set of deities hangs a yellow-painted wooden circle, marked with three red horizontal lines and decorated with red and white painted dots; this is the goddess inherited from Thanganne's mother, about which neither Thanganne nor Revathi know much else, but they both felt that they should "keep" this goddess.

Other deities who reside on the second shelf of this domestic shrine have joined the wider ritual family through pilgrimages the Thangavelus have made: Lakshmi from Udipi; Sharada Devi from Sringeri; Shiva from Palaghat. A flat brass *yantra* (intersecting, geometrical triangles) representing the goddess also resides on this shelf. Joining the deities in this cupboard shrine are three framed pictures of family elders who have passed on: Thanganne's parents, his paternal grandparents, and Revathi's parents; a vermilion dot has been placed on the forehead of each elder. Many families keep photographs of their ancestors hanging on walls outside, rather than in, the *puja* shrine; and these photographs are similarly honored with vermilion markings and often a garland of flowers. In this way, the ancestors are treated like deities; although they do not grant boons, they offer protection to the generations that follow them.

Thanganne often noted the familial connections between the deities: the Shiva *linga* requires the presence of Nandi; Hanuman is found wherever Rama and Sita are found; the roadside goddess shrines scattered throughout Hyderabad are all forms of Durga. Revathi, on the other hand, spoke of the requirements of ritually taking care of the deities. For example, she explained that the yellow wooden circle with three red lines would traditionally have been painted, or applied with turmeric and vermilion, on the wall of the home itself, but maintaining this is a "big job"; and so, she had it painted on a piece of wood. She went on to describe her responsibility of taking all the deities off the shelves and washing them every week, and then carefully putting them back in the particular places that her elders used to do, a ritual that preserves and maintains family ties and traditions through embodied practices.[12]

Domestic shrine of a Brahmin family in suburban Atlanta: Ravi and Sasikala Penumarthi immigrated to Atlanta from Andhra Pradesh in 1991. Ravi is an executive in a software engineering company and Sasikala a renowned Kuchipudi dancer and dance guru. The family's *puja* shrine (which Sasikala called a *puja mandiram*, lit., *puja* temple) is located in the kitchen, in an east-facing cabinet with glass doors that was specifically constructed for this purpose when they built their house in the Atlanta suburbs. Sasikala explained that she wanted the shrine close to where she prepared the food offered to the deities (rather than in an upstairs bedroom dedicated to this purpose, which is quite common in American Hindu homes), so that it didn't have to "pass over all kinds of floors and carpets to get to another room," which may result in the offerings coming into contact with impurities.

Sasikala identified the central deities of the shrine to be Venkateshvara and his two wives Padmavati and Bhu Devi. She explained that these

---

[12] With the encouragement of her adult children, when they have felt the *puja* shrine is becoming too crowded and it is being reconfigured or moved, Revathi has periodically taken off *murtis* that are not part of the patrilineal inheritance.

are family deities from both her husband's family and her own father's family. Before they moved to their newly constructed house, these deities had been represented by framed lithographs; but for the new house they purchased the metal images that are now installed. Other deities in the cabinet shrine, and the stated reasons they are present, include: Shiva and Parvati, her mother's side's family deities; the half-woman/half-man Ardhanarishvara form of Shiva, which, she explained, represents the centrality of the "couple"; Durga because her mother used to worship her; Rama, because her mother-in-law "liked him a lot"; Hanuman, because her father had told her that Hanuman gives strength and courage; a small Lakshmi, which was a wedding

Figure 1.6   Penumarthi domestic *puja* shrine, suburban Atlanta.

41

gift given by an aunt; and an unusual Ganesha made from laminated grains and lentils given to Sasikala by her sister. Prominent on the *puja* shelf is the dancing Nataraja form of Shiva; as Sasikala explained, "Shiva is my main god because of dance. He's my *ishtadevata*. I first pray to Shiva. Then [I think of] Venkateshvara." Her husband Ravi, on the other hand, said he thinks of Venkateshvara first.

An unusual framed lithograph of Hanuman with a very long tail marked with a line of vermilion dots leans against the inner side of the main *puja* shelf. Sasikala explained that this form of Hanuman came to reside in the shrine as the result of a particular vow to him that she has performed four times. When Sasikala's father had lost his job when she was a young girl, a friend had encouraged her mother to perform the vow; and the vow had subsequently become a family tradition. For 41 days (each day marked by a vermilion dot on his tail), the devotee eats only one time a day and recites the Hanuman Chalisa (a short devotional praise text to Hanuman) 11 times. Most recently, Sasikala had vowed to observe these rituals to bring successful fruition to an innovative Kuchipudi dance drama she had choreographed; after the highly successful performance, she fulfilled her vow of fasting and chanting the Chalisa for 41 days.

Sasikala and Ravi share in the responsibilities of service to the deities in their home shrine. Sasikala explained that when one keeps deities in the home, there should always be *prasad* in front of them – minimally, offerings of water and a silver coin. Every Friday, she makes special *prasad* of cooked rice and lentils for the deities and, Friday being a special day for the goddess, recites the Lalitasahasranama (the 1,000 names of the goddess). During the recitation, she places a series of flowers into a silver tray set in front of the goddess. Sasikala has trained her two children to recite Vishnu *suprabhatam* (verses recited to awaken a deity in the morning), which they chant to Venkateshvara before they go to school. Every Saturday, a day special to Venkateshvara, Ravi performs *abhishekam* for the god and his wives, a ritual that involves pouring milk and water over the brass images and reclothing and decorating them with a gold chains and vermilion and turmeric markings.

Sasikala explained the differences between worshipping a deity at home and in a temple: the temple is more powerful because the images are larger, they are worshipped by priests throughout the day (rather than only once a day at home), and there are no distractions of daily life all around you like there are at home. However, she knows some friends who think the home *puja* is more powerful, in part because of the intimate contact householders can have with these deities (feeding and dressing them) without a priest serving as an intermediary (as is the case in *puranic*-deity temples); and certainly, Sasikala affirms, every Hindu home *should* have a *puja* shrine of some kind.

Domestic shrine in rural Chhattisgarh: Many domestic shrines are much simpler than the two described above; they may be a simple wall shelf or a few framed and garlanded lithographs of deities hung above a doorway. Even if rural families are wealthy enough to purchase metal *murtis*, they often have only a few small ones and rely on lithographs for representations of their deities. One village domestic shrine of a Chhattisgarhi Kolta-caste, wealthy farming family consists of two simple stone shelves built into a brick wall of the interior of the house. When I asked if I could see their *puja* shelf, the female householder took me into a darkened room with no electricity, and only with my camera flash could I identify who was there. The top shelf held three large framed lithographs of Ganesha, Hanuman, and Lakshmi, all garlanded with a single string of pink plastic flowers. In front of them were smaller lithographs of Shirdi Sai Baba, Durga sitting atop her tiger, and a lithograph brought back from the pilgrimage site of Narsinghnath (see Chapter 4). The shelf below held three small brass images of Lakshmi, each wrapped with pink cloth, a lithograph of Narasimha, and ritual implements including a conch shell and small brass water vessel; several incense sticks lay in front of them.

Domestic *puja* shrines reveal the religious, regional, and personal networks within which particular families and individuals live. They are often crowded and even "messy" with ritual remains (such as vermilion and turmeric powder); they are constantly shifting, with the addition of deities with whom a worshipper may have had an encounter at a pilgrimage site or through a particular vow; and

43

Figure 1.7 Rural *puja* shelf, Chhattisgarh.

they reflect and help to create relationships between worshippers and particular deities, as well as materially embodying family relationships and histories.

*****

Ritual and narrative families of Hindu deities are both expansive and context-specific. Hindus do not live on a daily basis with the fullest possible pantheon of deities, or even all of those they have come to know narratively. They worship family and personal deities on a daily basis, may participate in rituals at the homes of friends whose *puja* shelves house another set of deities, and they may visit temples of still other deities weekly or on periodic pilgrimages.

With all this diversity, there also coexists for some Hindus the concept of the singular *brahman*, ultimate reality that has no shape, form, or mythology, that exists beyond the created world. And it is to this concept that Hindus are referring when they say, for example, "God is one," or "There are many forms and names of god, but there is only one." But "god" here is not the theistic reality that the term implies in English; rather, it is an Upanishadic concept developed by Vedantic philosophers who argue that reality is singular: the created and non-created worlds – and *brahman* is that singular identity that cannot be known except by yogis who follow strict discipline and practice. Thus, when a Hindu says "God is one," this is very different from a Muslim, Christian, or Jew who may say, "There is only one god."

References

Flueckiger, Joyce Burkhalter. 2013. *When the World Becomes Female: Guises of a South Indian Goddess*. Bloomington, IN: Indiana University Press.

Handelman, Don, and David Shulman. 2004. *Siva in the Forest of Pines: An Essay on Sorcery and Self-Knowledge*. New Delhi: Oxford University Press.

Recommended Readings

Dimmitt, Cornelia, and J. A. B. Van Buitenen. 1978. *Classical Hindu Mythology: A Reader in the Sanskrit Puranas*. Philadelphia: Temple University Press.

Hawley, John Stratton, and Donna Marie Wulff, eds. 1996. *Devi: Goddesses of India*. Berkeley: University of California Press.

Mazumdar, Shampa, and Sanjoy Mazumdar. 2003. "Creating the Sacred: Altars in the Hindu American Home." *Revealing the Sacred in Asian and Pacific America*, eds. Jane N. Iwamura and Spickard Paul, 143–157. New York: Routledge.

Shulman, David. 1980. *Tamil Temple Myths: Sacrifice and Divine Marriage in the South Indian Saiva Tradition*. Princeton: Princeton University Press.

Turner, Kay. 1999. *Beautiful Necessity: The Art and Meaning of Women's Altars*. London: Thames & Hudson.

2

Oral and Visual Narratives and Theologies

Hindus rarely learn or know religious narratives, such as those related in the previous chapter, by picking up a book and reading the stories privately, although there are hundreds of religious texts available in written form. Rather, Hinduism is primarily an oral and visual tradition; Hindus know their stories primarily by hearing them performed and seeing them through a wide range of visual mediums. Religious narratives are sung or recited by performers in village squares and temple courtyards or dramatically enacted at particular festivals; they are danced in classical Indian dance and dramatic forms such as Bharatanatyam, Kuchipudi, and Kathakali; they are painted on scrolls and carved onto the outside of temple towers, walls, and gateways. Ubiquitous brightly colored lithographs of deities often layer different narrative episodes of a deity into a single montage. Religious narratives are also frequently the subject of commercial films and television serials and may be referenced in advertisements for or labels on consumer goods as various as match boxes, packets of butter

Everyday Hinduism, First Edition. Joyce Burkhalter Flueckiger.
© 2015 Joyce Burkhalter Flueckiger. Published 2015 by John Wiley & Sons, Ltd.

and milk, rice, and saris. This chapter focuses on *how* Hindus know the stories of their gods and goddesses and their theologies.

Most audiences attend religious narrative performances not to "learn" the story nor to find out "what happens" – they already know the story – rather, they attend performances in order to gain merit, as an act of devotion, and/or to participate in a social event. V. Narayana Rao distinguishes between narrative performances that "communicate" (that is, tell the story for content) and those that create "communion" with the deity and/or the narrative community (oral communication). Audiences attend performances to relish the experience of a particular narrative rendition and its unique performative qualities and to establish communication and a relationship with the divine, and/or for religious merit.[1]

In this chapter, we will first take a "tour" of some representative oral and visual Hindu narrative performance genres. Then, in the second half of the chapter, we will focus on the wide array of genres through which the epic story of the Ramayana is performed and known.

Oral Performance Genres

Narrative performers: Professional performers of *puranic* and epic narratives are found throughout India. In the South Indian states of Andhra Pradesh and Telangana, a popular oral narrative performance genre is *hari katha* (lit., stories of god/Hari), during which performers play a stringed instrument (*tambura*) and cymbals, accompanied by a musician on the *mridangam* drum. In rural Chhattisgarh, similar performers are called *bahaks*, who walk up and down village streets while playing a large *dholak* drum, bells on their feet, and strong voices singing out *puranic* narratives. Traditionally, *bahaks* are male; but the rare female *bahak* attracts large crowds – and both unusually productive crops and failed crops have been attributed to the fact that a female *bahak* had performed in the previous year. Other Chhattisgarhi performers specialize in Mahabharata narratives

---

[1] Think of performances of Handel's Messiah as an equivalent for many Christians who know the Biblical stories that are performed.

called *pandvani* (named after the five Pandava hero brothers) that are localized in Chhattisgarhi physical and social landscapes. In Varanasi and elsewhere in the Gangetic plain, oral reciters and expositors of the Hindi *Ramcaritmanas* are called *kathavachaks* (lit., storytellers).

The Tirumala Tirupati Devasthanam (TTD) Music College in the South Indian temple town of Tirupati offers a two-year training program for professional performers called *purana pandits* (many fewer are female, *purana panditas*) – literally, scholars of the *puranas*. The training consists of listening to experienced *pandits* perform and give textual commentary, culminating in a written exam that tests the performers in various narrative genres such as Ramayana, Mahabharata, and Bhagavata Purana, followed by their own performances on stage. The Temple Endowments Department (a government-appointed body that manages temples whose income is above a certain amount and administers their endowments) hires performers from among these graduates to sing in various temples around Tirupati.

One Brahmin female performer explained that she performs for one month at a time at a given temple or series of temples in rotation (often traveling several hours a day between various sites) and may also be called to perform for specific temple-based festivals and rituals. While she sings with a book propped up on a wooden bookstand in front of her, she has a wide berth for creativity, weaving various narratives together and providing her own commentaries. She explained that she shapes her performances (choice of narratives and the language register in which she sings – Sanskritized Telugu or more colloquial Telugu) for specific audiences according to whether she is performing in villages or towns, whether the majority of the audience members are men or women, and the kinds of questions they may ask her.

Recitation of names: Hindus may also be reminded (directly or indirectly) of the stories, qualities, and theologies of their deities through recitation of their names, since many are drawn from their mythologies or their visual and theological qualities. For example, when Shiva is called Nilakantha, "the blue-necked one," a listener may be reminded of the story of the churning of the ocean in which the gods and *asuras* (opponents of the gods), who were constantly battling, each took one side of a churning rope (in the form of a snake) tied around Mount Mandara, which sat on the back of a tortoise at the bottom of the ocean, in order to churn up the elixir of immortality (*amrita*). But before the *amrita* was released, other substances from the ocean were thrown up, including potentially world-destroying poison. To save the world, Shiva drank the poison, which lodged in his throat – hence one of his names: the blue-necked one. Among his other names, Shiva is also known as Jagdish (lord of the universe), Nagabhushan (he who has serpents as ornaments), Pashupati (lord of the animals), and Gangadhara (he who holds Ganga River). The name Gangadhara is a reference to the narrative of the descent of the Ganga River goddess from heaven to earth, during which Shiva catches the river in his hair so that the power of her descent won't destroy the earth.

Similarly, Krishna's name Giridhar (the mountain-bearing one) references the story of Krishna saving the villagers of Braj from the wrath of the storm god Indra by holding Mount Govardhan above his head, under which they all took refuge from the violent storm. His name Murali (he who plays the flute) conjures the image of the god as a cowherd who played his flute in the jungle outside the village, the melodious sound of which drew the village women (*gopis*) out to dance with him. Krishna as Kamsantaka (slayer of the demon Kamsa) refers to Krishna's defeat of the world-threatening demon. The common ritual practice of recitation of the 1,000 or 1,008 names (*namajapa; sahasranama*) for a particular deity can thus be understood as an oral litany of his/her narratives, visual representations, and theologies.

Visual Narratives and Theologies

Hindus also know the stories of their deities through iconography of the deities that suggests or embodies their narratives.[2] For example, one image of Krishna depicts him dancing on the head of a serpent; for those who live in Hindu narrative worlds, the story is explicit.

---

[2]   Lest we think that coming to know narratives visually is uniquely Hindu, we only have to think about the narratives implied in the Christian crucifix and Christmas cards and carols, and the ways in which many Christians come to know these narratives.

Figure 2.1 Krishna dancing and overpowering the serpent Kaliya, ca. 1400–1500, Tamil Nadu. Courtesy of the Asian Art Museum of San Francisco, The Avery Brundage Collection, B65B72. Image © Asian Art Museum of San Francisco.

When Krishna was a prepubescent boy living in a village on the banks of the river Yamuna, the river became poisoned by the great snake Kaliya who lived in its waters; the trees and vegetation on the river's banks were dying, as were the cattle that drank from its waters. One day Krishna and his friends were playing ball at the river's edge when the ball went into the dangerous waters. To the dismay of his friends, Krishna jumped into the river to retrieve it. Amidst tumultuous waters indicating a battle, he emerged victorious, dancing on the hood of Kaliya.

The sculpture catches a moment of control, balance, and grace – a visual theology of the god revealing who he truly is. The narrative continues (and is portrayed in some lithographs and miniature paintings) with Kaliya's wives coming out of the water to beg Krishna for mercy, not to kill their husband. In his compassion, Krishna realizes that it is the very nature of the snake to emit poison; he agrees not to kill Kaliya, but rather banishes him to the ocean where his poison can be more easily absorbed. His footprint on Kaliya's hood is said to protect the snake from his natural enemy, Garuda the eagle.

Permanent sculptures and temporary clay festival images of Durga also imply her narratives. Also known as Mahishasuramardini, she who has killed the demon Mahisha, the final moment of Durga's battle with Mahisha is often depicted in these visual representations, as she spears the demon who has taken buffalo form. Like the sculptural portrayal of Krishna's victory over Kaliya, Durga's victorious stance is one of balance. Ganesha's unusual elephant head embodies the narrative of his father Shiva beheading the young boy he finds guarding entrance to his own house and subsequently bringing him back to life by replacing his head with an elephant's head (full narrative in Chapter 1).

Lithographs, called "god pictures" in some Indian languages, often depict fuller narrative episodes than do sculptures of the deities. These lithographs (framed or as calendar art) are ubiquitous in Hindu businesses and homes, often as a part of domestic *puja* shrines. Like sculptural representations, lithographs of deities convey not only narratives, but also theology. For example, the two lithographs in Figures 2.2 and 2.3 visualize the narrative of the descent of the river goddess Ganga Devi (narrated below) in two very different ways, one in which Ganga is dominant and the other in which Shiva is most central. The story is the "same," but its visualizations create different theologies and experiences for the viewers.

The Tirupati *purana pandita* mentioned above performed the following story of the descent of Ganga in response to my enquiry about whether she knew any stories about the *gramadevata* Gangamma. While their names are similar, the two goddesses are distinct; and yet the storyteller describes Ganga Devi as having the same excessive force as Gangamma. Her orally performed narrative below reflects

Figure 2.2   Descent of Ganga lithograph; Bhagiratha lower right; no Shiva visible. (Early twentieth-century lithograph.)

Figure 2.3   Shiva lithograph showing (lower right) Bhagiratha sitting in front Shiva *linga*, performing penance to call down Ganga. (Late twentieth-century lithograph.)

the theology of the lithograph in Figure 2.2, which is goddess-oriented, rather than the one in Figure 2.3, which is Shiva-centered.

There was a King Sagara who had 60,000 sons. He was performing a horse sacrifice when the horse was stolen by Indra (king of gods). Indra tied the horse up at Kapila Maharishi's hermitage (*ashram*). King Sagara's 60,000 sons started digging up the earth to find the horse. Their father warned that if they didn't find the horse and complete the sacrifice, their entire lineage would be destroyed. He sent his sons to every realm to search for the horse. Their digging caused a dreadful sound and the whole earth shook; all the 14 realms, seven above and seven below, were shaking; each of the four directions was crying; animals, snakes, and all living creatures were being killed. Bhu Devi (goddess of earth) went to Brahma to ask him to put a stop to this destruction. The god assured her that they would soon find the horse at Kapila Maharishi's *ashram*. The sons found the horse, thought the *rishi* had stolen it, and began to attack him; he opened his eyes and turned them into ashes.

When his sons didn't return, their father sent out his grand-sons, "Go find your fathers; they haven't come back." Five grand-sons went in search of their fathers, and they, too, died. But another grandson found the horse and the king was able to complete the sacrifice. The king wanted to purify all those who had died (by immersing their ashes in Ganga water). They were struggling in hell (*naraka*). So that the ancestors could reach *moksha* (liberation), someone had to bring Ganga down from heaven. Some of the (living) grandsons performed austerities, but they weren't able to bring her down; and they, too, died.

The last male in their lineage was Bhagiratha. He thought, "All my people are dead and I'm newly married [that is, without any sons yet to carry on his lineage]. Somehow or the other I need to bring Ganga down from heaven." He left his wife and kingdom in the care of his ministers and went to perform austerities. After many years, Brahma appeared to him and asked, "What do you want? Ask for any boon."[3] And he replied, "I want Ganga Devi to come down to earth and purify my fathers. They are struggling in hell and they need release (*moksha*)."

Brahma said, "I'll send Ganga. But who has the *shakti* (strength) to bear her? Only Shiva has that power; you'll have to perform austerities to call Shiva." So Bhagiratha performed austerities for many more years, and Shiva finally appeared to him. Shiva agreed to bear Ganga Devi as she made her descent to earth, to break her destructive flooding. But Ganga Devi taunted, "Will Shiva bear me?! Does he have the *shakti* to bear me? I will send him, too, to the underworld. It's not an easy thing to bear me. It's impossible." And she tried to stomp on Shiva, pushing him to the underworld. Shiva spread out his matted hair, protecting the earth. Ganga flowed down with a great sound, along with small and big fish, snakes, and other living things, including flowers, trees, and animals. As she fell from above, it was as though there was thunder, as though mountains were crashing down with great speed. Shiva tied her up in his hair and let out just one strand of hair, one small stream of Ganga's waters. Even this stream came down with great force and everything in the way flowed along with her. She reached the *ashram* of Kapila Rishi; and as soon as she touched the ashes of Bhagiratha's ancestors, they went to heaven, and Bhagiratha performed their last rites. [The narrative performance ended, as many do, by bringing the story into the present, with the performer asserting:] And today, too, Hindus immerse the ashes of their ancestors in the waters of the Ganga, so they may achieve immortality (shortened version of narrative as appears in Flueckiger 2013, 124–132).

---

[3] The performance of austerities (*tapas*) and the power it generates creates instability in the world and is potentially dangerous, so the god asks what Bhagiratha wants, so that he will stop his ascetic practices.

During the violent flooding of the Ganga River as she descended from the high Himalayas in June 2013, which wreaked havoc on the mountains and their inhabitants, an image of Shiva that had been installed in the Ganga River at the pilgrimage town of Rishikesh (where the great river enters the plains from the mountains) was destroyed by the raging river. The image (depicting the god seated in meditation) was a relatively new, approximately 15-foot-high, construction sitting on a platform that extended from the river bank into the middle of the river. The collapse of the image under the onslaught of the river was an event significant enough for many Indian viewers that at least one television news show interrupted its programing with "breaking news" to report the collapse.[4] Some who witnessed the image battered by the rising waters of the river thought of the narrative above, of Ganga's first violent descent to earth. Many internet comments made reference to the power of Shiva (before the image collapsed), and then, after the collapse, some asserted that the god exists beyond his physical image; others commented on the power of the river goddess. However, scholar of religion Brian Pennington reports that in his interviews with local inhabitants after the flooding, the dominant narrative he heard was not mythological or cosmological, but one that faulted climate change, unregulated development, and government negligence for the degree of destruction the floods caused – forces that some Hindu internet commentators attributed to the Kaliyuga (the last of the four *yugas*, in which *dharma* is not – in fact, cannot be – fully observed).

While Hindus may hear oral performances of the narratives of their deities and references to these narratives are commonly made in idiomatic spoken conversation, proverbs, and songs, they do not rely solely on these for "knowing" their stories. Narrative visual images are all around them, in temples and shrines, on domestic walls and in *puja* shrines, in advertisements and labels of consumer products, entering their imaginations as though by osmosis. As A. K. Ramanujan has said about Ramayana and Mahabharata epic traditions, a Hindu

---

[4] Numerous still images and videos of the collapse of this Shiva image are available on the internet; these can be accessed through a Google search of "Shiva image Rishikesh flooding." Many of these sites include viewer comments about and interpretations of the collapse of the image of Shiva.

never reads the story for the first time: "The stories are there, 'always already'" (1991, 46); and this statement can be extended to other well-known religious narratives recounted in this book.

Verbal and Visual Together

In many regions of India, oral and visual performances come together in traditions of scroll paintings, which are themselves considered to be sacred, like a deity and his/her shrine. In such scrolls, narratives are painted in episodic scenes and a professional storyteller points to the particular episode she/he is singing; some long scrolls are unrolled and rolled as the narrative proceeds, to reveal only the episode being performed; others are rectangular canvases that are rolled up only after the performance is complete. In Bengal, the scrolls are called *patas*; in Telangana, Cheriyal paintings; in Rajasthan, *pars*. The *pars* are large canvases (which can be as large as five to six feet wide and 16 to 20 feet long) that lay out the regional epics of Pabuji and Devnarayan in episodic panels that are arranged non-chronologically. Not all episodes that are performed are visualized, and not all that are painted on a scroll are sung during any single performance; the singer assumes audience knowledge of the key episodes of the epics.

Rajasthani *kavads*, brightly painted storytelling boxes (traditionally about two feet high) are similar to scroll paintings in the episodic character of their paintings, but on a much smaller scale. Their doors fold out in sections to reveal key moments of the Ramayana and the stories of Krishna from the Bhagavata Purana, each story on one side of the box's paneled doors. The doors fold in on themselves, "performing" the reflexive nature of many Hindu narratives.[5] The performer holds the box between his knees, pointing with a peacock

---

[5] Two examples of this narrative reflexivity taken from orally performed Ramayanas are: when the Ramayana figure of the monkey-formed Hanuman accidentally drops a ring into the ocean and dives down to retrieve it, he finds a whole pile of such rings from other Ramayanas; and when Ram tries to dissuade his wife Sita from accompanying him to his forest exile, she retorts that she must, that there's never been a Ramayana where Sita doesn't accompany him to the forest (Ramanujan 1991, 33).

Figure 2.4 Rajasthani *kavad*, closed and fully opened, revealing images of Rama, Lakshmana, and Sita in its deepest interior (main box 7.5 × 3 inches).

feather to the episode he is singing. The size of the boxes themselves implies an intimate, small audience – compared with the much larger painted narrative scrolls. At the end of the performance, the doors of a small "room" at the center and most interior space of the box are opened, to reveal the deities whose lives have been sung – Rama, his wife Sita, and brother Lakshmana – suggesting that (at the end of a narrative performance) one purpose of telling stories is to know and see god. Rajasthani scrolls and storytelling boxes are thus visual narratives, visual theologies, and traveling shrines. Some of these traditional modes of storytelling are losing favor to other media such as television and film; however, the *par* and *kavad* visual traditions are being kept alive (if not always their oral accompanying traditions) as products for foreign and domestic tourist consumption.

A newer genre through which many middle- and upper-class Hindu children in urban India and the Indian diaspora come to know Hindu deities and their mythologies is the Amar Chitra Katha (lit., "Immortal Picture Stories"; hereafter ACK) comic books (published in both regional Indian languages and English), founded in 1967.[6] The creator of ACK, Anant Pai, attributes his motivation for creating the comic series to have been a children's quiz show on television, in which the upper-class participants could answer questions about Greek mythology, but seemed to know little about their own Hindu mythologies (Pritchett 1995, 76). The range of topics that the comics narrate, now numbering in the hundreds, is wide-reaching: mythologies of specific deities; the epics of the Ramayana and Mahabharata; hagiographies of devotional poet-saints such as Andal, Mira Bai, and Surdas; biographies of Indian historical "heroes" such as Mahatma Gandhi and Ambedkar; stories of non-Hindu religious figures such as Buddha and Jesus; and well-known Indian folktales such as the Panchatantra.

Since its inception, Anant Pai's editorial vision for ACK has been influential in determining the subject matter of the comics and their artistic design and representation. He self-consciously attempted to create a national canon of mythological and historical heroes for Indian

---

[6] All the comics are first written in English and then, as demand is perceived, some are translated into Indian regional languages; but the primary sales are the English versions.

children, in which they could take pride. However, as Karline McLain has observed in her book *India's Immortal Comic Books* (2009), the ACK canon reflects a particular view of what it means to be Indian, and more specifically, what it means to be Hindu – who "counted" in India's history and how their stories should be told (52). McLain observes that the selection of heroes and their portrayal reflects a "modern," middle-class, upper-caste, and Vishnu-centered worldview (208), in which women are self-sacrificing and Islamic orthodoxy is an "enemy" (that is, there are "good Muslims" and "bad Muslims") (208). When ACK sales started dropping in the late 1980s and 1990s with the serialization of the Ramayana and Mahabharata on television (see below), the publisher of ACK, India Book House, decided to cease regular production of new issues and, instead, reprint earlier "best-sellers," both in their original form and in deluxe packaging of various thematic series.

While most Hindu children in India (with the exception of the quiz show participants mentioned above, and perhaps some of their English-educated upper-class cohort) already know many of the mythological stories they read in ACK through other means (including storytelling by their grandmothers, public festivals, and other mediums discussed in this chapter), for many children in the diaspora, the ACK have been the primary way through which they learn the stories of their deities. And the comics have become authoritative texts, homogenizing the wide number of regional-language and other context-specific variants of various stories that are available in Indian contexts.

Commercial mythological films are another popular venue for Hindu narrative performances – including the Ramayana and Mahabharata and *puranic* stories – as well as stories of contemporary lives in which deities intervene and perform miracles. In the latter category, a particularly influential film was the 1975 *Jai Santoshi Maa* [sic] ("Hail to the Mother of Satisfaction"). The film centered on the goddess Santoshi Ma, said to be the daughter of Ganesha and associated with his powers to remove obstacles, in this case obstacles toward contentment or satisfaction (*santosh*). At the time the movie was released, Santoshi Ma was a relatively "new" goddess in North India whose reputation had been growing for a decade before the release of the film through women's oral testimonies of her powers to bring contentment and the growing practice of Santoshi Ma's *vrat* (ritual vow) on Fridays. But her popularity grew exponentially with the wide viewing of the film. Philip Lutgendorf describes the opening of the film:

> The film opens with a still of a carved temple image of Santoshi Ma, stained red-orange with sindur (a paste made of vermilion and oil), and adorned with jewelry and fabric. The smoke of incense rises, and an unseen narrator announces:
>
> "The greatness of Santoshi Ma is limitless. Each devotee has extolled her greatness in a unique way. This film's story is likewise based on some religious books and on popular stories (*lok kathaem*). We hope that you will accept it in a proper spirit. Hail to Santoshi Ma!" (Lutgendorf 2002, 26).

Another example of this genre of film is the popular 1995 Telugu film titled *Ammoru* (lit., mother, in reference to a village goddess), which centers on the goddess and a human family in whose lives she directly intervenes. I was conducting fieldwork in the city of Hyderabad at the time of the film's release; for many viewers, attendance was a devotional act, and the theaters showing the film were packed. I heard many reports of audience members making ritual offerings to the goddess on screen or becoming possessed by the goddess at particularly powerful moments of the film, when the goddess reveals her full power. In this context, the boundaries between film and everyday life were permeable, and its viewing became a religious experience through which audience members took *darshan* (lit., sight) of and interacted with the goddess.

The internet is another source of narrative knowledge for many Hindus, primarily in diasporic communities where, in the absence of family elders who know and can transmit their traditions and the lack of ubiquitous narrative images and references in the dominant culture, some Hindus need help in performing domestic rituals and festivals and learning the narratives behind them. Summaries of most well-known Hindu narratives can be found on the internet, along with descriptions of festivals and rituals. This mode of transmission to a transnational audience tends to singularize the many regional, caste, and gendered variations of narrative and ritual.

Where Does the Narrative Lie?

Many Hindus who worship the visual image of a deity in sculpture or lithograph or hear the recitation of his/her story do not know the specific textual source (when it exists) from which the story is drawn; that is, although many Hindu narratives may have written sources, the stories circulate beyond, outside, and back into many of these textual traditions. These narratives exist in oral traditions *about* the narrative, their non-performative retellings, performance traditions (such as those described above), and recorded written texts (Sears and Flueckiger 1991, 6); and the three spheres often relate in interesting, complex ways. V. Narayana Rao uses the terms "recorded" and "received" texts to distinguish what is recorded on a page and what is received or heard by an audience when that text is performed orally, which often includes additions and commentary by the oral performer (2007, 114).

One example of the ways in which oral, written, and performance traditions interact, and an example of the distinction between recorded and received or performed texts, can be found in the performance of an episode from the Ramayana. In this episode – commonly portrayed in lithographs, sculptures, and dramatic performances – to demonstrate his devotion, the friend and helpmate of Rama, the monkey-imaged Hanuman, tears open his chest to reveal Rama and Sita seated in his heart. Many North Indian audiences assume this story of devotion is found in the sixteenth century text of Tulsidas's *Ramcaritmanas*, although it does not actually appear in the written text; but the oral tradition of the episode has entered many performances of that text (the received text). However, for the majority of Rama and Hanuman devotees who view the visual representation of this episode or hear its oral performance, the distinctions between oral, performance, and written traditions, or written and received texts, are not relevant.

Finally, for those narrative traditions that have written texts, Wendy Doniger has made a performative distinction between the interior and exterior of a text:

> To use the inside means to use the text in a fluid way, as we might use an oral text: to interrupt the recitation in order to ask about the

meaning … or to choose only appropriate passages to recite on a particular occasion. However, to use the outside of a text means to use it in a rigid way, to read or recite it without necessarily knowing its meaning at all, or to recite it with no regard for the choice of an appropriate message. …. Indeed, the "outside" of the text may be used even more rigidly. The book may be set down but never opened, making a silent statement about status or community …. (1991, 32)

A *purana pandita* usually places in front of her a text laid on a wooden book stand; and yet she may never actually read from it, but rather weave various *puranic* narratives together with her own commentary. The *Ramcaritmanas* physical text similarly appears on a book stand in some performance contexts, with ritual remains of flowers and/or vermilion powder staining its pages; or the text may be read, verse by verse, so rapidly from beginning to end (a process called *akhand* Ramayana, lit., Ramayana without breaks) that audience members can barely distinguish individual words and sentences. In the latter case, it is the sound and the ritual efficacy of recitation that is most important, rather than the content of the recitation. These are instances of using the exterior of the text. On the other hand, members of one women's Ramayana recitation group (*mandali*) assert that everything they sing is in the *Ramcaritmanas*, but they use no physical text; and when they elaborate on Rama and Sita's wedding by singing local Chhattisgarhi wedding songs, the interior of the text is creatively performed. These variations in performed and received texts or the interior and exterior of a text are lost when we read only the written texts of Hindu narratives.

The Ramayana Tradition Performed

We shift now to a focus on the story and selected performance genres of the epic of the Ramayana as an example of the fluidity and creativity of Hindu narrative traditions. The Ramayana is the story of Rama – prince, hero, and the eighth incarnation (*avatara*) of the god Vishnu – that can be described more accurately as an epic *tradition* rather than a text. It is known and performed across India in numerous regional textual variants and oral and visual performance genres. It can be found in printed texts, heard through recitations and devotional songs, seen in theatrical enactments, dance, television serials and movies, and visualized in scroll paintings, sculptures, lithographs, and comic books. A. K. Ramanujan has characterized the Ramayana tradition as "almost a second language of the whole culture area ..." (1991, 45–46); like a language, it is fluid, finds many forms, and is used creatively.

The basic story – which can be told in a few sentences, a few hours, or even over the period of 30 days (as is the case for one Ramlila annual performance in Varanasi) – is one of royal succession, palace intrigue, exile, kidnapping, battles with demons, and the triumphant return of Rama to his rightful throne. And for most Hindus, it is also understood to be the story of the deity Vishnu taking human form in order to restore *dharma* in a world threatened by the 10-headed Ravana, a learned king whose father was a Brahmin and mother a *rakshasa* (demon). A summary follows:

King Dasharatha was a righteous king who had no heir, and so he performed a great sacrifice that resulted in his three wives giving birth to four sons: Rama, Bharata, and the twins Lakshmana and Shatrughna. Meanwhile, in a neighboring kingdom, a baby girl was found in a plowed field by King Janaka; he named her Sita (lit., furrow) and raised her as his daughter. When she became of marriageable age, Sita's father held a *svayamvara*, a ritual during which she could choose her own husband. Her criterion was that her husband would be the man who would be able to lift her father's great bow, given to him by Shiva. The only suitor who could pass this test was Rama, and Rama and Sita were married.

When Dasharatha decided to cede his throne to his oldest son Rama, his wife Kaikeyi asked him to fulfill a boon he had earlier granted her: she demanded that Rama be sent into forest exile for 14 years and that her son Bharata be given the throne. Dasharatha was heartbroken, but felt he had no choice but to be true to his earlier promise.

Rama, his brother Lakshmana, and (with great reluctance on her husband's part) Sita accompanied him to the jungle. For his part, Bharata was horrified at his mother's manipulations and agreed to serve only as a regent, not king. The threesome in exile had many adventures in the jungle, including battles with various demons who threatened the sacrifices of the sages who lived in the forest. One of these demons was Surpanakha, sister of the great king of Lanka, the ten-headed Ravana. She approached the two brothers, attempting to seduce them; when she was rejected and then threatened to kill Sita, Lakshmana humiliated her by taunting her and cutting off her nose.

Ravana heard about this humiliation and vowed to defend his sister's honor and destroy Rama and Lakshmana. Through complicated manipulations involving disguising himself as a mendicant and sending a golden deer to distract Rama, he was able to kidnap Sita and carry her away to his palace in Lanka. There, he kept her guarded in one of his gardens, waiting for her to willingly marry him, since he had been cursed that his head would explode if he forced any woman to be his wife. Meanwhile, Rama and Lakshmana realized that they had been duped and set out to find Sita. In their search, they met Sugriva, the ruler of a monkey kingdom, and his general, Hanuman. Hanuman, who has special powers of flight, strength, and changing size, offered to fly over the ocean to Lanka to locate Sita and to assure her Rama was on his way to rescue her.

There were many battles between Ravana's armies and Rama's monkey- and bear-army allies (the Ramlila dramatic enactments of the narrative love to depict these battles). Finally, Rama and Ravana came face-to-face. Rama proceeded to cut off Ravana's heads, one after the other, but a new head sprouted in their place, and he did not die. Rama was perplexed. Some versions narrate that Ravana had once practiced a severe form of asceticism (in

Hindu myths, demons, too, can practice asceticism), for which the god Brahma had rewarded him the nectar of immortality, to be housed in his navel. Only when Rama learned this secret from Ravana's brother Vibhishana and proceeded to strike Ravana in his navel did the great demon king die.

After Ravana's defeat, Sita was brought into Rama's presence. However, thinking that she had lived in the palace of another man, before Rama was willing to accept her back, he forced her to undergo a test of purity by entering a fire (the test of *agnipariksha*); protected by the god of fire himself, Agni, Sita emerged unscathed. And the couple returned to the capital Ayodhya amidst great celebrations, where Rama reclaimed his throne and *dharma* was reestablished in the realm.

Some variants of the Ramayana narrative end here. Others variants continue, as follows:

Sita soon became pregnant. However, Rama heard whisperings from his subjects about her potential lack of faithfulness while in captivity in Lanka, and he decided that to maintain *dharmic* order in his kingdom, he must banish Sita to the jungle. He deputed Lakshmana to take Sita to the jungle on the pretense of an outing and then to leave her there. Alone in the jungle, Sita eventually found her way to the *ashram* of Valmiki, the composer of the Ramayana, where she gave birth to her twin sons. Raised in the *ashram*, they learned from Valmiki to sing the narrative of their own father (the Ramayana). Their performance reputation grew and Rama called them to his court to sing for him. Only as they began singing his own story did Rama recognize his sons. He called Sita to his presence with the intention of reinstalling her as queen and wife; but he required one more test of fidelity from her, at which point she prayed to the earth to swallow her as proof of her faithfulness and purity.

Valimiki's Ramayana: The first textual source we have for the Ramayana narrative is said to have been composed as the first Sanskrit *kavya* (poem) by the poet Valmiki between 200 BCE and 200 CE. Regional language textual versions often refer to their texts as "translations" of Valmiki or otherwise refer to it as a source. While most variants of the Ramayana follow a shared narrative grammar with that of Valmiki, there are often significant narrative and theological differences in these Ramayanas; and some performative variants purposefully defy that grammar to suggest very different ideologies and politics to those of the dominant Sanskrit and regional-language written Ramayana texts.

Tulsidas's Ramcaritmanas: The dominant textual tradition of the North Indian plains is the composition of the sixteenth-century poet Tulsidas, the *Ramcaritmanas* (lit., lake of the acts of Rama). This is an explicitly devotional text whose purpose is to praise Rama as a god, and many ambiguities and complexities in Rama's character found in earlier textual traditions such as Valmiki are smoothed over or omitted. Chanting and hearing the *Ramcaritmanas* creates religious merit for performers and their audiences. In the context of *akhand Ramayana*, in which the text is recited without stopping, its content is secondary to its ritual benefit. Another performance genre called *katha* (lit., story) focuses on under-standing, as the performers provide elaborate exegesis and commentary to various verses and narrative episodes (Lutgendorf 1991, 84).

Ramlilas: A popular performance genre in Hindi-speaking regions, often authoritatively attributed to Tulsidas's text, is the dramatic form of Ramlilas (lit., the play of Rama) performed during the festival of Dashera. The actors are treated as gods (*swarups*), and particular scenes are often held in suspension to enable audience members to come forward and worship Rama, Sita, Lakshmana, and Hanuman. At these moments, the boundary lines between theater and audience are permeable. Similarly erasing the boundaries of performance and the social world of its audiences, in one village Ramlila performance, at the moment when King Dasharatha was performing his sacrifice for progeny, infertile women in the village came forward to partake of the sacrificial remains (a sweet pudding) in hopes that they, too, would become pregnant.

Everyday language: Fragments of Ramayana themes and images also enter proverbs, many folksongs, and everyday conversation. For example, the term Ramraj (lit., the rule of Ram) may be used to refer to good governance or an effective, ethical government. The phrase *lakshman rekha* – referring to the line that Lakshmana drew around the forest hermitage to protect Sita when he left her alone to find Rama, whose voice they had heard calling out for help – is used in everyday language to refer to any kind of "line" that shouldn't be crossed. For example, the phrase has been used to refer to politicians who are "crossing the line" in their behavior or in their comments about another politician (see, among many others, the English-language newspaper *The Times of India*'s 2014 article with the headline "BJP hits back at Mamata, says she is crossing 'lakshman rekha'"). The phrase has also found its way into discussion of male violence against women in an *Economic and Political Weekly* article titled "Men and Their Lakshman Rekha" (Roy 2013).[7]

Two Telugu proverbs serve as examples that rely on knowledge of the Ramayana, even though its characters are not named. The first is: Divulge the secrets of a house, you will destroy the house. This makes reference to Ravana's brother Vibhishana revealing to Rama the secret of the nectar of immortality housed in Ravana's belly, a revelation that ultimately led to the downfall of Lanka. The second is: Ask him to go look and tell you; he goes, burns it, and comes back. This proverb is used in contexts where an assistant or servant (positively) exceeds the requests of his/her superior; its understanding depends on knowledge of the Ramayana episode in which Hanuman was sent by Rama to find Sita in Lanka. Hanuman did so, but he did much more; he also set Lanka on fire.[8]

---

[7] The day I wrote this paragraph on *lakshman rekha*, I went to an Atlanta Indian grocery store and saw a packet at the checkout counter with a label that read Lakshman Rekha; the checkout clerk explained the packet contained a powder that deterred cockroaches from crossing it.

[8] I thank V. Narayana Rao for these orally transmitted examples.

Female-centered Ramayana performances: While written textual traditions of the Ramayana give us primarily male perspectives on the actions described, women perform Ramayana songs, narratives, and recitations that offer female perspectives. For example, in Raipur and other Chhattisgarhi towns, women's Ramayana *mandalis* (groups) gather regularly to perform the epic story as they understand and experience it.[9] One kind of *mandali* takes place in the homes of upper-caste women who sponsor the performance in fulfillment of a vow, in celebration of a birth or marriage, or for "passing time;" they come from families that may own a copy of the *Ramcaritmanas* or that have sponsored textual readings of the epic by a Brahmin *pandit* – that is, who participate in the literary tradition of Tulsidas. While these women assert that they are singing the "Ramayana of Tulsidas," there is no visible text and one well-known performer told me that what she was singing could be found in no text. A given afternoon's performance focuses on a particular short episode of the narrative, expanding its *bhava* (emotion) through repetition of a chosen refrain, inclusion of wedding and birth folksongs at appropriate moments, elaboration of the episode from a female character's point of view, and performance of devotional songs from outside the narrative itself. One lead singer explained that the women sang parts of the story of which they were most fond and with which they could most closely identify: birth, marriage, issues of family dynamics, and devotion to Rama. Significantly, these did not include battle scenes or the episode from some textual traditions in which Rama banishes his pregnant wife Sita to the jungle in order to quiet rumors that she had had sexual relations with Ravana during her captivity. The elderly woman simply said, "We don't sing that part because we don't think god would have done that [unfairly exile his pregnant wife]."

The second and increasingly popular context for women's *mandalis* in urban Chhattisgarh is temple courtyards, scheduled for a given day each week. Here, the physical text of the *Ramcaritmanas*

---

[9] This section about Chhattisgarhi women's *mandali* performances is drawn from Flueckiger 1991; however, I have observed these kinds of *mandalis* in recent years.

is the center of the performance, with several copies lying open on book stands, so that participants can follow along. The *mandalis* sing through the entire epic, a few verses (seven, nine, or 11) each week, until it is finished and then they start again. *Mandali* members take turns introducing a particular tune to which the group will sing the verses that follow; the sung verses are interspersed with the reading of a colloquial Hindi commentary printed beneath them, or, if there is a woman so qualified, the commentary may be given extemporaneously in the local Chhattisgarhi dialect, drawing upon relevant images and issues of everyday life. Women's voices are also heard in wedding and birth songs that focus on Ramayana themes and characters; for example, a bride and groom may be compared to the "ideal" couple Rama and Sita, or birth songs may reference Sita giving birth to her twins in the jungle.

While some traditional female-centered, female performance genres such as folk songs are losing popularity with increasing rates of female literacy and the ubiquitous presence of televisions even in lower-class homes, new forms that offer female perspectives are emerging through written poetry, novels, film, and essays in women's magazines. A recent example is the graphic novel *Sita's Ramayana*, published in 2011, which tells the story from Sita's perspective. The author, Samhita Arni, draws on a Bengali sixteenth-century variant of the epic composed by Chandrabati, who herself likely drew on women's songs and stories. The graphics of the book were drawn by Bengali scroll painter Moyna Chitrakar, who adapted the traditional scroll painting art to fit the contours of a printed book. Another example is the animated film *Sita Sings the Blues*, released in 2008, that weaves together Sita's perspective of her ordeal of testing by fire and banishment to the jungle in the Ramayana with the contemporary break-up story of the writer, animator, and producer Nina Paley (the film is available for viewing on sitasingstheblues.com).

TV Serialization of the Ramayana: One of the most influential variants of the Ramayana in contemporary Hinduism is the 1987–1988 television serialization, still available and widely viewed in video format. An episode was aired every Sunday morning over 78 weeks, when it seemed as if India "shut down" while millions were sitting in front of the television; the original series was followed by a sequel of another 26 episodes. This was at a time when televisions were still a luxury in most homes, and neighbors without televisions would gather, seated on the floor, in front of televisions in their wealthier neighbors' homes. The television was often garlanded as Rama first appeared on screen, incense was lit, and at the end of the hour-long show, *arati* (flame offering) was performed; for many, viewing this serial was a *religious* event. A simultaneous audience was created throughout India by virtue of the popularity of the narrative itself and the fact that there was, at that time, only a single government-supported television channel (Doordarshan). The television narrative was created by Ramanand Sagar, who drew its primary inspiration from the Hindi *Ramcaritmanas*, but it also included elements of Valmiki's Ramayana and other regional variants of the epic.

Philip Lutgendorf observes that the *style* of the television version was similar to other more traditional Ramayana performance genres, such as the narration style of *katha*, in which "the source text serves merely as an anchor for an improvised verbal meditation that may include almost endless digressions and elaborations" (1995, 227). And like the dramatic performances of Ramlilas, the television version was episodic, slow-moving, and sometimes came to a "stop" in order that its viewers could take *darshan* of its divine characters as they "posed" in a still tableau. Periodically, the camera zoomed in to focus on the face of Rama or Sita, pulled back out, and zoomed in again, with appropriately dramatic music accompanying these sequences. Lutgendorf writes, "The emphasis in *Ramayan* [the televised version] was squarely on 'seeing' its characters … drinking in and entering into visual communication with epic characters" (1995, 230).

The television serialization created a new and powerfully influential version that for many Hindus became *the* authoritative version; like the comic books discussed above, this medium singularized the epic story for many of its viewers who lived in contexts in which they were not exposed to its many variants. Videotapes of each episode became readily available in Indian grocery and video stores throughout the diaspora, and many parents relied (and continue to do so) on these, like they did and do with the ACK comic books, to introduce their children to a narrative tradition that they, as children growing up in India, simply "knew" because it was visually and verbally "all around them."

*****

Some variations and performance genres of Hindu narratives described above are shifting, even being lost altogether, with the emergence of expanding literacy, contemporary media, middle-class values and sensibilities, and globalization. However, narratives such as the Ramayana continue to be flexible and responsive to their newly forming narrative communities through new mediums and performance contexts; and for the majority of Hindus, visual and oral narrative performances, rather than the "book," continue to be the mediums through which they come to know the stories of their deities and help to create their theologies.

References

Arni, Samhita, and Moyna Chitrakar. 2011. *Sita's Ramayana*. Toronto: Groundwood Books.

Doniger, Wendy. 1991. Fluid and Fixed Texts. In *Boundaries of the Text: Epic Performances in South and Southeast Asia*, eds. Joyce Burkhalter Flueckiger and Laurie J. Sears, 31–41. Ann Arbor: Center for South and Southeast Asian Studies, University of Michigan.

Flueckiger, Joyce Burkhalter. 1991. Literacy and the Changing Concept of Text: Women's Ramayana *Mandali* in Central India. In *Boundaries of the Text*, eds. Joyce Burkhalter Flueckiger and Laurie J. Sears, 44–60. Ann Arbor: Center for South and Southeast Asian Studies, University of Michigan.

Flueckiger, Joyce Burkhalter. 2013. *When the World Becomes Female: Guises of a South Indian Goddess*. Bloomington: Indiana University Press.

Lutgendorf, Philip. 1991. *The Life of a Text: Performing the Ramcharitmanas of Tulsidas*. Berkeley: University of California Press.

Lutgendorf, Philip. 1995. All in the (Raghu) Family: A Video Epic in Cultural Context. In *Media and the Transformation of Religion in South Asia*, eds. Lawrence Babb and Susan Wadley, 217–253. Philadelphia: University of Pennsylvania Press.

Lutgendorf, Philip. 2002. A Superhit Goddess/A Made-to-Satisfaction Goddess: *Jai Santoshi Maa* and Caste Hierarchy in Indian Films. *Manushi: A Journal about Women and Society* 131, 10–16: 24–37.

McLain, Karline. 2009. *India's Immortal Comic Books: Gods, Kings, and Other Heroes.* Bloomington: Indiana University Press.

Narayana Rao, V. 2007 [2004]. *Purana.* In *The Hindu World*, eds. Sushil Mittal and Gene Thursby, 97–115. New York: Routledge.

Paley, Nina. 2008. *Sita Sings the Blues.* http://sitasingstheblues.com/watch. html (accessed September 2014).

Pritchett, Frances W. 1995. The World of *Amar Chitra Katha.* In *Media and the Transformation of Religion in South Asia*, eds. Lawrence A. Babb and Susan S. Wadley, 76–106. Philadelphia: University of Pennsylvania Press.

Ramanujan, A. K. 1991. Three Hundred Ramayanas: Five Examples and Three Thoughts on Translation. In *Many Ramayanas: The Diversity of a Narrative Tradition in SouthAsia*, ed. Paula Richman, 22–49. Berkeley: University of California Press.

Richman, Paula, ed. 1991. *Many Ramayanas: The Diversity of a Narrative Tradition in SouthAsia.* Berkeley: University of California Press.

Roy, Rahul. 2013. Men and Their Lakshman Rekha. *Economic and Political Weekly.* XLVIII: 8. Mumbai.

Sears, Laurie J. and Joyce Burkhalter Flueckiger,. 1991. Introduction. In *Boundaries of the Text: Epic Performances in South and Southeast Asia*, ed. Joyce Burkhalter Flueckiger and Laurie J. Sears, 1–16. Ann Arbor: Center for South and Southeast Asian Studies, University of Michigan.

Times of India. May 10, 2014. BJP hits back at Mamata, says she is crossing "lakshman rekha." Delhi.

Recommended Readings

Rinehart, Robin. 2004. Hearing and Remembering: Oral and Written Texts in Hinduism. In *Contemporary Hinduism: Ritual, Culture, and Practice*, ed. Robin Rinehart, 67–98. Santa Barbara: ABC-CLIO, Inc.

Whitmore, Luke. 2012. The Challenges of Representing Shiva: Image, Place, and Divine Form in the Himalayan Hindu Shrine of Kedarnath. *Material Religion* 8, 2: 216–243.

3

Loving and Serving God: *Bhakti, Murtis,* and *Puja*

Bhakti, Devotion

The primary mode of worshipping god or the goddess in contemporary Hindu traditions is through practices of *bhakti* (devotion). The word *bhakti* is derived from the Sanskrit verbal root *bhaj*, literally, to share; and it has come to mean sharing in the divine presence, entering a relationship with a loving, compassionate deity. Historically, *bhakti* traditions developed in what is called the medieval period (circa the seventh to seventeenth centuries CE), in response, in part, to Vedic *brahminic*, ritual religion conducted in Sanskrit from which women and low castes were excluded, in favor of the possibilities of unmediated access to the deity. However, it is important to point out that Hindu traditions tend to be aggregative; that is, while new traditions and modes of expression may be added, older ones are rarely totally dropped, so that Vedic rituals are still part of Hindu practices even after the development of *bhakti* traditions.

Everyday Hinduism, First Edition. Joyce Burkhalter Flueckiger.
© 2015 Joyce Burkhalter Flueckiger. Published 2015 by John Wiley & Sons, Ltd.

One of the primary ways in which *bhakti* was articulated and pro-
mulgated was through songs composed in regional languages by
"poet-saints" (Hindi, *sants*; Alvars in Tamil Srivaishnava tradition;
Nayanmars in Tamil Shaiva tradition). Songs of the poet-saints
continue to be sung today in both domestic and temple contexts; and
many of these poet-saints have themselves been deified and their
images appear in some temples.[1] Their poetry describes the beauty and
physical characteristics of deities who have such qualities (*saguna*) or
the nature of the deity without physical qualities (*nirguna*), the deities'
stories, and/or the emotional quality of the poet's relationship with the
deity. Almost any emotion has the potential for creating intimacy with
the deity: the pain of separation from the god (when he is imagined as
a lover), the love a mother feels for her child, the sheer joy of gazing
at the beauty of the deity, and arguments with or teasing the deity. A
few examples of the kinds of relationships with the deity expressed
by *bhakti* poets and the emotional quality of their songs follow.

The Tamil poet Appar (circa 570–670 CE) describes the beauty of
Shiva in his manifestation as Nataraja, King of Dance:

> If you could see
> the arch of his brow
> the budding smile
> on lips red as the kovvai fruit
> cool matted hair,
> the milk-white ash on coral skin,
> and the sweet golden foot raised up in dance,
> then even human birth on this wide earth would be a thing worth
>   having.
>
> (Peterson 1989, 118)

Fifteenth-century Telugu poet Annamayya sings of the mutually
dependent relationship between god and human, teasing the god
by asking "imagine that I wasn't here?"

---

[1] For example, the Alvar female saint Andal (whose *murti* is distinguishable by the
side hair bun she wears) appears in many Srivaishnava temples, including the
Hindu Temple of Atlanta, where she is one of Sri Venkateshvara's two wives and is
also considered to be an incarnation of Bhu Devi (goddess of earth).

Imagine that I wasn't here. What would you do with your kindness?
You get a good name because of me.

I'm number one among idiots. A huge mountain of ego.
Rich in weakness, in giving in to my senses.
You're lucky you found me. Try not to lose me.

>   *Imagine that I wasn't here.*

I'm the Emperor of Confusion, of life and death.
Listed in the book of bad karma.
I wallow in births, womb after womb.
Even if you try, could you find another like me?

>   *Imagine that I wasn't here.*

Think it over. By saving someone so low,
you win praise all over the world.
You get merit from me, and I get life
out of you. We're right for each other,
god on the hill.

>   *Imagine that I wasn't here.*

> (Narayana Rao and Shulman 2005, 27)

In a very different voice, North Indian sixteenth-century poet Surdas relies on Krishna mythology in the poem in which he sings in the voice of Krishna's mother, Yashoda. She urges her toddler Krishna (here called Gopal) to drink some milk, promising him that if he does, his hair will grow and he will be strong like the other boys in the village. Her voice is filled with maternal love and joy in her child; and one form of love between god and devotee can be this maternal love (*vatsalya bhakti*).

"If you drink the milk of the black cow, Gopal,
    you'll see your black braid grow.
Little son, listen, among all the little boys
    you'll be the finest, most splendid one.

75

> Look at the other lads in Braj and see:
> > it's milk that brought them their strength.
> So drink: the fires daily burn in the bellies
> > of your foes – Kans and Kesi and the crane."
> He takes a little bit and tugs his hair a little bit
> > to see if his mother's telling lies.
> Sur says, Yashoda looks at his face and laughs
> > when he tries to coax his curls beyond his ear.
>
> (Hawley and Juergensmeyer 1988, 105)

In contemporary Hinduism, *bhakti* practices are the dominant mode of worship. The goals of *bhakti* rituals are to establish an intimate relationship with the deity; or, through serving the deity, to gain her/his favor so she/he may then intervene in a positive way in the human lives of devotees. Devotional acts create good *karma* and the deities to which they are offered can crosscut and reverse the karmic cycle of action and its consequences (see Chapter 6 for *vrats* [ritual vows] as a mode of *bhakti* that produces tangible results).

Singing to God and the Goddess

One way to establish a relationship with the deity, love and worship him/her, and evoke his/her blessings is to sing to him/her in genres called *bhajans or kirtans* (sometimes these words are conflated and other times distinguished by content or performance context; I will use the term *bhajan* hereafter). Many *bhajans* are the sung poetry of the poet-saints mentioned above; others repeat over and over the names of a particular god. While *bhajans* may be sung alone by individuals, their performance is most often a communal activity that helps to create a devotional community; they may be performed in front of images (*murtis*) of a deity in domestic or temple contexts, or without the *murti*. In communal contexts, *bhajans* are performed in a call-and-response style in which a lead singer sings out a line that is then repeated by the group. Individual lines may be repeated over and over, with the aim of intensifying the emotional (often ecstatic) quality of the relationship with the deity, rather than to communicate "content."[2] The use of instruments (such as drums – *tabla*, *pakhawaj*, or *mridangam* – cymbals, and harmonium) augments the emotional intensity of *bhajan* ritual performances.

Bhajans can adapt longer narrative and poetic traditions, such as Tulsidas's *Ramcaritmanas* or *Hanuman Chalisa* (praise poem to Hanuman), to this devotional call-and-response style. For example, many women's Ramayana *mandalis* (singing groups) in Chhattisgarh sing through the entire Tulsidas text over the period of many months, with its verses interspersed with lines of *bhajans*. The *Ramcaritmanas* verses relating the episode of Rama asking a boatman to take him across a river, for example, are interspersed with the Chhattisgarhi *bhajan* lines: "On the banks of the Yamuna River, Rama called to the boatman, 'Brother, bring the boat to the bank.'" Other episodes are interspersed with simple praise lines such as "Praise to Lord Ganapati," "Praise to Lord Hanuman," "Praise to Santoshi Mata" (the latter is an interesting inclusion given that this goddess does not appear in the Ramayana narrative) (Flueckiger 1991). After every three or four verses, a Hindi commentary that is included in printed texts of the *Ramcaritmanas* is read; or, if the *mandali* leader is qualified, she gives an extemperaneous Chhattisgarhi or Hindi commentary.

Worshipping Deities in Material Form

The primary mode of *bhakti* worship is through rituals offered to physical forms (*murtis*) that embody (or are the body of) a deity. The two most common Indian-language terms for the image of a deity, *murti* and *vigraham*, give us ways to begin to understand Hindu views of the physical mage.[3] A *murti* is, literally, anything that has a definite shape or form. When used to identify the image of a deity, the implication is that the *murti* is the shape, embodiment, or manifestation of a specific god or goddess. The term *vigraham* comes

---

[2]   In Indian Muslim traditions, a similar genre is *qavvali*.

[3]   The term *vigraham* is rarely used in everyday speech in the North, while it is more commonly used in the South. However, *murti* is also commonly used in the South in reference to festival images (*utsava murtis*) and the primary image of a temple (*mula murti*).

from the Sanskrit verbal root *grh*, which means "to grasp, catch hold of." Thus, the material *vigraham* can be understood to be a form that enables the worshipper to "grasp hold of," know, and enter a relationship with the deity.

There are two primary Hindu interpretations of the nature of the physical image: the deity is there in physical form, or the form is a *representation* of the deity and a means through which human worshippers can imagine and concentrate upon god or the goddess but is not *actually* the deity. An example of the latter interpretation can be found in the ritual text of the *Vishnu Samhita*:

> Without a form (*vigraham*), how can God be meditated upon? If (He is) without any form, where will the mind fix itself? When there is nothing for the mind to attach itself to, it will slip away from meditation or will glide into a state of slumber. Therefore the wise will meditate on some form, remembering, however, that the form is a superimposition and not a reality (cited in Eck 1998, 45)

Worshippers at The Hindu Temple of Atlanta often explain to non-Hindu visitors (including many university students), if the topic comes up, that the image is only something to concentrate on through which one can show reverence to the god, and that the worshippers are not actually worshipping the physical *image*. These kinds of statements are made, in an American context in which Christian and Jewish views of image worship are dominant, to help non-Hindus "make sense" of what they are seeing (note that in India itself, few Hindus, Muslims, or Christians would ask a Hindu what the image means since images are around them all the time and they have their own assumptions). But when one observes these same Hindus feed their *murtis* at home or temple priests massage the limbs of a temple *murti* with oil, the rituals seem to imply that the *murti* is more than a symbol or point of concentration.

The more common interpretation of the *murti* is that it is a literal embodiment of the deity. The deity is willing, through his/her grace, to take this manifest form, a form which is dependent upon the worship of the devotee, in order to make him/herself accessible to the devotee. For example, in the Vaishnava text *Paramasamhita*, the god Brahma asks Vishnu:

> You have told me that the Highest God Vishnu is the ultimate cause of creation. ... Then how should humans worship him and meditate on him? For he is not ever limited by any conditions, and his form cannot be ascertained through direction, place, time, or shape. So how should one who hopes to be successful worship Him?
>
> [Vishnu answers] He can be worshiped in embodied form only. There is no worship of one without manifest form. ... Thanks to my benevolence toward all beings, there are manifest forms of Vishnu, intended for the purpose of ritual action. Therefore humans should construct the Imperishable One in human form and worship him with utmost devotion, in order to gain success (cited in Davis 1999, 30).

In Srivaishnava traditions, the temple image is called the *arca avatara*, literally, the "incarnation in a worshipable form."

Speakers of Indian English usually translate *murti* or *vigraham* as "idol," and this term is commonly used in American temple brochures and on their websites. When Hindus use the term, they are thinking *murti* or *vigraham*; but when non-Hindu English speakers hear the term, they are likely to think "idolatry," a pejorative term. It is possible that Hindus born and brought up in American and other English-speaking diasporic communities and whose first language is English may, over time, internalize this negative view of image worship and their experience may come to be that they are not actually *worshipping* the image, but that it is a symbol, focal point for concentration and meditation. Because no English word fully connotes this interpretation of the physical image as a *living* form, I prefer to use the indigenous term *murti* even when speaking English, rather than English translations such as image, statue, idol – none of which connote a living entity (perhaps the closest translation would be icon, as the term is used by Eastern Orthodox Christians).

Narratives of God in the *Murti*

Numerous oral traditions narrate the complexities and multivalency of the relationship between the *murti* and deity, implying that she/he is both in and beyond her/his physical image. For example, one common narrative motif is of a wounded god whose physical *murti* bears the scars of that wound. The *murti* of the god Simhadri Appanana (the local name for the man-lion [Narasimha] incarnation of Vishnu) in Simhacalam, Andhra Pradesh, carries such a wound. A local story tells of the god in his boar *avatara* (Varaha) rooting in a forest when he was struck by a hunter's arrow. When the hunter realized, too late, that the boar was god, he applied a balm to the wound, but it never fully healed. And today, the temple *murti* carries that wound, which is covered with soothing sandal paste throughout the year, except for one day when the paste is totally removed and the wound is visible (Handelman, Krishnayya, and Shulman 2013, 141). Another common narrative motif identifies the *murti* with the god when a devotee asks a deity, as present in a *murti*, to indicate his/her answer to a particular question – often asking the deity for permission to do something – by dropping a flower from his/her *murti* form.

A Rajasthani narrative performed during a female *vrat* (vow) ritual similarly performs some of these complex dynamics between god and image (Gold 1994, 166–167).[4] A summary follows:

> There was a Brahmin girl who used to worship the *murti* of the deity Ganesha every day; but instead of using traditional "pure" devotional offerings, she used fire from the cremation ground and butter from Ganesha's own navel (both items considered to be polluting). Ganesha was pleased, however, with her devotion; and responding with a joke, he put his

---

[4] Gold tells the story as an illustration of the power of women's devotion and the use of *purdah* (lit., curtain) to create a space for women to act (167–168).

finger on his nose (trunk). Now when a *murti* moves and changes his/her iconography, it is considered very inauspicious, and the worried villagers went to report this to the local king. He, in turn, called on Brahmin priests from Varanasi to perform powerful sacrifices to remedy the situation. However, none of their rituals were efficacious; Ganesha's finger stayed on his nose. The Brahmin girl asked her mother-in-law to go to the king and ask what he would give to her if she could cause Ganesha to move his finger. The king promised many villages and to make the girl "great."

The Brahmin girl asked that a curtain be placed in front of the *murti*. The girl first made her (polluting) offerings to the god, reminded him of her devotion, and then threatened him: "Now take your finger down; if you don't, then I will take this stick and break your icon into little pieces" (166). Ganesha laughed and acknowledged her devotion; he took down his finger and auspicious flowers rained down from above. The king fulfilled his promise and gifted the girl five villages.

The storyteller ends her performance saying, "O Lord, Great Ganeshji, as you satisfied that Brahmin girl, so satisfy me, and satisfy the world, O Lord" (167).

This narrative provides an indigenous commentary on the nature of the *murti*: it is alive, it can move, it has agency; god is there, but he is not *only* there – to destroy the *murti* may be disrespectful (although in this story, Ganesha is amused by the threat of his *murti's* destruction), but its destruction would not destroy god.

Another narrative (with many oral and written variants) that confirms the presence of the deity in the image is the well-known story of the (circa ninth-century) South Indian female saint Andal (the only female among the 12 Alvar Srivaishnava poet-saints). Andal was raised in the family of a priest who served Vishnu at a local temple and whose responsibilities included making and offering flower garlands daily to the god. Andal grew up imagining herself to be Vishnu's bride, and, unbeknownst to her father, used to try on Vishnu's garlands before they were offered to the god. One day her father noticed a long black hair in the garland he was about to put on the god. This hair would have been considered polluting and Andal's father scolded her for trying on the garland, begged the god's pardon, threw the polluted garland away, and made a new one for that day. However, the god refused the new garland and asked for the "polluted" one, whose scent he preferred and that had been worn by Andal in such devotion. Then Andal's father realized the intensity of his daughter's devotion.

Andal's hagiography concludes with the Andal merging with the image of the god whom she considered her husband; the *murti* is the god, with the ability to take in (absorb) his human devotee. Similarly, the (circa sixteenth-century) North Indian poet-saint Mira Bai – who, like Andal, considered the god to be her husband – is said to have merged with the *murti* of Krishna in front of whom she was worshipping.

Finally, the oral tradition about the (circa eleventh-century) Telugu poet Bhimakavi provides another narrative commentary about the relationship between god and his image, in this case Shiva and his stone *linga*. Bhimakavi's mother was a widow who, seeing other pilgrims praying to the god Bhimeshvara-Shiva for certain boons, prayed for a son. The god complied and she gave birth to a son. However, because his mother was known to have no husband, the son was teased for being a bastard. He ran to his mother and threatened to hit her with a rock if she didn't tell him who his father was. She replied, "That rock in the temple is your father; go ask him." The boy then threatened the god in the temple, to hit *him* with a rock, if he didn't tell him who he was. The god appeared in his "true form" and acknowledged he was, indeed, the boy's father. The boy made the god promise that if this was true, then whatever he (the boy) said would come to pass. And so it came to be: whatever Bhimakavi pronounced came to be, but he was also able to take back those results with a simple verbal command (Narayana Rao and Shulman 1998, 11–13).

The Deity without Form

Critiques of image worship within Hindu traditions come primarily from two directions: philosophical schools such as Advaita Vedanta and *nirguna bhakti* poets who worship god without tangible qualities (*nirguna*, as opposed to *saguna*, with qualities), both of which continue to shape some contemporary Hindu views of the *murti*. These views range from the view that image worship is acceptable as a step on the path to full knowledge that does not require or depend on images, to objection to image worship as empty ritual (Davis 1999, 47).

Advaita Vedanta, Shankara: The leading proponent of Advaita Vedanta, the (circa eighth- or ninth-century) philosopher Shankara, argued (based on Upanishadic thought) for the singularity of all reality (without duality, *advaita*), including the created world and ultimate reality identified as *brahman*, which has no qualities. However, Shankara accepted that *brahman* could take on qualities in order to be accessible to humans for worship, that deities could take on bodies (*vigraham*) if they so choose. The goal of "a true aspirant to nondualist knowledge should [be to] turn progressively inward, toward ever more 'subtle' forms of practice, and finally to modes of mental practice that dispense altogether with the dualities of self and other, worshiper and worshipped, knower and known" (Davis 1999, 47–48). That is, Shankara argued, while image worship may be needed "on the way," ultimately it should not be necessary or even desired. This Vedantic view has been particularly influential in some North American diasporic families and communities.

Bhakti voices against empty ritual: The twelfth-century South Indian poet and social reformer Basavanna, who gave impetus to the development of what became the Virashaiva sect, objected to the idea that god could be fixed in one place through a temple *murti*. He affirmed Shiva as the supreme being, whose *linga* was the form through which to worship the deity; but the *linga*, like god himself, is not stable. Thus, Basavanna advocated that rather than keeping it in a temple, the *linga* (in miniature form) should be worn around the necks of devotees – that is, where it would be a moving form. One of Basavanna's poems mocks the wide range of everyday physical objects that were being worshipped as god, asserting at the end that there is only one god, Shiva, here called Lord of the Meeting Rivers.

> The pot is a god. The winnowing
> fan is a god. The stone in the
> street is a god. The comb is a
> god. The bowstring is also a god. The bushel is a god and the
> spouted cup is a god.
>
> Gods, gods, there are so many
> there's no place left for a foot.
>   There is only
> one god. He is our Lord
> of the Meeting Rivers.
>
>   (Ramanujan 1973, 28)

Another strong *bhakti* voice against image worship, as one among many empty ritualistic practices, can be found in the poetry of the fifteenth-century North Indian poet Kabir.

> Saints, I see the world is mad.
> If I tell the truth they rush to beat me,
> If I lie they trust me.
> I've seen the pious Hindus, rule-followers,
> Early morning bath-takers –
> Killing souls, they worship rocks.
> They know nothing.
> …
> And posturing yogis, hypocrites,
> Hearts crammed with pride,
> Praying to brass, to stones, reeling
> With pride in their pilgrimage,
> Fixing their caps and their prayer-beads,
> Painting their brow-marks and arm-marks
> Braying their hymns and their couplets,
> Reeling. They never heard of soul.
> …
> Kabir says, listen saints:
> They're all deluded!

Whatever I say, nobody gets it.
It's too simple.

(Hess and Singh 2002, 42–43)

Ironically, even as they were vociferous in their objections against institutional religion, the followers of Kabir and Basavanna have formed sects, known as Kabir Panth and Lingayyats (Virashaivas), respectively, and their ritual practices have become institutionalized.

Reform movements: In the nineteenth century, in response, in part, to British colonial critiques of Hindu practices, some Hindus made an effort to "reform" or transform Hindu traditions, to return to what they considered the more pure and ancient Vedic religion. They argued that later "accretions" to Vedic religion – such as *puranic* deities and narratives, image worship, festivals, and pilgrimage – were only "superstition" and that social customs such as child marriage and *sati* (immolation of widows on the funeral pyres of their husbands) were not true Hindu practices. The religion these reformers articulated was more in line with colonial, Christian worldviews and practices, even as they explicitly rejected Christianity. One major proponent of these reforms was the Bengali intellectual Ram Mohan Roy (1772–1833), who founded the Brahmo Samaj (Society). Dayananda Sarasvati (1824–1883), influenced by Roy, founded the Arya Samaj (particularly successful in its early years in Punjab, Northwest India), which made an effort to convert back to Hinduism low-caste converts to Christianity and Islam and had a wider geographic and social spread than did the Brahmo Samaj. Today, adherents of both Samaj groups do not worship *murtis*; however, the majority of Hindu communities were not immediately impacted by these reform movements, and worship of *murtis* is one of the dominant ways of worshipping and loving the deity.

Modes of Worshipping the *Murti*

We return now to dominant modes of worship of the deity as embodied in physical form, the *murti*, in homes and temples.

Enlivening a murti: Not every image of a deity is considered to be an embodiment of a deity; some are just that, images, such as sculptures in museums or the many Ganesha images, whose collection is so popular among middle-class Hindus, which hang on living room walls outside the *puja* shrine of these families. These images are treated respectfully, but are considered to be representations, rather than full embodiments, of the god or goddess; for example, I've observed Hindus at American museums respectfully fold their hands in *namaste* in front of the sculpture of a deity or touch their hands to his/her feet. Most of these museum sculptures were either at one time actively worshipped in temples or graced the outsides of temples, but now, without regular worship, the deity is not believed to be there – it is just an image, not god.

In *brahminic* traditions, before a *murti* is worshipped, a ritual called *pranapratishta* (lit., to establish the life-breath) is performed to call the god or goddess into the form. In temples, this is a one-time ritual for any given *murti*; in domestic *brahminic* rituals, the deity is called each time *puja* is performed. For temporary clay or plaster-of-paris festival images (such as those established for the festivals of Durga Puja or Ganesha Chaturthi), too, the deity is invoked by asking him/her to come take up residence in the image (*avahana*); and at the end of the ritual or festival, deities are "dismissed" or given permission to leave the form before the images are immersed in a body of water (*visarjana*). Further, it is assumed that the deity leaves even permanent images and lithographs that are damaged or fall into disuse; as a matter of respect, these are often taken to a temple, lining up against its walls, but are no longer actively worshipped.

However, the situation is less clear in non-*brahminic* traditions. These worshippers do not perform a specific ritual like *pranapratishta* to call the deity to the *murti* or lithograph being worshipped. Rather, the worshipper minimally garlands the image, offers it water, and/ or lights incense and/or an oil lamp in front of it: these rituals themselves may be interpreted as calling the deity, or they may assume the deity is already present at the moment of worship.

Worshipping the deity through adornment: Adornment of a *murti* is a form of devotion – a mode of loving god – and enables devotees to "see" and experience the nature of the deity. In domestic shrines, adornment may be simply with flowers or vermilion or turmeric powders; but some domestic *murtis* lend themselves to adornment through clothing and jewelry, such as Bala Krishna (the crawling baby *murti*). In small shops selling ritual accoutrements, for example, one can find sets of sequined clothing for baby Krishna, in different colors, with different styles of crowns and a tiny flute included in each packet; a worshipper may also purchase a swing or small throne for him to sit on. Temple-*murti* adornment is generally much more elaborate than that of domestic *murtis*. A particularly powerful moment in worshipping the deity in a temple is when, after the ritual of *abhishekam* (anointing with a series of liquids; see Chapter 4) of the *murti*, it is adorned by a priest behind a closed door or curtain, and after waiting expectantly, the curtain is drawn back and the worshippers see the fully adorned image (i.e., they "take *darshan*").

Figure 3.1 An adorned domestic *puja*-shelf, brass Bala Krishna (two inches high).

In Indian languages, the closest equivalent to the English word "ornament" is *alamkara*. The term is made of two Sanskrit verbal forms, *alam*/adequate and the verbal root *kr*/to make; so *alamkara* becomes "that which makes a thing adequate." Without *alamkara*, a *murti*, building (adorned through architectural features), or person is, by implication, inadequate or incomplete. *Alamkara* is not just an embellishment; it is integral to whatever it adorns. Adornment may create identities – such as when it, quite literally, "makes a bride" (see Chapter 7) – or its loss may entail loss of identity – such as when a widow breaks her bangles and takes off her ornaments. Similarly, *alamkara* of a deity both reflects and "makes" who she/he is or how she/he is known.

Certain deities are known to like certain kinds of adornment: At his home temple in Tirupati, Sri Venkateshvara is said to be adorned with up to 120 different jeweled and gold ornaments every day; on special days, the ornaments are all pearls, or diamonds, or rubies. Srinathji (Krishna) at Nathdvara, Rajasthan, is famous for his wide array of adornments and sets of clothing, and calendars often portray him in different *alamkara* every month. *Gramadevata* goddesses are often adorned (covered) with turmeric powder. Flower sellers at Gangamma's Tatayyagunta temple in Tirupati compared the turmeric application on the *murti* of the goddess to "make-up" (using the English word), explaining that it both beautifies the goddess and accentuates her features, enabling worshippers to more clearly "see" her. One female temple employee elaborated:

> *Pasupu* (turmeric) gives beauty and radiance to the face. Look at this stone. If you leave it just like this, it won't look good. Only when we do *alamkara* does she look like an auspicious woman (*muttaiduva*). Married women, too, wear *pasupu-kumkum* (Flueckiger 2013, 59).

The turmeric masking covers the fangs of Gangamma's stone-head images, and thus ameliorates her excessive and potentially destructive nature (*ugram*); it is said to make her *shantam* (peaceful, content). The comment above suggests that the application of turmeric not only beautifies, but has the potential to change the nature of the goddess, who is, in fact, not married and not traditionally identified as a *muttaiduva*.

The Services of *Puja*

The ritual of *puja* (sometimes called *seva*, or service, to the deity) – modeled after traditional hospitality shown to a guest or honored person (or, one could also say guests are treated as gods) – is offered to domestic deities every morning and/or evening and in temples throughout the day. The series of rituals performed to a deity vary from the textually prescribed elaborate 16 *upacharas* (services) performed in *puranic*-deity temples by temple priests, to a simple offering of water, flowers, and incense performed at domestic shrines. Domestic *pujas* may be very brief, lighting an oil lamp and incense, or elders of a family may spend an hour or two in front of their deities, offering *puja* and reciting ritual texts and the names of god. In temples, deities may be fed fruits and sweets, garlanded with flowers, offered *arati* (a flame offering), bathed and offered fresh clothes, offered a bed for rest, awakened with or served through song – and in some temples, on special occasions, served with performances of dance.[5] In all contexts, *puja* is accompanied by a worshipper's bodily gesture of humility (varying from a simple gesture of hands together in *namaste*, a deep knee bend

[5]   Dancing in temples fell out of practice with legislation (particularly the Madras Devadasi Act of 1947) outlawing the practice of dedicating women (*devadasis*, lit., servants of god; dancers, courtesans) to temples. Not all *devadasis* performed in temples; many performed in private salons and at public events such as weddings (Soneji 2012). While Indian legislation in the mid-twentieth century effectively curtailed *devadasi* performance, both within and outside *puranic* temples, the practice of dancing in the temple has recently been reintroduced in both Indian and American contexts. At numerous Indian *puranic* temples today, classical Indian dancers may perform in pavilions on the temple grounds. In some temples in United States, such as the Hindu Temple of Atlanta, on special festival days, dance has been reintroduced inside the temple itself as one of the *upacaras* offered to the deities.

holding ones ears [a sign of humility], bending one's head to the ground, to a full prostration). Many Hindus speaking English equate *puja* with the English term "prayer," a term with which non-Hindus will be more familiar. However, while one may pray while performing *puja*, the ritual is unique and implies making tangible offerings to the image of a deity.

An array of offerings: Hindu deities have individual desires, even demands, when it comes to ritual offerings they receive. The lanes and gullies leading up to large temples are filled with small stalls selling the appropriate offerings to that temple's main deity. For example, if it is a goddess temple – such as that of Padmavati (wife of Sri Venkateshvara) on the outskirts of Tirupati – worshippers may purchase baskets filled with flowers, a piece of cloth representing a sari or with which to make a sari blouse, or spangled, netted red scarves, and turmeric and vermilion powders (*pasupu-kumkum*). More recently, these goddess offerings – "women's things" – have been packaged in small plastic bags and often include two red glass bangles, a comb, mirror, a packet of *bindis* (forehead mark stickers), kohl, *kumkum-pasupu*, perfume, and (in South India) a *tali* (wedding pendant) turmeric-colored thread. Wealthier worshippers may offer the goddess a full-size sari on a festival day or on the occasion of a particular ritual that their family is sponsoring; after the goddess has worn the sari, it is, along with others, sold (often at auction) and the proceeds used for the upkeep of the temple. Shiva prefers milk offerings, *bilva* (wood apple tree) leaves, and ash. Some goddesses (including Kali and *gramadevatas*) require non-vegetarian offerings (animal sacrifice, *bali*).

Arati (harati): *Puja* is concluded with the clockwise circling of an oil lamp or camphor flame in front of the *murti*, a ritual called *arati* or *harati*. (Sometimes the entire ritual of *puja* is also simply called *arati*.) The flame is presented by the ritual officiant (temple priest or, in domestic *pujas*, the householder) to others present for the *puja*, who hold their hands over the flame and bring their hands to their eyes, as a mode of bringing the blessings of the deity to themselves.

Figure 3.2   *Arati* being offered to temple worshipper, Tirupati.

In North India, *arati* is often accompanied by the singing of a very popular Hindi *bhajan*, titled by its first line: "Jai Jagdish Hare." The first of several verses, with transliteration of the Hindi, is:

jai jagdish hare	Victory to the lord of the universe,
swami jai jagdish hare	Victory to the lord of the universe.
bhakt janon ke sankat	The difficulties of all devotees,
das janon ke sankat	The difficulties of all followers [lit., servants],
kshan me dur kare	In a mere second, distance them.
om jai jagdish hare	Om, victory to the lord of the universe.

Prasad: The water, food, flowers, gift packets described above, *pasupu-kumkum*, and other offerings given to a deity in *puja* are returned to worshippers as *prasad*, which is believed to have absorbed the blessings of the deity who has partaken of the offerings.[6] *Prasad*

---

[6]   If someone receives *prasad* but chooses not to partake of it for one reason or another, it should not be simply thrown away with the trash; rather, because it is sacred, it should be disposed of by placing it under a tree or in a body of water.

may be shared with family members and/or friends who have not actually participated in the *puja*, but who, nonetheless, share its benefits through *prasad*. Worshippers at pilgrimage temples often take some of the *prasad* they have received to share with family members and neighbors back home. For example, the renowned *prasad* from the Venkateshvara temple in Tirupati-Tirumala, unusually large *laddus* (ball-shaped sweets),[7] is often carefully wrapped to take home to family members and friends.

Forehead markings: After having performed *puja* at home or participating in temple rituals, most worshippers apply vermilion powder or ash (in Shiva temples) to their foreheads before they leave the temple or the *puja* shrine. The forehead marking (*tilaka* in Sanskrit, *bindi* in Hindi, *bottu* in Telugu) is particularly important to most Hindu women, who these days often apply a "sticker" forehead marking, available in all sizes, shapes, and colors; many women feel not fully dressed or incomplete without a forehead marking. After worship in a temple, however, women would also apply vermilion powder or ash to their foreheads. If a non-Hindu asks a Hindu woman what her forehead marking or sticker means, she will often answer that it is a form of adornment that is not necessarily "religious." Sometimes, the *bindi is* just cosmetic; and as such may also be worn by non-Hindu Indians. But the preceding comment may also reflect an assumed definition of religion and the saying "Hinduism is not a religion; it's a way of life" (see Introduction for an expanded definition of "religion"). For most women who apply *bindis* in India, it is an embodied practice about which they do not often think explicitly; in the diaspora, however, they may be more reflective about their practice, since they are often asked by non-Indians about the meaning of their forehead markings. Male devotees may apply a *tilaka* after

---

[7] In 2009, this particular form of sweet, both in its size and ingredients, received an international patent, as the *Times of India* reported September 16, 2009: "Here's some sweet news. The famed Tirupati laddu – the most sought-after prasadam for lakhs of pilgrims who throng Tirumala – too joins the ranks of Darjeeling tea, Madhubani paintings and Goa feni after it was granted the Geographical Indication (GI) patent rights. This bars others from naming or marketing the sweetmeat preparation under the same name" (accessed online July 28, 2014).

worship, but fewer of them leave these *tilakas* on all day; those who are particularly ardent devotees may apply markings that cover their entire forehead – a white 'U' with a slender red mark in the middle for Vaishnavas and three horizontal lines marked by ash for Shaivas.

A grammar of devotion: What does the performance of *puja* imply about the deity to whom it is offered? Does the deity *need* the food, or is making offerings of food, clothes, flowers, and so on primarily a human mode through which to express honor and devotion? Does the deity actually partake of the food and water offered him or her? Hindus may answer these questions in a variety of ways. Some Hindus will answer that the deity has put him/herself in a position to be accessible to human devotees and *does* rely on human service. For example, one Hindu friend always travels with her little brass image of child Krishna (Bala Krishna), along with various ritual ingredients with which to serve him, explaining that there would be no one at home to feed him were he to be left alone, and the god would be hungry. Others may answer that the deity does not actually *need* the food and services, but that *puja* is a way to show devotion. *Puja* follows a *grammar* of devotion through which humans make a connection with the deity – showing him/her devotion and love – in the ways that they know best, through modes of hospitality and care-taking (Eck 1998, 48).

Online, Cyber *Puja*

The relatively new phenomenon of online or cyber *puja* implies that *puja* can be efficacious without the direct mediation of the human body,[8] but it raises questions about the nature of the body of the god or goddess and what it is that devotees are seeing when they take *darshan* of the deity on screen (either live through recordings from temples themselves or pixelated images of the deity) and the power of that *darshan*. Online "live *darshans*" are available

---

[8] A related phenomenon is for a worshipper to pay temple employees to perform *puja* on his/her behalf. This suggests that the ritual itself is efficacious whether or not its sponsor is present.

for large Indian temples such as Somnath (Gujarat), Shirdi Sai Baba Samadhi Mandir (Maharashtra), Kashi Vishvanath Mandir (Varanasi), and Shree Mahakaleshwar temple in Ujjain (Madhya Pradesh), among many others. (I encourage readers to look up some of these sites to see the kinds of rituals that are available online.) Other sites give the option for on-demand webcasts of particular rituals and processions (such as the Sri Jagannath Temple in Puri offering a webcast of the annual Ratha Jatra chariot festival); still others (such as the Shirdi Sai Baba Samadhi Mandir) give the option of the viewer offering *arati* and other services to the on-screen image of the deity.

Devotees who access these sites have different views of the power and legitimacy of these cyber *darshans*. Some articulate the view that since god is everywhere, he is also here, on screen; or that since *murtis* can be made of multiple forms (including that in the mind), this cyber form is just one more; or that it is devotion that creates a *murti,* and that if one views online images with devotion, they are, then, *murtis*. Others argue that because the *murti* online is unstable – the internet can go down and the image suddenly disappear – or because the online image is not three-dimensional and has not undergone the ritual of *pranapratishta*, it is not a "real" *murti*. Nicole Karapanagiotis argues for "a new category for the study of Hindu forms of God (cyber-forms in particular): namely, that of the *'worshipable form.'* … although – in the theoretical sense – virtual Visnu is Visnu and cyber Siva is Siva, these cyber-forms need to evoke adequate sentiment in devotees in order for devotees to *see them as God and to worship them as God"* (2013, 74; italics in original). She identifies three criteria that create a "worshipable form": "framing, aesthetics, and image histories/ associations of devotional power" (74). What is missing, however, from these *darshans* and devotional experience is the power of the geographic place itself associated with many temples (see Chapter 4); and most Hindus who participate in cyber *darshan* (mostly those living in Hindu diasporic communities) would prefer to visit the temple itself if they were able.

*****

Hindus show their love and devotion to god or the goddess through a wide variety of rituals, including ornamentation of the *murti, puja, bhajan*, and recitation of the stories of the deities and litanies of their many names. These rituals may be attenuated (performed quickly before one goes to work) or may be more elaborate and more time-consuming (on festival days, or performed by elders who have more time). We turn in the next chapter to similar rituals performed in temples where, in *puranic*-deity temples that are served by fulltime Brahmin priests, the rituals are performed throughout the day, with or without the presence of other (lay) worshippers.

References

Davis, Richard. 1999. *Lives of Indian Images.* Princeton: Princeton University Press.

Eck, Diana. 1998. *Darsan: Seeing the Divine Image in India.* New York: Columbia University Press.

Flueckiger, Joyce Burkhalter. 1991. Literacy and the Changing Concept of Text: Women's Ramayana *Mandali* in Central India. In *Boundaries of the Text: Performing the Epics in South and Southeast Asia*, eds. Joyce Flueckiger and Laurie Sears, 44–60. Ann Arbor: South and Southeast Asian Center Publications, University of Michigan.

Flueckiger, Joyce Burkhalter. 2013. *When the World Becomes Female: Guises of a South Indian Goddess.* Bloomington: Indiana University Press.

Gold, Ann Grodzins. 1994. Purdah Is As Purdah's Kept: A Storyteller's Story. In *Listen to the Heron's Words: Reimagining Gender and Kinship in North India*, Gloria Goodwin Raheja and Ann Grodzins Gold, 164–181. Berkeley: University of California Press.

Handelman, Don, M. V. Krishnayya, and David Shulman. 2013. Growing a Kingdom: The Goddess of Depth in Vizianagaram. In *One God, Two Goddesses, Three Studies of South Indian Cosmology*, Don Handelman, 115–143. Leiden: Brill Academic Publishing.

Hawley, John Stratton, and Mark Juergensmeyer. 1988. *Songs of the Saints of India.* New York: Oxford University Press.

Hess, Linda, and Shukdeo Singh. 2002. *The Bijak of Kabir.* New York: Oxford University Press.

Karapanagiotis, Nicole. 2013. Cyber Forms, *Worshipable Forms*: Hindu Devotional Viewpoints on the Ontology of Cyber-Gods and Goddesses. *International Journal of Hindu Studies* 17, 1: 57–82.

Narayana Rao, Velcheru, and David Shulman. 1998. *A Poem at the Right Moment: Remembered Verses from Premodern South India.* Berkeley: University of California Press.

Narayana Rao, Velcheru, and David Shulman. 2005. *God on the Hill: Temple Poems from Tirupati.* New York: Oxford University Press.

Peterson, Indira Viswanathan. 1989. *Poems to Siva: The Hymns of the Tamil Saints.* Princeton: Princeton University Press.

Ramanujan, A. K. 1973. *Speaking of Siva.* New York: Penguin Books.

Soneji, Davesh. 2012. *Unfinished Gestures: Devadasis, Memory, and Modernity in South India.* Chicago: University of Chicago Press.

Recommended Readings

DeNapoli, Antoinette. 2014. *Real Sadhus Sing to God: Gender, Asceticism, and Vernacular Religion in Rajasthan.* New York: Oxford University Press.

Packert, Cynthia. 2010. *The Art of Loving Krishna: Ornamentation and Devotion.* Bloomington: University of Indiana Press.

Pinkney, Andrea M. 2013. Prasada, the Gracious Gift, in Contemporary and Classical South Asia. *Journal of the American Academy of Religion* 81, 3: 734–756.

Ramanujan, A. K. 2005. *Nammalvar: Hymns for the Drowning.* New York: Penguin Books.

Shacham, Ilanit Loewy. 2014. Divine and Human Agency in Kṛṣṇadevarāya's Retelling of the Story of Āṇṭāḷ. *Journal of Vaishnava Studies* 22, 2: 103–124.

Shulman, David. 1980. *Tamil Temple Myths: Sacrifice and Divine Marriage in the South Indian Saiva Tradition.* Princeton: Princeton University Press.

4

Temples, Shrines, and Pilgrimage

Hindu deities live in a wide variety of big and small shrines and temples, as well as in domestic shrines and *puja* shelves (discussed at the end of Chapter 1). I distinguish shrines as abodes that are not enclosed or very small enclosures and temples as larger structures that have walls and roofs, but the distinction is slippery, and numerous shrines have become or are becoming more permanent structures that we may call "temples" in English. And of course, rivers who are the goddess are contained in neither shrine nor temple; and mountains are often considered the abode of a deity, beyond the temples that may be there (such as the Himalayas being called "the abode of the gods" and, more specifically, Mount Kailasha as the dwelling of Shiva). Other distinctions are the levels of service offered to the deity housed in shrine or temple and whether or not there is a full-time professional attendant at the site whose responsibility it is to offer rituals whether or not there are devotees present. Further, it is difficult to clearly distinguish what makes a particular

Everyday Hinduism, First Edition. Joyce Burkhalter Flueckiger.
© 2015 Joyce Burkhalter Flueckiger. Published 2015 by John Wiley & Sons, Ltd.

temple a pilgrimage site, since most major temples are, on some level, the destination of a journey to a powerful place – that is, pilgrimage. For our purposes, a pilgrimage temple draws from a wider "catchment" area than do temples that may draw from only the immediate neighborhood; but again, these distinctions are slippery.

Indian-language words for abodes of god do not make these distinctions between temple and shrine hard and fast either. The general Sanskrit term (also used in South Indian languages) for abode of god is *alaya*, which may also refer simply to a general abode (hence Himalaya literally means "place or abode of snow [*hima*]"). The term for temple in Hindi is *mandir*, but it may also be used to identify domestic *puja* shrines, as in *puja mandir*; the Telugu word for temple is *gudi* and Tamil is *koil*, which may refer both to shrines and to temples. One of the most common words for a pilgrimage site is *tirtha* (lit., crossing-place or ford at a riverbank); however, all shrines and temples are, at some level, "crossing places" where divine and human worlds meet.

Temples

Visiting temples is not a ritual obligation for Hindu practitioners (such as Friday prayers in the mosque may be for Muslim males, for example). Neither is temple worship congregational in the sense of Christian, Jewish, or Muslim worship on Sundays, Saturdays, and Fridays, respectively. However, certain days are special to certain deities (such as Tuesdays and Fridays for the goddess), and their temples will be more populated on these days. And in the United States, temples tend to be busier on weekends due to the American work and school schedules and the distance some worshippers live from the temple, which precludes their visits on weekdays before or after work.

So why do Hindus visit temples rather than simply worshipping at their home shrines? If god is omnipresent, taking different forms in different places, why is one localized form "better" than another? If asked, Hindus would give many different answers: the image of the deity is bigger (the main image [*mula murti*] at the Venkateshvara

Tirumala-Tirupati temple is, for example, a little over nine feet tall) and thus more powerful than those kept in domestic shrines; the deity may be too powerful to keep at home (in the case of some *gramadevatas*); or the temple provides refuge from the distractions of everyday life at home, and so on. But the primary reason for visiting a temple is the power of the *place* itself (particularly for large temples), where the deity has manifest him/herself in unique ways.

Sthala Puranas

The power of the place is narrated in a genre called *sthala puranas* (lit., ancient stories about a specific place), which may be performed only orally or may be preserved in manuscripts and/or printed pamphlets; today many *sthala puranas* are summarized on internet sites for particular large and well-known temples. These *puranas* narrate the stories of how the main deity of the temple came to be in that place (either whose *svayambhu* [self-manifesting, rather than man-made] image was miraculously found or stories of the acts of the deity at that site, for example), and explain the relationship between the main deity and other deities who may be housed in the temple and environs, the kinds of worship that should be done at that specific sacred place (temple), and the particular benefits that may result from having worshipped here (Shulman 1980, 17–18). While most Hindus do not worship one deity to the total exclusion of another, *sthala puranas* tend to praise the deity *of that place* as most powerful, whose worship is most efficacious.

Cidambara sthala purana: One example of a *sthala purana* that extols the power of a specific place is the Cidambara Mahatmya. It is important to note that the narrative of how god came to *this* place is a Shaiva myth, narrated by Shaiva devotees who see Shiva as supreme, and Vishnu is represented as a devotee of Shiva; Vaishnava myths narrate a very different hierarchy of gods. The story tells us that Cidambaram is the only place on earth that can bear the tremendously powerful dance of Shiva, and the temple is the only one in India in which the central image is Shiva in his form of the Lord of Dance (Nataraja).

The story is embedded in a series of conversations, the primary one being between Vishnu and the great snake Anantha (upon whom Vishnu lies on the ocean of milk; see image in Chapter 1).

Shiva decides to test the devotion of a group of sages performing rituals in the Pine Forest. He asks Vishnu to take the form of a woman, Mohini, to witness what he is about to do. He takes the guise of a beautiful wandering mendicant called Bhikshatana Murty (with whom Mohini subsequently falls in love). Shiva as the shining, beautiful mendicant enters the village where the sages' wives have been left behind; his beauty is so overcoming that the wives' saris and bangles fall off of their own accord; they fall in love with him. When the sages return from having performed their sacrifices in the forest and see the state of their wives, they are furious with the mendicant who has threatened the women's chastity. They curse the mendicant, to no effect; they then light a fire and chant *mantras*, and from the fire emerge, one by one, a tiger, a great snake, and finally a menacing dwarf. Bhikshatana rips the tiger's skin off with his nails and wraps it around his waist, he grabs the snake and ties it around his chest, and finally he subdues the dwarf and begins to dance on him. Seeing his powerful dance, the sages fall to the ground; even Shiva's wife Parvati, watching from the distance, is afraid; and Vishnu, having returned to his original form, reports that, "I worshipped him; I was alive as never before, my mind melting. He gave me an eye with which to see. … I was fully absorbed in the dance of the black-throated god, and I no longer needed the sadness we call sleep" (Smith 2003, 73). Only when he begins to dance do the spectators realize who the mendicant is – god himself.

When Ananta hears this story, he wants to see Shiva's dance and begins to perform austerities that will call the god to him, so he can make his request. Shiva appears to him and explains that the forest in which he had danced could not bear the power of the dance, and so, in compassion, he stopped dancing.

However, Shiva continues, there is *one* place on earth that is capable of bearing his dance, and where Ananta can witness the dance: Cidambaram. And from that day, Shiva dances continuously in that place, manifesting himself as Nataraja, King of Dance (Smith 2003; Handelman and Shulman 2004).

On a different level, there are numerous oral narratives (not called *sthala puranas*, but which fit the genre) of how particular *gramadevatas* came to be at the places where they reside. See Chapter 1 for the narrative of Gangamma in Tirupati, a goddess who was brought up as a human girl by a Reddy-caste family of that place and who revealed her divinity at that very place.

Temple Architecture

Puranic-deity temples are laid out according to textual prescriptions, specifically modeled on the body of the "cosmic man," Purusha (details of which few lay worshippers are aware of). However, there are many regional variations in the materials used to build temples – depending on local resources, weather, and local building codes – and in their layouts. Nevertheless, one can generalize some distinctions between North and South Indian temple architecture.

Many North Indian temples are characterized by their temple towers called *shikaras* (lit., mountain peak), which stand above the *garbagriha*. South Indian temples with historical royal patronage are characterized, in part, by their tower temple gates, *gopurams*. *Gopurams* are covered with carved images of deities and figures from the human and animal world; some are brightly painted and others covered with white paint. Because of the power of place, royal patrons often expanded older temples rather than build new ones, adding bigger and taller *gopurams* (gateways connected by walls enclosing the temple proper) and other architectural changes that visually displayed their power. The series of walls and *gopurams* that have built up

Figure 4.1 One of the *gopurams* at Thillai Nataraja Temple, Cidambaram, Tamil Nadu.

around some of the largest South Indian temples dwarf the inner temple itself and the dome above the *garbagriha* (see Figure 4.2).

In the largest temples, worshippers often have to negotiate what can feel like, quite literally, mazes of walkways, courtyards, and small shrines until they reach the *garbagriha* (lit. womb room), the innermost shrine where the primary deity lives. In North Indian temples, the deity (if married) appears with his/her spouse in the *garbagriha* (for example Parvati and Shiva, or Krishna and Radha); whereas in the South, the deity often appears alone in the *garbagriha*

Figure 4.2   Series of *gopurams* at Sri Ranganathaswamy Temple, Srirangam, Tamil Nadu.

and his/her consort resides in a different shrine in the same temple complex (or, in the case of Venkateshvara in Tirupati, in a different temple altogether, at the bottom of the hill).

Other regional differences include the materials from which temple *murtis* are made. The preferred material in the South is black granite, whereas in many parts of North India, the *murtis* (except for Shiva, who appears as a black stone *linga*) are often carved from white marble and their facial features (such as eyes) are painted on the *murti*; the images of Krishna, his sister Subhadra, and brother Balarama in the Jagannath temple in Puri, Odisha, are made of wood, and are remade and replaced every 12 years. The materials from which *murtis* are made contribute to some distinctions of the kinds of rituals offered to the deity (see *abhishekam* below).

American temples were first housed in non-traditional temple spaces, such as community centers that also served other functions for local Indian communities. The ritual families of deities in many of these temples were much more expansive than those housed in temples in India (see Chapter 1), in order to satisfy a wide spectrum of worshippers from different sects and regions of India. As more Hindus arrived, they became more settled and financially secure, and there were more worshippers from a given region and language-area, regionally identified temples (both through their architecture and the deities housed therein) began to be constructed.

Temple Worship

Darshan: Hindus often use the phrase "taking *darshan*" for their visits to and participation in temple rituals; the term is rarely used for participation in domestic *puja*. The word *darshan* derives from the Sanskrit verbal root *drish* meaning "sight," but its everyday usage in religious contexts implies much more than literal sight.[1] The entire body of the worshipper and all the senses are involved in what is referred to as *darshan*: the worshipper bows or prostrates, hears chanting of *mantras* and ringing of bells, smells burning incense and camphor, and tastes the *prasad* (fruits, spiced water, nuts) offered to worshippers at the end of *puja*. The ambience of temples, too, helps to shape the *darshan* experience. Most temples in India are very busy places – multiple rituals taking place at the same time at different shrines, chanting, comings and goings, children running around or crying. Many Hindus who first visit a temple in the United States comment on the silence, particularly in those temples where there are strategically placed signs indicating "Quiet Please."

Someone may ask a friend or family member who has returned from a temple visit (particularly when it is not made daily, such as at a pilgrimage site), "Did you take *darshan* today," or "did you have good *darshan* today?" The latter question implies a question both about literal sight (were you able to see – for example, at a busy

---

[1] In secular contexts, the term *darshan* may be used to describe having sighted a politician or other important person; one may also use *darshan* to talk about seeing a beautiful, well-known landscape such as the Himalayas or the ocean.

temple such as that of Venkateshvara in Tirumala-Tirupati, where worshippers are afforded only a few seconds in front of the primary *murti* in the *garbagriha* due to the long lines of pilgrims behind them) and about the experiential quality of the worship.[2]

Temple daily services: *Puranic*-temple rituals are much more elaborate than those conducted at domestic and public shrines, including an expanded set of *puja* rituals laid out in Sanskrit ritual manuals. Deities in these temples are served full-time by professional Brahmin male priests; whereas *gramadevata* shrines are served by either non-Brahmin lay devotees or members (including women) of non-Brahmin hereditary families, and their rituals are less elaborate. The rituals expanded in and/or unique to temple rituals described below are those offered to *puranic* deities.

The first ritual of the day is that of awakening the deity, often with a "morning song" (*suprabhatam*).[3] *Puja* is offered throughout the day, with its primary ingredients of flowers and fruits, turmeric and vermilion powder, and coconuts often contributed by worshippers. When cooked food (*naivedyam*) is offered, the curtain or door in front of the deity is closed, to give him/her privacy to eat.[4] Worshippers may pay a fee to have the priest offer the ritual of

[2] When I went to Tirupati one year for the *gramadevata* Gangamma's annual festival, I took the opportunity to go "uphill" to the grand Venkateshvara temple. When I returned to the hotel after having "taken *darshan*," the desk clerk asked, "So how was god today?" His question implied that god has his own moods *and* that I, as someone who had taken *darshan* of him, would be able to experience his shifting moods.

[3] Before the days of voice recordings, this song was heard only at this specific time of awakening the deity and in a specific place in front of the deity; however, these days, one can play recordings of the *suprabhatam* at home or in one's car at any time of day. Particularly popular is the recording of Venkateshvara's *suprabhatam* by M. S. Subbulakshmi, readily available on YouTube and other voice recordings.

[4] In a domestic context, observing offerings of cooked food to a *gramadevata*, I was given permission to photograph the offering and then leaned against the doorsill between the kitchen, where the goddess was being served, and the living room to which the female family members had withdrawn. Not having fully absorbed the protocol, I had to be reminded to come with them into the living room where I couldn't see the goddess; after all, my friend's said, "We shouldn't watch her eat." It should be noted that in traditional contexts, eating has not been the social occasion it has become in middle-class urban contexts.

archana, the recitation of the deity's 1008 names, during which the priest sprinkles *kumkum* or rice grains at the feet of the deity with each name. *Prasad* is offered by temple priests to worshippers witnessing any of these rituals. If the temple is built in such a way that the *garbagriha* is an independent structure within the temple, worshippers circumambulate the inner shrine before leaving, and then, in South India, traditionally worshippers sit for at least a few minutes after worshipping the deity.

At the end of the day, in many large temples, a series of rituals are performed that "put the deity to bed" – in Shiva temples called *ardhajama aradhanai* (evening ritual), or in Vishnu temples called *sayana utasava* (lit., laying down ritual), or more generically *ekanta seva* (last service). These night rituals are often accompanied by evening *ragas*[5] or soothing lullaby-type songs. At the Shiva cave temple on the Rock Fort Hill in Tiruchirappalli, Tamil Nadu, this is an elaborate affair. On the evening I witnessed the series of rituals, my friend and I were about to leave the temple after having taken *darshan*, when we were stopped by a priest who told us we must stay for the *ardhajama aradhanai* ritual that was to begin shortly. The ritual began at about 8:30 p.m. in front of the shrine of Shiva (here named Thayumanavar Swami, lit., the lord who is a mother) where he appears as a *linga*. [6] Evening songs were sung to the deity and a lit oil lamp placed in front of the *linga* before the doors to the *garbagriha* were shut. Then his processional metal image (*utsava murti*), clothed in a fresh silk garment and anointed with sandalwood paste, was carried in a palanquin to the shrine of his wife (some distance away), led by a small group of women and some elderly men (many of

---

[5] Classical *ragas* are composed to be performed at particular times of day; and the assumption is that those specific contexts influence the experience of the music.

[6] The story is told of a devout, pregnant woman who had visited the temple and was caught late in the evening on the other side of the Kaveri River from her home, due to sudden flooding. She went into labor, alone in the darkness on the banks of the river and prayed to Shiva for help. Shiva came to her as her mother and helped deliver her baby. Later, her mother came to find her, and mother and daughter realized then that it was Shiva who had come to her aid. This is the god in the cave temple on the hill that overlooks the Kaveri River.

whom said this was their favorite ritual and that they came every evening to participate in it). The women sang to the god as they escorted him to his wife. The *utsava murtis* of both god and goddess were placed on a swing, which was pushed gently for a few minutes by a priest; and the deities were served (sleep-inducing) warm, sweetened milk, which was then offered as *prasad* to the small group of worshippers that sat in front of the swing. Finally, the doors to the swing room were closed, and the attendees slowly made their way out of the temple, with the priests locking the series of temples doors behind them as they exited.[7]

Abhishekam: One ritual that is largely unique to temple worship is *abhishekam*, the anointing of the image of a deity with a series of auspicious liquid substances, including water, milk, honey, yogurt, and turmeric water. Often translated as "consecration," Richard Davis offers a translation of *abhishekam* as "affusion":

> Affusions in Indian ritual idiom are rites that add powers and capacities to a subject [including, in earlier days, kings] by pouring various substances over it. … The idea behind the repetitive, cumulative procedures of affusion is to concentrate within the body of the subject all the auspicious substances of the world (1997, 36).

Abhishekam has also been interpreted as a protective rite, protecting the king, and by extension, the deity, from sin and inauspiciousness (Geslani 2012). The ritual is performed in most South Indian *puranic* temples on a weekly basis, but is not commonly performed to North Indian marble *murtis* since the liquids would wear down the soft stone (the exception is the Shiva *linga* that is also dark stone in the North). Like ornamentation, *abhishekam*, too, enables the features of

---

[7] At Venkateshvara's temple in Tirumala-Tirupati, this evening ritual is very late, after midnight; and the *suprabhatam* is performed at about 2:30 in the morning. There are simply too many pilgrims waiting for his *darshan* to give the god a full night's sleep. Several years ago, there was even discussion about whether the evening ritual should be dispensed with altogether; but the suggestion was quickly rejected. After all, god, too, needed some rest.

dark stone *murtis* to be seen more easily, as the milk or turmeric water runs over them.[8]

Most images housed in *puranic*-deity temples are served directly only by Brahmin priests; the priests perform rituals of service whether or not worshippers are present, and if worshippers are present, the priests offer ritual services on their behalf. However, Shaiva, Vaishnava, and goddess temples differ in the levels of direct access a worshipper may have to the deity, with Vaishnava temples tending to be more restrictive in access than Shaiva temples. For example, one can hardly imagine seeing at a Vaishnava temple the renowned and intimate ritual (called *ghi malish*, lit. massage with clarified butter) performed at the high-mountain pilgrimage temple in Kedarnath (Uttarakhand), in which pilgrims themselves apply *ghi* to and "massage" the temple's *linga* (Whitmore 2012). Similarly, in the Hindu Temple of Atlanta complex, the Vaishnava temple to Venkateshvara is strikingly more formal than the Shaiva temple sitting next to it, where various children's performances are held and where the goddesses (each in her own small shrine) can be approached directly by worshippers who wish to leave offerings at their feet.

Festival processions: Many temples celebrate annual festival processions, during which a small (approximately two-foot-tall) metal festival image of the deity (*utsava murti*) is processed outside the temple on more or less elaborate "chariots," ranging from massive wooden temple carts to a simple wooden chair onto which the *murti* is tied in Chhattisgarhi villages. Perhaps the most famous (to the non-Hindu world) of these processions is the Jagannath Rath festival of Puri, Odisha – a procession from which the English word *juggernaut* derives, referring to something whose momentum cannot be stopped, as the large wooden temple chariots sometimes cannot be once they start moving. Many ISCKON (International Society for Krishna Consciousness) Krishna-worshipping communities outside of India perform this Jagannath procession through the streets of cities like London, Atlanta, and Toronto.

---

[8] A video of Ganesha *abhishekam* at the Hindu Temple of Atlanta can be seen on Emory University's Michael C. Carlos Museum website, carlos.emory.edu.

The annual nine-day processional festival for Venkateshvara in Tirumala-Tirupati, called *brahmotsavam*, draws hundreds of thousands of pilgrims. On each day, the *utsava murti* is decorated differently (given a different guise) – with a different *vahana* accompanying him – drawing on Vaishnava mythologies of the different *avataras* or manifestations of Vishnu. For example, on the sixth day the god is decorated to be Rama and his *vahana* (on this day) is Hanuman; on the seventh day, he is decorated as Govardhanadhari (Krishna who holds up the Govardhan Mountain); on the eighth day his *vahana* is a white horse, implying that the god is Kalki, Vishnu's *avatara* still to come (Reddy 2012, 32–37). Interestingly, two of the *brahmotsavam* processional forms are female: the goddess Sarasvati on the second day and Vishnu's female guise Mohini on the fifth day (for photographs, see Reddy 2012, 80–81; 93–95). Temple processions bring deities directly into the human world, giving them more visibility than is possible when they stay in their interior temple shrines;[9] and in cities where Hindus are a minority, temple processions also bring visibility to the Hindu community itself.

Shrines

The worship sites I am identifying as shrines are less elaborate architecturally than temples. Sometimes there is no enclosing structure at all; the deity may be simply a stone marked with vermilion or turmeric, under a tree or at the edge of a paddy field. *Gramadevata* shrines housing the protective deity in the form of a rock or a row of tridents may be found on the outskirts of many villages – such as the Seven Sisters in South India or Thakur Dev in Chhattisgarh. Other common open-air or simple-structure shrines are the sites of a Shiva *linga* at the side of local water tanks, Hanuman brightly painted with orange paint or adorned with vermilion, or a goddess

---

[9] In the days when the lowest castes in India were not allowed in *brahminic* temples (a tradition that is now unconstitutional in India), these processions were occasions for members of these castes to take *darshan* of the deity who otherwise lived behind walls that these castes could not enter.

protecting a forest road (Figure 4.3). These kinds of shrines are served by non-Brahmin practitioners, who are often women and members of lower castes. The small white shrine in Figure 4.4 sits on the main street of a small village on the borderland between Chhattisgarh and Odisha; the Oriya goddess Samlai Devi is a simple uncarved rock on which is applied vermilion powder, and a small oil lamp is lit every morning and evening by the householder in front of whose home the shrine sits.

Pilgrimage

Pilgrimage or *yatra* (lit., journey) implies travel to particularly powerful dwellings of god or the goddess, the power of which is recited in their *sthala puranas*. They are associated with mythological events and acts of deities that occurred *at this very place*, such as the land of Braj where Krishna grew up, or Cidambaram where Shiva dances, or Rameshvaram where Rama crossed the ocean to Lanka. Pilgrimage sites are often located on riverbanks and are called *tirthas*, a term that refers, quite literally, to a boat-crossing at a river bank (Eck 1998, 63–64).

Pilgrimage is not required of Hindus, as is Hajj pilgrimage for Muslims, for example; rather, Hindus go on pilgrimage for a wide range of reasons: for the experience and joy of powerful *darshan*, as a devotional act that builds merit, for the promise of release (*moksha*) from the cycle of birth and rebirth that some *sthala puranas* assert, to immerse the ashes of one's ancestors in the waters of particularly powerful rivers, for specific benefits offered by a particular deity at a particular site or the fulfillment of a vow (*vrat*), or for tourist-pilgrimage – almost always for some combination of these reasons (see Gold 2000, Chapter 4).

Identifying and sacralizing space: Different sets or networks of pilgrimage sites help to give identity to and sacralize space on different scales, from local regions to networks of regions, and even to the Indian subcontinent itself. For example, the *char dham* (lit., four seats) outline the subcontinent: Badrinath in the northern

Figure 4.3   Forest open-air shrine to Satyamma Tali, Andhra Pradesh.

Figure 4.4   Village shrine to Samlai Devi, Chhattisgarh.

Himalayas, Puri in the east on the coast of the Bay of Bengal, Rameshvaram on the southernmost tip of the subcontinent, and Dvarka in the west on the coast of the Indian Ocean. Other "sets" include the five South Indian temples dedicated to the Shiva *lingas* made up of one of the five elements – water, fire, wind, earth, air/ether – and the 12 *jyotirlingas*, or *lingas* of light. The variously numbered – 4, 18, 51, or 108 – *shakti pithas* (lit., seats of the goddess/*shakti*) mark the places where pieces of the goddess Sati's (Shiva's wife, incarnation of Parvati) body fell as a mourning, devastated Shiva carried her dead body on his shoulders, unwilling to give her up. Shiva had not been invited to his father-in-law Daksha's sacrifice; and, humiliated, Sati immolated herself in the sacrificial fire. To stop Shiva's inauspicious wanderings with the dead body, Vishnu cut off parts of the body with his discus, and where these body parts landed became the *shakti pithas*.

Other pilgrimage sites are more singular, "centers," if you will, such as Varanasi (also known as Kashi) on the banks of the river Ganga, itself a goddess. It is said that if one dies in Kashi, after death, she/he will attain liberation, and many pilgrims travel there on a one-way journey, to die there. Like many pilgrimage sites, the power of the place is intensified by a layering of significance. For example, the famous Kashi Vishwanath Temple is the site of one of the *jyotirlingas*. The Ganga River at Varanasi is also a particularly powerful place (among others, such as Gaya and Rishikesh) to immerse the ashes of one's ancestors (and most Hindus living outside of India make an effort to immerse their relatives' ashes in such a sacred site). But both Kashi and Ganga replicate around India; rivers such as the Godavari and Kaveri in the South and the Mahanadi in Central India are identified with Ganga and are believed to replicate her powers.

As we have read, each pilgrimage place is unique, having unique narratives, powers of place, and rituals that should be performed there. I provide more detailed descriptions of two pilgrimage sites below. The Venkateshvara temple in Tirumala-Tirupati is particularly important for Hindus from South India, but is also a pan-Indian and transnational site; the Oriya site of Narsinghnath, in contrast, is known only regionally, on the borderlands of Chhattisgarh and Odisha.

The journey: Traditionally, the journey to a pilgrimage site has been considered to be part of the ritual act and helps to create its benefits. Rajasthani pilgrims on a long bus journey to the seaside Jagannath-Puri temple told anthropologist Ann Gold that though pilgrimage to certain sites may promise pilgrims *moksha*, one could never be guaranteed of this. Nevertheless, pilgrims agreed that pilgrimage had other benefits,

> because the cumulative effect of being removed from daily routines and attachments at home, of taking many powerful *darshans* of all the gods, of voluntarily enduring hardships on the road, and above all of putting out money both for the sake of these experiences (the initial fare) and during them (the constant drain of rupees and paisa into the outstretched hands of *pandas* [priests who perform requisite rituals on behalf of the pilgrims] and beggars) is decidedly good for the soul. The effect is one of lightening: the returning pilgrim should be thinner and poorer (Gold 2000, 263).

The difficulties of pilgrimage journeys help to loosen ties to this world and "sweep the road ahead" to *moksha* (288), but do not guarantee it.[10]

For all pilgrims, the pilgrimage is not considered to be complete without *darshan* of the deity at the end of the journey, whether it be easy or difficult. But even in the presence of the powerful images of Jagannath, the goddess Ganga, and others that one Rajasthani

---

[10]   Having read Ann Gold's *Fruitful Journeys*, from which the above quotation is taken, a worried Hindu Emory University student who had made a pilgrimage to Tirumala-Tirupati wondered whether the benefits of his pilgrimage had been mitigated because his journey had not been difficult. His family had been driven up the mountain in an air-conditioned car instead of walking the footpath up the mountain; and his parents had had inside contacts at the temple who took them directly to the *garbagriha*, bypassing the long, long *darshan* lines. One can imagine the Rajasthani pilgrims answering that there would, of course, be benefit, but perhaps not as much as had the student suffered more difficulties.

pilgrim took *darshan* of, he often commented to fellow traveler Ann Gold, "I miss God," referring to his home *murti* of the local deity Niranjani (a manifestation of Vishnu), with whom he had an intimate relationship (Gold, 2000, 277).

Tirumala, a Southern, Pan-Indian, and Transnational Pilgrimage Site

The reader has already been introduced to the god who lives on the mountain in Tirumala-Tirupati, Venkateshvara (a manifestation of Vishnu), through numerous references in earlier chapters. Here we focus on the pilgrimage journey itself, the physical site, and the kinds of rituals pilgrims perform at this site. Pilgrims are drawn primarily from across South India and its international diaspora: many toddlers are brought to the temple for their first tonsure (*mundan*); many newly married couples make it a point to visit Tirumala shortly after their wedding to receive the blessings of the god on their marriage; numerous vows are taken to the god that are fulfilled through pilgrimage; and politicians from throughout India come to take *darshan* of the god, but also to be seen doing so by their constituencies.

Pilgrims who come to Tirupati by train, bus, and car (there's also an airport) recognize that they're coming near when the land begins to swell from the paddy fields, and then they see the mountain's rock face that anchors Tirupati and on which the great god lives. The mountain range is called Saptagiri (lit., seven hills), which reaches to a height of about 3,500 feet; god lives on the seventh range, Venkatagiri. Before taking up permanent residence on the mountain, Venkateshvara asked permission to do so from Varaha (Vishnu's boar *avatara*), who was already residing there; in return, Venkateshvara mandated that any pilgrimage to Tirumala would not be considered complete until the pilgrim visited the temple of Varaha. A full pilgrimage also includes visiting the temples of Venkateshvara's wife Padmavati (an incarnation of Lakshmi; locally known as Alamelumanga)

Figure 4.5 The beginning of the footpath to Tirumala; women lighting camphor flames and beginning application of turmeric-vermilion on each step.

and his brother Govinda Raja Swamy, both of which are on the plains, downhill from Venkateshvara's temple.

In an unusual living situation, Padmavati lives independently of her husband in a temple in a small town named Tiruchanur, a few miles outside of Tirupati. (As is typical of Hindu traditions, imaginatively she is multiple; she simultaneously resides downhill in Tiruchanur *and* on the stone chest of her husband's temple *murti*, so what I am talking about here is specifically her independent temple, where pilgrims go specifically for *her darshan*.) Several different explanations circulate that explain this separate living arrangement, including Padmavati's jealousy over the god letting Lakshmi (a goddess both distinct from and identified with Padmavati) reside along with her on his chest. Whatever the reason for separate residences, it is said that it is incumbent on Venkateshvara to come down from the mountain to visit his wife every night, rather than

115

her going uphill; and all the walking up and down wears out his sandals, which have to be replaced daily. At the beginning of the footpath going uphill is a small temple whose worshipped *murti* is the feet of the god. Pilgrims here place a pair of brass sandals on their heads as they circumambulate the god's feet, showing humility towards the god as well as embodying a reminder of the distance covered nightly by the god, as he visits his wife.

Venkateshvara's brother Govinda Raja Swamy's temple, whose temple *gopuram* dominates the Tirupati skyline, is located in the heart of the town near the bus and railway stations. The story is told that when Venkateshvara wanted to get married, he borrowed money for his wedding from his brother (other versions say he borrowed from Kubera, god of wealth). He is still paying interest on that loan even today, and pilgrims' offerings placed in the temple *hundi* (cash box) uphill are said to be applied towards interest on that loan. *Hundi* cash contents are conspicuously counted in public view at the end of every day, visible to pilgrims on their way out of the temple complex after having taken *darshan* of the indebted god. On his part, Govinda Raja Swamy downhill is a reclining *murti* that rests its head on a vessel he has used to measure the cash interest he's been paid by Venkateshvara; he's tired out from expending so much energy on this task.

Before the car road was constructed and hundreds of buses, taxis, and private vehicles began to transport pilgrims to the top of the mountain, they walked. And today thousands of pilgrims continue to do so, believing that to walk up the mountain brings more merit than riding a motorized conveyance. The approximately six-mile-long footpath begins at the base of the Seven Hills; 3,350 cement steps have been built into the footpath, much of which is covered by galvanized-tin roofing to provide shade and cover from rains. Each of the steps is marked with layers of turmeric and vermilion (*pasupu-kumkum*), the result of thousands of individual back-breaking vows by female pilgrims to so mark each step. The visual contrast of looking at the steps going up or going down is dramatic – the vertical portion of each step brightly colored on the way up and the horizontal portion of the steps visible on the way down a somber gray. Depending on their health and the number of rituals they perform on the way up, most pilgrims take three or four hours to reach the top of the mountain.

Upon arrival at the top of the mountain (locally called "uphill"), these days one of the first matters of business is to obtain *darshan* tickets. In earlier years, pilgrims could stand in a no-charge line or purchase tickets for a range of costs and stand in proportionately much shorter lines. When I first visited Tirumala in 1992, waiting time in the no-cost line was about 12 hours, whereas other lines' wait times were between two-and-a-half and five hours. In an effort to lessen the burden of waiting for hours on end, the Tirumala Tirupati Devasthanam (TTD) instituted the "Sudarsanam" (lit., good *darshan*) scheme that opened *darshan* ticket counters at three different places uphill. Pilgrims, whether or not they pay for their tickets, are given wristbands on which are stamped computer-determined timings indicating when they should report to the appropriate line entrance, leaving the pilgrims free to visit other shrines, sightsee, or simply rest and socialize until that time. When I visited Tirumala after this scheme was instituted, the wait time for a Rs. 50 *darshan* ticket, after appearing at the line entrance at the appropriate time, was about two-and-a-half hours.

Ultimately, all lines come together in the vestibule immediately in front of the *garbagriha*. The pilgrims cry out, "Govinda! Govinda!" (an appellation of Vishnu) as they press forward for a glimpse of the god. Right in front of the doorway to the *garbagriha*, in an effort to keep pilgrims' lines moving, worshippers are given only seconds to take *darshan* before they are pushed on by young male temple volunteers; even if every pilgrim took only a minute or two for *darshan*, the wait times for those behind would be extended by hours. One way to avoid the pressing crowds and long wait times and to have longer *darshan* is to purchase special tickets to attend the famous Venkateshvara *suprabhatam*, which, due to the god's busy schedule meeting the crowds that wait to see him, occurs at about 2:30 in the morning. (At the Hindu Temple of Atlanta, in contrast, *suprabhatam* is performed at 9 a.m.) Or, one can also purchase special tickets for the weekly *abhishekam* on Saturdays; however, demand for tickets to these rituals is high, and pilgrims need to buy the tickets many months ahead of the date they plan to make their pilgrimage.

One of the rituals for which pilgrimage to Tirumala is most well-known actually occurs outside the temple and its courtyards, and that is head-shaving (tonsure). Hundreds of pilgrims standing in line for *darshan* and waiting at bus and train stations have shaved heads, smeared with cooling sandalwood paste; some pilgrims speak of the humility and surrender to god implied through the ritual of tonsure. These days, the air-conditioned tonsure-center, built specifically for this purpose by the TTD, is extremely efficient, although one has to wait in relatively long lines to get in there, too. The center is a large room lined by barbers with their tools of trade, and individual pilgrims squat in front of them for their tonsure. The hair is collected by TTD workers and (much later) sold, the proceeds of which go back into TTD service institutions.[11]

Other rituals performed outside the *darshan* lines include sponsoring the (almost) daily *kalyanam* (wedding ritual) for the god and goddess, which employs *utsava murtis*; *porludandalu* (Telugu) or *angapradaksina* (Sanskrit), rolling the body over and over, clockwise, around the temple, often an auspicious 108 times; and *tulabharam*, offering coins or food equal to the weight of the person (particularly children) for whom the now-fulfilled vow was performed.

A successful pilgrimage to Tirumala is never assured. Numerous oral narratives circulate among pilgrims and their families about a particular group's thwarted efforts to get to Tirupati: trains are canceled, cars break down, family members become ill. But just as many

---

[11]   Most of the hair offered to the god (from a distance) is sold to international entrepreneurs for use in making wigs. In the 1990s, a controversy erupted in the Orthodox Jewish community (particularly in the United States) about whether or not Jewish women could wear wigs made from Indian hair, the majority of which comes from Tirumala. The legal question was whether the hair had physically been offered to the physical image of the deity; if so, according to rabbinic law, Jewish women could not wear it. But since it is cut/offered at a distance, way out of eyesight of the deity, ultimately the rabbis determined wigs made from Tirumala hair were permissible.

stories tell of miraculous arrivals, being taken out of the long *darshan* line by an unidentified temple employee to go right to the front (as happened to a friend and me), or unexpectedly long *darshans* (when the young male "pushers" seem to have forgotten the pilgrim is standing there). The assumption is that either god calls you or not; and if he calls, you will find your way to his doorstep regardless of impediments that would seem to keep you away; but if you make an effort and it isn't your turn or time – that is, if god hasn't called you – no matter how hard you try, you will not arrive.

Narsinghnath, a Sub-regional Pilgrimage Site

Narsinghnath,[12] whose temple is in western Odisha (formerly called Orissa), near the border with Chhattisgarh, is a pilgrimage site of very different scale than that of Tirumala; it identifies a sub-region and few Hindus outside of that area would know about it. I first came to know of the god Narsinghnath when I saw a lithograph of the Vishnu *avatara* Narasimha (half-man, half-lion) on a village *puja* shelf in an Oriya home in eastern Chhattisgarh. The lithograph had printed on it (in Hindi) the name of the pilgrimage site – Narsinghnath Tirtha. When I asked the female householder where this temple was, she explained it was a "very famous" temple two or three hours by bus from the village and encouraged me to try to visit it, which I did. The bus took me through acres of paddy fields with very few villages in between, jungle, and scrubland. The site itself was not easy to get to, and during the time of my visit, in the rainy season, there were very few pilgrims. But, I learned, during the temple's annual festival called Baisakhi (on the fourteenth day of the bright moon of the month Baisakh, May/June), hundreds of thousands of pilgrims find their way to the isolated jungle temple.

---

[12] English-language pamphlets about the temple transcribe the god's name as Nrusinghnath; I am using standard academic Roman transliteration for the name as it appears in Oriya and Hindi scripts.

When I asked several temple priests for the story of the temple, assuming it would be that of the *puranic* Vishnu *avatara* Narasimha, I heard a very different story about the uniqueness of this place and its deity:

> A certain demon named Musika Daitya (mouse demon) was terrorizing the communities of the area where the temple now stands. To save them, Vishnu took the form of a cat, named Marjara Kesari (lit., a lion of a cat; also known as Narsinghnath; who becomes associated with Narasimha). The cat chased the mouse, who ran into a small crack in the rock face behind where the current temple is standing. And god has been waiting at this rock face ever since, waiting for the mouse demon to emerge.

The temple image of Narsinghnath is not that of the half-man, half-lion Narasimha, but rather two uncarved stones to which have been attached silver eyes, a nose, whiskers, and cheek outlines (showing his feline features), topped by silver halos. In this context, the two feline *avataras* of Vishnu who have come to earth to restore *dharma*, Narsinghnath and Narasimha, both are and are not the "same."

Other narratives have accrued to this powerful place: Rama and Sita are said to have stopped here during their 14-year forest exile, as did the five exiled Pandava brothers of the Mahabharata. The rock face at which the god is waiting is at the bottom of a mountain named Gandhamardhan, said to be a piece of the mountain that Hanuman carried to the Lanka battlefield where Lakshmana lay grievously wounded. Rama had sent Hanuman to the Himalayas to find a particular healing herb; when he couldn't identify it, Hanuman simply carried the entire mountaintop down to Lanka, so that Rama himself could identify the appropriate herb. A piece of this mountain fell off as Hanuman was flying over western Odisha and it is said to be filled with these same healing herbs, which local villagers harvest and sell at the base of the path leading to the temple. The power of the site compounds: the power of a very local form of Narasimha and the

120

mountain associated with the Ramayana narrative. More recently, the Ramayana aspect of the site has been accentuated with the creation of a sculpture park at the entrance to the site; the most visible sculpture is a 20–25-foot-high modern sculpture of Hanuman; other smaller sculptures include Gopala (cowherd) Krishna hiding in a tree with the clothes he has stolen from village girls bathing in a pond; they stand in the pond under the tree begging Krishna for their clothes.

Like Tirumala and other pilgrimage destinations, this one, too, has numerous sites that a pilgrim should visit, among them: Gokund Ghat (where any crimes committed against cattle are expunged), the Samaleshwari temple (a uniquely Oriya goddess), and Binjhai Ghat (temple of goddess Vindhya Vasini). Minimally, one should dip in the Papharini (lit., destroyer of sins) River (more like a stream in the hot season), locally called Odisha's Ganga River, with her equivalent powers to destroy sins (*papa*).

*****

Temples and pilgrimage sites beckon worshippers with their unique powers of place (*sthala*) and their deities who have strong powers of attraction (*akarshana*) and whose *darshan* is particularly strong. And yet, these are not the deities with whom Hindu worshippers experience the most intimate *bhakti* relationships; these gods and goddesses are those who live in domestic *puja* shrines where they are intimately accessible and served by householders and which embody family and personal histories. Some of these domestic *murtis* are themselves brought back from pilgrimages and temples and, on some level, are domesticized. And so there is an interesting dynamic between domestically housed and temple and pilgrimage deities, each calling the worshipper for different reasons.

References

Davis, Richard. 1997. *Lives of Indian Images*. Princeton: Princeton University Press.
Eck, Diana. 1998. *Darsan: Seeing the Divine Image in India*. New York: Columbia University Press.

Geslani, Marko. 2012. Santi in the Development of Puranic Rajyabhiseka. *Indo-Iranian Journal* 55, 4: 321–377.

Gold, Ann Grodzins. 2000 [1988]. *Fruitful Journeys: The Ways of Rajasthani Pilgrims*. Prospect Heights, IL: Waveland Press.

Handelman, Don, and David Shulman. 2004. *Siva in the Forest of Pines: An Essay on Sorcery and Self-Knowledge*. New Delhi: Oxford University Press.

Reddy, D. Ravinder. 2012. *Tirumala: The Hill-Shrine of Hindu God Lord Venkateswara*. Hyderabad: D. Ravinder Reddy & Ravi Press Photo.

Shulman, David. 1980. *Tamil Temple Myths*. Princeton: Princeton University Press.

Smith, David. 2003. *The Dance of Siva: Religion, Art and Poetry in South India*. Cambridge: Cambridge University Press.

Whitmore, Luke. 2012. The Challenges of Representing Shiva: Image, Place, and the Divine Form in the Himalayan Hindu Shrine of Kedarnath. *Material Religion* 8, 2: 216–243.

Recommended Readings

Bhardwaj, Surinder M., and James G. Lochtefeld. 2004. *Tirtha*. In *The Hindu World*, eds. Sushil Mittal and Gene Thursby, 478–501. New York: Routledge.

Eck, Diana. 2012. *India: A Sacred Geography*. New York: Three Rivers Press.

Haberman, David. 1994. *Journey to the Twelve Forests: An Encounter with Krishna*. New York: Oxford University Press.

Kolapen, Mahalingum, and Sanjay Kolapen. 2002. *Hindu Temples in North America: A Celebration of Life*. Winter Park, IL: Titan Graphics and Publications.

Michell, George. 1988 [1977]. *The Hindu Temple: An Introduction to Its Meaning and Forms*. Chicago: University of Chicago Press.

Nanda, Vivek, and George Michell, ed. 2004. *Chidambaram: Home of Nataraja*. Mumbai: Marg Publications.

Narayanan, Vasudha. 2004. *Alaya*. In *The Hindu World*, eds. Sushil Mittal and Gene Thursby, 446–477. New York: Routledge.

Sax, William. 1991. *Mountain Goddess: Gender and Politics in a Himalayan Pilgrimage*. New York: Oxford University Press.

5

Festivals

There's a common aphorism in rural Chhattisgarh: "Twelve months, thirteen festivals." The Hindu calendar is crowded with festivals – each one associated with particular rituals, narratives and/or songs, special foods, and family visits. Festivals vary considerably in the ways they are celebrated – or whether they are celebrated at all – by region, caste, gender, and family. Several festivals, such as Divali (Dipavali; festival of lights) and Navaratri (Nine Nights of the Goddess), are celebrated throughout India, but the rituals, myths, and foods associated with them differ significantly between regions. Other festivals are celebrated only locally and may not be known beyond a few villages or a geographic region. Because of the deep significance of festivals to many of their participants and the considerable variations in the ways each festival is celebrated, some festival participants may find exceptions to the descriptions below or their favorite aspect of a festival may have been left out.

Everyday Hinduism, First Edition. Joyce Burkhalter Flueckiger.
© 2015 Joyce Burkhalter Flueckiger. Published 2015 by John Wiley & Sons, Ltd.

Most Hindu festivals are based on the lunar calendar, which is adjusted to the solar calendar every three years by adding an extra lunar month (*adhika masa*), so that the lunar year stays in sync with the solar year, agricultural cycles, and seasons. This is similar to the Jewish lunisolar year, but unlike the Islamic, purely lunar calendar, which cycles through the solar year so that festivals like Ramadan also cycle through the year. There are at least two kinds of lunar monthly reckonings in India: in North India the month is calculated from full moon to full moon, whereas in South India the month begins with the new moon. Even if not marked by particular festivals, new and full moons (*amavasya* and *purnima*) are acknowledged by special rituals and/or fasting.

Many festivals coincide with the agricultural cycle of seasons: hot season, rainy season, and cold/winter season – plowing, planting, first fruits, and full harvest. In the autumnal harvest season of North India, the festival season becomes particularly active with festivals of Navaratri, Dashera, and Divali. In South India, the harvest is celebrated for four days at the time of the winter solstice (a set date, January 14) during the festival of Pongol (also called Makar Sankranti). Householders clean out their homes, discarding old pots and pans, baskets, and clothes, which they burn in specially lit bonfires; small temporary domestic shrines are constructed with freshly cut sugarcane and loaded with fresh vegetables and fruits – a performance of renewal, abundance, and auspiciousness, much like Divali in the north. Sankranti is also celebrated in North India as a festival of kite-flying.

Most Indian urban dwellers are not so cut off from the rural agricultural cycle so as to have forgotten the agricultural associations of festivals such as Divali, which, in North and Central India, coincides with the rice paddy harvest. They may have family ancestral lands and homes in the village, to which they return regularly, and the seasonal fruits of harvest are readily visible in urban markets. However, these agricultural associations are lost in the diaspora, where Hinduism is practiced outside of the seasonal and agricultural cycles of India, and Divali as a celebration of the goddess of wealth Lakshmi, for example, is no longer specifically associated with the wealth of the newly harvested rice paddy.

Some festivals mark the births or marriages of gods and goddesses: for example, pan-Indian Ramanavmi, Rama's birth; and Chhattisgarhi Gaura festival, Shiva and Parvati's wedding. In August 2013, the Sanatan Mandir of Atlanta sent out the following email to its mailing list to announce the wedding of Krishna and Rukmini:

Wedding Invitation

The Sanatan Mandir devotees will be giving away their beloved Rukmani as bride to Lord Krishna who is accompanied by Acharya Baal Shuk Shri Gopeshji from Braj on Friday. Please come in your wedding attire to bless this occasion. And yes, the bride and groom do expect gifts.

Other festivals celebrate particular mythological narrative events, although the same festival may celebrate different events depending on region. For example, in South India, Dashera (also known as Vijaya Dashami) celebrates the victory of the goddess Durga over the demon Mahishasura; but in North India, the same festival is most commonly associated with the defeat of Ravana by the god Rama. In some Telugu-, Kannada-, and Marathi-speaking communities, the same festival commemorates the Mahabharata event when the epic Pandava hero-brothers retrieved the weapons they had hidden in the *sami* tree for the duration of the year in which they were forced to live in disguise; the brothers prayed to the tree for victory in the upcoming battle with their Kaurava cousins. Villagers (and their vehicles of all kinds, to be blessed) gather at and circumambulate the *sami* tree, plucking its leaves and exchanging them one with the other as blessings.

The Hindu calendar has several traditional New Year's days that vary according to region. Many regions celebrate the New Year in the lunar month of Chaitra (Tamil, Chitterai; March–April); some Hindus believe this is the day when the god Brahma created the universe. Celebrated on the new moon closest to the vernal equinox, this New Year is called Ugadi in Telugu-speaking communities and

125

in Karnataka, Maharashtra, Goa, and Kerala. The importance of festival foods is exhibited in this festival through the requisite Ugadi *paccadi*, a relish made from six ingredients that are individually bitter, sweet, peppery hot, salty, sour, and tangy – representing the basic emotions of life – sadness, happiness, anger, fear, disgust, and surprise. The Tamil New Year is determined by the solar rather than lunar calendar and so falls on the same day each year, April 14. In North India, Divali marks the beginning of the financial New Year, when businesses begin a new financial ledger.

Finally, in contemporary India and Indian diasporic communities, the Gregorian New Year's day of January 1 has been added to the repertoire of ritual New Year celebrations. On January 1, many city and village streets are lined with auspicious *rangolis* (rice flour and/or colored powder designs) in front of domestic and commercial doorways; some large *rangolis* include the English greeting "Happy New Year." The Gregorian New Year is also marked at numerous temples; the numbers of pilgrims visiting Tirupati to worship Sri Venkateshvara, for example, swell to their largest numbers all year on January 1. At the Venkateshvara Hindu Temple of Atlanta, Georgia, January 1 festivities draw thousands of Hindus (some years estimated to be as many as 10,000, requiring buses to ferry visitors to and from the temple from off-site parking lots) from throughout the southeastern United States. Celebrants come for *darshan* of the god, but celebrations continue all day in the large social hall of the temple, filled with stalls selling curios, saris, books, and food; there are also continual dance and other performances in the temple auditorium.

Many festivals are domestically oriented, while others are primarily associated with temples and large processions of temple deities (see Chapter 4); still others that were traditionally celebrated in domestic contexts have expanded into more public spaces. For example, the spring festival of Holi, during which colored powders are thrown joyfully between celebrants, was traditionally celebrated in domestic courtyards among family and friends. However, in contemporary India, male celebrants have taken to the streets to barrage passersby with color and to set off fireworks.

I describe three festivals in more detail below to illustrate the great variety in celebration of any one of them and the differences between different *kinds* of festivals: pan-Indian and local, domestic and public.

Divali: Festival of Lights

Divali (also called Dipavali, lit., row of lamps, *diyas*) is celebrated on the darkest night of the auspicious lunar month of Kartik (October-November). The central ritual of the festival is to throw light, quite literally, into that darkness by lighting oil lamps to drive away inauspicious forces, and more importantly, to invite in auspiciousness in the form of the goddess of wealth and prosperity, Lakshmi. As mentioned above, in North India, Divali also celebrates the occasion of Rama's return to Ayodhya after having conquered the demon king Ravana – the lights and fireworks celebrate Rama's return and are testimony to *adharma*, or evil, having been conquered by *dharma*. In South India, Divali is more commonly associated with the mythical event of Krishna's killing of the demon Narakasura.

In Central and North India, Divali falls at the end of the monsoons when the rice paddy has been (or is being) harvested; even for those who do not own or work on the land, there is a feeling of abundance. The monsoons are hard on houses and general maintenance and, in keeping with the theme of auspicious renewal, the days before Divali are a time of house cleaning and repair, new plastering and/or paint, and new *rangolis* on the floors, walls, or courtyards. Female householders busy themselves with preparing special sweets and other foods; they also have the responsibility to make sure the household has sufficient numbers, often dozens, of *diyas* (small unglazed clay lamps) and to soak them in water before they are filled with oil. On the darkest night itself, small *diyas* are placed in rows along window sills, balcony ledges, verandah boundaries, and walkways. A line of flames often lights the path into the most interior part of the home, to the *puja* shrine – or, for merchants, to the safe of their stores – welcoming Lakshmi. These days, the exterior lights are frequently candles or strings of small electrical lights; however, in the very interior of the home – at the *puja* shrine – or at the front entry to the home, there is always at least one traditional clay lamp. The dark night is also frequently punctuated with the brilliance (and sound) of fireworks.[1]

Divali is celebrated for five days; the most important day, Lakshmi Puja, is celebrated on the third day – *amavashya*, the darkest night. The fourth day is Govardan, named after the mountain that the deity Krishna lifted up above his village to protect its inhabitants and cattle from the fierce storm god Indra. On this day, Lakshmi in the form of the wealth of cattle is celebrated; cattle owners decorate their animals' horns, daub their backs with vermilion powder, and feed them special food out of brass plates. The fifth and last day is Bhai Duj (lit., brother's second), which celebrates the wealth of family and kinship through rituals in which girls and grown women give gifts (and often perform *arati*) to their brothers, who, in turn, are responsible for protecting their sisters.

In villages on the Chhattisgarh-Odisha border, month-long rituals during the auspicious month of Kartik take precedence over Divali itself and its association with lines of oil lamps. Women told me that it was only in "cities" (such as Raipur, four hours away) that people lined their porches with *diyas*, and even then, only wealthy families who could afford the oil required to fill so many *diyas* observed the tradition. Here in the village, the women explained, they draw *rangolis* and light only one *diya* inside, at their *puja* shrines. Every Thursday in these Oriya villages, female householders draw *rangolis* at the thresholds of their homes in the early morning light; these *rangolis*, like the Divali oil lamps, attract the gaze of Lakshmi, inviting prosperity into the household and deflecting inauspiciousness and the evil eye. Women often draw cattle footprints to direct Lakshmi into the centers of their homes. Another Kartik ritual, Kartik *snanam* (lit. bath), in these same villages is performed by unmarried girls at dawn every Monday. Directed by a village female elder, the girls knock on each other's doors in the hour before sunrise and gather to walk down to the village tank or river to immerse in

---

[1] Many cities are making an effort to reduce the "noise pollution" of these fireworks.

its cold waters and perform rituals on the water banks. They bring back brass pots filled with this water, carefully balanced on their heads, to their homes – the blessings of their rituals. Most married women join the girls only on the last Monday of the month.

Divali is now recognized around the world as "the" quintessential Hindu festival, particularly in the diaspora. Indian stores encourage Divali gift-giving, offering "specials" and decorating their windows; Divali greeting cards (both paper and electronic) are becoming more popular; and the festival is often celebrated (particularly in the diaspora and upper-class communities in urban India) for several weeks before the actual auspicious five days of Divali with parties and socializing. Divali in American diasporic Hindu communities engages with an American repertoire of "festivals of lights," including Christmas and Chanukah. Some Indian activists in the United States have made an effort (as of this writing, unsuccessful) to get a Divali stamp issued by the US Postal Service, for the festival to take its place with Christmas, Chanukah, Id, Kwanzaa, and Chinese New Year in commemorative stamps.

Ganesha Chaturthi: Domestic, Neighborhood, and City-Wide Celebrations

The elephant-headed deity Ganesha is worshipped by many Hindus at the beginning of any endeavor, such as a journey or ritual, to clear any obstacles in the path; he is often placed near or at entrances of temples, to clear the path towards successful worship of other deities in the temple that will follow. (The story of how Ganesha got his elephant head can be found in Chapter 1.) Ganesha's primary festival is Ganesha Chaturthi (also known as Vinayaka Chaturthi, Vinayaka being another name for Ganesha), which begins on the fourth day of the waning moon of the month of Bhadra (Bhadrapada; August-September). Domestic festival rituals are observed for an uneven number of days, depending on different families' traditions and resources; however, temporary clay or plaster-of-paris images installed in public shrines are seated for ten full days and immersed on the eleventh day. The festival is most often represented in the media by urban, public shrines (*pandals*) and the large processions, at the end of the festival, that carry the Ganesha images to a body of water for immersion. However, Ganesha Chaturthi is also a domestic, intimate festival, and we start our descriptions in the home.

Domestic shrines: I was told by several women in Hyderabad that all domestic Ganesha images used to be made by the women of the family, but that these days, few women have time (or the inclination, or, living in apartment buildings, easy access to clay) to do so, and so they buy Ganesha images in the bazaar to bring home; and the commercial centers and streets of Hyderabad are lined with push-carts and temporary stalls selling these smaller Ganeshas. However, the matriarch of a Mudaliar-caste, middle-class family still makes their own Ganesha, albeit much smaller, she says, than it used to be when she was growing up. Her family used to keep the much larger images in the home for the full ten days of the festival, and relatives and friends would come to see and worship the image throughout the festival. But now, the family keeps the smaller images for only three days, because the god requires *puja* twice a day – with specially prepared food offerings; the younger generation of the family are all professionals working outside the home and, the matriarch explained, they don't have time to sustain this level of worship for the full ten days. The custom of friends and neighbors going around to see as many Ganeshas as they can continues, however, as time permits; and when householders hear a Ganesha procession passing in front of their homes, they go out to the street to take *darshan* and pay respects.

On one Ganesha Chaturthi I observed with this Hyderabadi family, the female matriarch began making her Ganesha from clay dug up from her garden in the early evening. From a lump of moistened clay, she carefully formed a seated Ganesha, with one leg crossed over his opposite knee, and created the outline of a trunk. Before beginning Ganesha's adornment, the matriarch ritually anointed him with milk and pieces of softened banana. She then wrapped the image with strips of silk cloth for his clothing and

Figure 5.1   Domestic shrine Ganesha, Hyderabad (12 inches tall).

decorated him with carefully selected pieces of her own jewelry and a multitude of flowers. The creativity allowed the householder in both form and adornment creates a certain intimacy between devotee and god that is lost with the purchase of commercially made images. Ganesha and his temporary altar were fully "ready" and adorned only three hours later; a visiting friend told me that even when using a purchased image, it often takes one to two hours to prepare the entire "*puja* scene."

The matriarch's full concentration during this creation was broken by periodic commentary and laughter with her daughter-in-law who was making her own (very small) Ganesha and his mouse *vahana* for the first time. She told me, "In the old days, women used to cook, cook, cook. But they also took time to do this, and it gave them a break and gave them peace of mind." For the three days during which Ganesha sat enthroned in their house, he was fed sweets and offered incense and *arati* (flame offering) twice a day. On the third day, the main image (along with the daughter-in-law's much smaller images) was placed on a stainless steel plate and the women of the household carried it out to the garden well. The ornaments were carefully taken off before the images were dropped into the deep well, as the women joyfully cried out "Jai Ganesha, jai Ganesha!" (Victory to Ganesha!). The matriarch explained the significance of immersion of temporary images: "Immersion can mean immersing one's sins, mistakes, etc. of the last year – to start anew with fresh slate." Rather than taking their Ganeshas individually for immersion, many families take their domestic Ganesha *murtis* to a close-by neighborhood shrine (*pandal*), placing them at the feet of the larger image, to be taken in procession for immersion along with this image at the end of the full ten days of celebration.

Neighborhood and city-wide celebrations: In rural villages, village headmen and/or wealthy landowners may set up a Ganesha shrine on the verandahs of their homes – where the god sits under a canopy of fresh bamboo, strung with leaves, flowers, and sometimes fruits

Figure 5.2 Ganesha seated on back of bicycle, ready for procession, rural Chhattisgarh.

and vegetables – open to public viewing and worship. In Chhattisgarhi villages, girls who intend to formalize ritual friendships (called *bhojali* or *mahaprasad*) often plant wheat seeds together in baskets placed at the feet of Ganesha. The bright green seedlings that grow over the ten days (to a height of 8–10 inches) are carried by the girls in procession to a body of water (tank or river), along with the village Ganesha image. The seedings are washed off and exchanged between the friends as *prasad* from the ritual; and the girls are now *mahaprasads* (lit., great *prasad*) and are obligated to each other like kin.[2]

In large cities such as Hyderabad, large Ganesha images (10, 15, 20 feet tall) are housed in public *pandals* that are most often sponsored by neighborhood organizations, organizations of young men, or

Figure 5.3 Ganesha procession led by girls carrying *bhojali* seedlings, rural Chhattisgarh.

[2] This ritual exchange of seedlings may be celebrated at any ritual or festival, but Ganesha Chaturthi is a favorite.

labor unions. A couple of weeks before the festival begins, members of these organizations go out to begin to collect donations from passersby and households within particular neighborhoods to be used to buy a Ganesha image for the neighborhood *pandal* and to support the daily rituals incumbent upon them once the image is installed. Some groups are particularly well-organized and give receipts for donations. The largest Ganesha in Hyderabad (60 feet tall in 2014) is sponsored by a local "government servant," as he self-identified, with donations from hundreds of businesses to meet the cost of close to Rs. 15–20,000 *lakhs*.[3] The sponsor of this Ganesha told me he began

Figure 5.4   Largest Ganesha in (Khairatabad) Hyderabad, 2007.

[3]   1 *lakh* = 100,000.

the tradition as a young man in 1954. His first Ganesha was only one foot tall, he said, and the size of the image grew every year until it reached a height of 60 feet. The city government has now informed him that this is the maximum height that will be allowed, and he has promised to begin to decrease its height. He proudly told me that, in 2007, he had hired 200 security personnel for the immersion day, when a large crane would come to remove the Ganesha and join the city-wide procession to Hussein Sagar lake.

In 2007, one neighborhood *pandal* in Hyderabad was supported by the Tulja Bhavani Youth Association. When my Hyderabadi friend asked who Tulja Bhavani was, the two 21-year-old men (studying hotel management) attending the deity for the evening teased her about her ignorance: "This is in every ninth grade curric-ulum," they said, "He is the person who gave [the seventeenth-century general and founder of the Maratha empire] Shivaji his sword." They said the costs of their *pandal* this year were: Rs. 8,000 for the image, Rs. 8,000 for the shrine lighting throughout the ten days, and Rs. 10,000 to rent the small truck that would take Ganesha to the local lake, joining a long line of such trucks. The young men estimated that most households from which they asked for dona-tions gave Rs. 501 or Rs. 1001 (the "extra" one rupee is an Indian tradition of cash gifts, signifying potential for growth). The actual *puja* to this image was performed by a Brahmin priest from a nearby temple. Every evening, a policeman stood watch at the *pandal* and slept in front of it; these services were provided by the Hyderabad Police Department to deter any potential communal violence (see below for further discussion). I asked the young men when this tradition of public *pandals* had begun in Hyderabad. They estimated in the 1940s or 1950s, saying that people saw what kind of celebra-tions were held in Bombay (Mumbai) and thought that they, too, could do this. They explained that these *pandals* were associated, in particular, with male youth groups – and these spaces are, indeed, very male spaces where young men often spend their evenings. They added that similar *pandals* were created for the goddess during Durga Puja (a festival later in the autumn), but that she has spe-cial "superstitions" (using the English word), such as prohibitions

Figure 5.5 Neighborhood Ganesha shrine (*pandal*).

Figure 5.6 Ganesha on his way to be immersed.

against smoking and drinking in her presence. When I asked whether Ganesha allows these behaviors, they answered in English, "No, no. It's not like that; but *she's* very strict, very powerful."

The large urban processions that now characterize Ganesha Chaturthi are attributed to innovations made by the Marathi nationalist leader Bal Gangadhar Tilak at end of the nineteenth century. Tilak "revived" the festival by introducing public processions for Ganesha's immersion, hoping that the processions would help to reinforce Hindu nationalist identity and solidarity (Courtright 1985, 188). While the British colonialists had made the gathering of large groups for political purposes illegal, religious processions were allowed, and Tilak was convinced they could serve both religious and political ends. Maharashtra, particularly the mega-city of Mumbai, is still famous throughout India for its elaborate Ganesha displays and huge processions.

Hindu and Muslim religious processions (such as Muharram processions) have historically been, and continue to be, one way for different communities to claim public space and perform communal identities; and these processions have periodically created tensions (even violence) between communities. To prevent such violence, in Hyderabad, all processions must procure a city permit and let the authorities know their exact route, along which policemen stand guard. In the 1990s, after the destruction of the Babri Masjid and following communal violence throughout India, I remember standing on one of Hyderabad's biggest thoroughfares watching long lines of trucks and auto-rickshaws taking Ganesha images of all sizes to be immersed in Hussein Sagar lake in central Hyderabad. Teenage boys were riding the trucks, wearing saffron headbands indicating their Hindu identities, throwing small packets of *prasad* to and pink powder (*gulal*) on passersby. (I asked the young men described above whether or not they, too, wore these headbands when they accompanied their Ganesha image for procession. They responded, in English, "Yes, that's our Hinduism; it's compulsory.") Most stores along the route were shuttered and policemen lined the route, prepared for any trouble that may erupt along the procession route.

Eco-friendly Ganeshas: In contemporary India, most Ganesha images are purchased in the bazaar, even for domestic worship, and these are made of plaster of paris (rather than clay) and are brightly painted with chemical-based paints (which include mercury, zinc oxide, chromium, and lead). While traditional clay images that were immersed in local bodies of water disintegrated with no adverse effects, these non-organic images pollute the waters and often do not fully disintegrate. In many cities, there is a movement to promote the use of eco-friendly clay images decorated with natural dyes, rather than the plaster-of-paris, chemical-paint decorated Ganeshas.

Place-Bound Festivals: Tirupati's Gangamma Jatara

While many festivals, such as Divali and Ugadi, may be transposed to new geographic settings as their celebrants move to different cities, regions, and even across the oceans, others are very local, tied to the very land upon which they are celebrated. In Telugu, these festivals are called *jataras*, distinguished from transportable festivals called *pandagas*. Most *jataras* are dedicated to village goddesses (*gramadevatas*) who protect the communities and land upon which they live. These goddesses have local names and narratives of their appearance at a particular place, even as they may attract participants from beyond that "place." *Jataras* are not solely domestic or temple-focused, although they may include both temple and domestic rituals. They are often celebrated at sites at the edge of villages or at their central crossroads or temples, from where they expand into surrounding streets and gullies. Gangamma Jatara, traditionally celebrated by artisan and non-landowning castes at the height of the hot season in Tirupati, is an example of this kind of place-bound festival (descriptions of the *jatara* below are drawn from Flueckiger 2013).

Beginning on the fourth Tuesday after the Tamil New Year (April 14), *jatara* rituals call the goddess out of her local shrines and temples to protect the community from hot season-associated illnesses (such as various poxes and childhood fevers) and to bring rains to the sun-baked paddy fields. Gangamma is an *ugra* (excessive, fierce) goddess who has "excessive" demands of service by her devotees. The rationale of festival rituals is motivated by the modulation of Gangamma's *ugram* (excessive power), building it up to become powerful enough to banish the hot-season illnesses and then satisfying it so that it does not *cause* the very illnesses from which the goddess protects. The goddess becomes present throughout Tirupati through a proliferation of her forms in both domestic and public contexts, outside of her shrines and temples.

The most unique and dramatic forms Gangamma takes are through the bodies of men of a particular weaving-caste (Kaikala) family. Every day of the festival, a man from this extended family takes on the guise of the goddess – through clothing and

Figure 5.7 Gangamma in her most powerful festival form, embodied in Kaikala guise.

ornamentation – reenacting Gangamma's primary local story (see summary in Chapter 1). The early guises taken by the Kaikalas are double – guises of the goddess who herself is guised as she chases her protagonist, the Palegadu (local chieftain). Only after Gangamma finally beheads the Palegadu, who has been threatening the young women of his domain, does she show her true identity; and on the last three days of the festival, the Kaikala guises are of the goddess revealed (performatively, a single guise). All of these Kaikala guises of the goddess – who *are* the goddess herself – perambulate the gullies and lanes of Tirupati, where female householders meet her at their doorways, worship, and receive her blessings.

Gangamma also appears in domestic kitchens in the form of small turmeric mounds created by female householders – a particularly intimate form for such a powerful, demanding goddess. She also appears as lines of turmeric and vermilion drawn on walls, as decorated coconuts sitting on the mouth of small brass pots, and as a yogurt-millet mixture that householders then distribute to passersby outside their doorways. Gangamma is also the small "1,000-eyed clay pots" that are held over children's heads by their mothers as they walk to the temple. Here, the pots are smashed against the stone pavement behind the temple, performing the dual nature of the goddess: she who protects from illness, but who may also become that illness if left unsatisfied. The goddess is, quite literally, "everywhere."

Gangamma's growing presence through multiple and expanding forms requires greater-than-normal rituals and service. During the early days of the *jatara*, the courtyard of Gangamma's largest Tirupati temple is filled with women cooking *pongal*, a boiled rice-lentil mixture that should overflow the sides of the cooking vessels. Gangamma's cement feet outside the temple are laden with fruits and flowers, vermilion and turmeric powders. However, as the goddess's *ugram* grows, a female *jatara* participant told me, these vegetarian offerings are not satisfying to her growing hunger; and on the last few days of the *jatara*, family groups begin to offer chicken (and a few goat) sacrifices in the temple courtyard, cooking the ritual remains right there over little open hearths, to be consumed by festival celebrants as Gangamma's blessing. A fine balance of intensifying/multiplying the goddess and then feeding/satisfying her growing forms creates the primary rhythms of the *jatara*.

While Tirupati's streets and homes and Gangamma's temples are filled with an array of rituals throughout the week-long *jatara*, one ritual in particular has caught the public imagination: men taking female guise (*stri vesham*) – saris, ornaments, breasts, braids. These men have made a vow to the goddess (or their mothers have made one on their behalf when they were young) that if their entreaties are fulfilled by Gangamma (for healing from one of the Gangamma-related illnesses, the welfare of their businesses, admission into a particular educational institution, etc.), then they will take *stri vesham* during her *jatara*. The vow itself is fulfilled by taking *stri vesham* only once; but many men continue to do so year after year. I asked several men why this particular, unusual vow was made to Gangamma rather than any number of other vow possibilities. One man ventured that when the goddess is in her most *ugra* (powerful, excessive) state during the *jatara*, men should

Figure 5.8   Men in female guise, Gangamma *jatara*, Tirupati.

appear before her only as a women. The answer of a Brahmin man in his sixties was more expansive. He said that he had been sickly as a child and, asking for full strength and healing, his mother had made the *stri-vesham* vow on his behalf. After he had fulfilled the vow once, as a pubescent boy, his grandmother had told him that he should continue to do so, and he had – taking *stri vesham* for 35 years. Her rationale: "Taking *vesham*, just once a year, you can get a corner on women's *shakti* [power]." During the week of the *jatara*, ultimate reality is imagined as female, a world in which the goddess is triumphant, and *stri vesham* enables men to more fully participate in that world.

Women, on the other hand, do not need to take *stri vesham* to appear before or experience the *shakti* of the goddess since they already embody this female quality. On the last day of the *jatara*, an eight- to ten-feet tall clay face (*ugra mukhi*) is built in front of each of Gangamma's two largest Tirupati temples. Several men had told us that these *ugra mukhis* are particularly powerful and that we should not look directly at them.

Figure 5.9 *Ugra mukhi*, final day of Gangamma Jatara, Tirupati. Courtesy of K. Rajendran, K. R. Studio, Tirupati.

I asked a female sweeper at the guesthouse where I was staying if she was afraid of the power of the *ugra mukhis*, as men seemed to be. She answered, "No, we're not afraid. That's because she [the goddess] is *shakti*, and we [women] have *shakti*. But men are different. They don't have it, so they're afraid." Women do not change who they are through *vesham*; they simply intensify what they do already – cook, for the goddess; cooking and guising are equally satisfying to her.

Gangamma's *ugra mukhis* are believed to be too powerful to be left in place for long and are dismantled by the final Kaikala guise of the goddess early on the last morning of the festival, drawing it to conclusion. Several male participants said that Gangamma now leaves Tirupati and crosses the seven seas. One woman concurred that the goddess is sent off: "By the last day, we can't bear her any-more. We would have to give her piles of food every day; we wouldn't be able to bear that. So, saying 'Next year we'll worship you,' we send her off." However, when I asked the flowersellers at one of Gangamma's temples where this place was, exactly, to which the goddess went – across the seven seas – they responded in aston-ishment, "She doesn't go anywhere. Don't we worship her [in her temples] every Tuesday and Friday [days special to the goddess]?!" Gangamma is both "here" and "not here." Her expanding, multi-plying *jatara* forms have been enlivened; she has fulfilled her mission of banishing illness and bringing rains; her growing forms (and hence needs) have been ritually satisfied; and she now returns to the dark stone forms of her temples and shrines, forms that can be borne more easily on a regular basis by her human worshippers.

The *jatara* world is time- and place-bound. At the end of the *jatara*, participants return to their daily lives, which include worship of a wide array of gods and goddesses among whom Gangamma is no longer the center; and *stri veshams* return to being men who work in businesses or in the fields. And yet, the *jatara* leaves traces of new gender possibilities, having performed and reminded women of their shared qualities with the goddess of agency and *shakti* and having reminded men of masculinity whose potentially aggressive nature can be transformed to include just a corner of female *shakti*.

*****

Festivals

Festivals are an important means of activating, celebrating, and entreating deities; they are also a means through which their human participants come to know these deities. They order and mark the passage of time through the ritual year; and they help to create and reflect family, caste, and regional identities.

References

Courtright, Paul. 1985. *Ganesa: Lord of Obstacles, Lord of Beginnings*. New York: Oxford University Press.
Flueckiger, Joyce Burkhalter. 2013. *When the World Becomes Female: Guises of a South Indian Goddess*. Bloomington: Indiana University Press.

Recommended Readings

Gold, Ann Grodzins. 2014. Sweetness and Light: The Bright Side of Pluralism in a North Indian Town. In *Religious Pluralism, State and Society in Asia*, ed. Chiara Formichi, 113–137. London: Routledge.
McDermott, Rachel Fell. 2011. *Revelry, Rivalry, and Longing for the Goddesses of Bengal*. New York: Columbia University Press.
Narayanan, Vasudha. 2000. Diglossic Hinduism: Liberation and Lentils. *Journal of the American Academy of Religion* 68, 4: 761–779.
Narayanan, Vasudha. 2011. The Many Flavors of the Hindu New Year. *Huffington Post:Religion*. http://www.huffingtonpost.com/vasudha-narayanan/the-flavors-of-the-hindu-_b_849113.html (last accessed October 16, 2014).
Pintchman, Tracy. 2005. *Guests at God's Wedding: Celebrating Kartik among the Women of Benares*. Albany: State University of New York Press.

6

Vrats: Ritual Vows and Women's Auspiciousness

Vrat[1] literally means vow, specifically a vow made to a deity to undertake a particular ritual, series of rituals, or pilgrimage in order to achieve a particular end through the intervention of the deity *or* to mark the fulfillment of that end. Both the vow of intention itself and the ritual fulfillment of that vow may be called a *vrat*. *Vrats* may also be performed for general well-being, without a specific request (such as the monthly Satyanarayan Vrat often performed in thanksgiving or for general blessings on a new home, newly married couple, etc.). Many *vrats* are individual, one-time vows taken or fulfilled at a religious shrine or pilgrimage site; and various sites are particularly well known for certain kinds of vows. Other *vrats* are performed exclusively in domestic contexts. Members of all classes and castes participate in these kinds of vows, and many vow participants may step outside of their own

---

[1] Sanskrit *vrata*; Hindi *vrat*; Telugu *nomu, vratam*; Tamil *nompu, vratam*, or *viratam*.

Everyday Hinduism, First Edition. Joyce Burkhalter Flueckiger.
© 2015 Joyce Burkhalter Flueckiger. Published 2015 by John Wiley & Sons, Ltd.

religious tradition to make a vow at a well-known site of another religious tradition – such as Hindus making vows for fertility at the grave shrines of Muslim saints, and Christians, Muslims, and Hindus all making vows for healing at temples of the goddess Mariamma (Raj and Harman 2006). (See Chapter 8 for further description of healing practices.)

Temple *Vrats*

One well-known *vrat*-fulfilling deity is Sri Venkateshvara, whose primary temple is in the South Indian pilgrimage town of Tirupati. Thousands of pilgrims visit the famous temple to initiate and fulfill of a wide range of vows – college students asking the god to help them with admissions to medical school or to find employment, mothers seeking aid in finding a spouse for their children, women asking for fertility, family members asking for the health of a relative, movie directors bringing their film footage for successful completion, politicians asking the god for positive election results. These vows are marked through a range of different kinds of rituals (already described in Chapter 4).

But *vrat*-fulfilling deities are not limited to those with such wide fame and wealth as that of Sri Venkateshvara. Goddesses at many smaller shrines and temples are well known for granting fertility, and the trees in the courtyards of these shrines or temples are filled with hanging "cradles" offered by petitioners (see Chapter 8 for photographs); or one may see women performing vows through circumambulation of sacred trees outside temples, winding lengths of cotton thread around the trees to mark their rounds. More recently, several temples have become known for the power of their deities to facilitate granting of visas to travel to the United States. At these temples, petitioners may make vows to send a determined percentage of the American salaries back to the temple or to return on pilgrimage to the temple if the visa is granted.

Figure 6.1 Women fulfilling vows at Ankalamma goddess temple, Tirupati. Threads wrapped around tree upon each circumambulation.

Domestic *Vrats*

This rest of this chapter focuses on domestic *vrats*, votive rituals that involve some kind of discipline (such as fasting, cooking of special foods, performing particular rituals), recitation of a story relating the efficacy of that ritual, worship of the deity (*puja*), and petition to the deity for fulfillment of a specific request or general well-being. Some women who regularly participate in these *vrats* distinguish everyday worship of a deity (*puja*) and *vrats* primarily by the intensity of their performance and the specificity of their requests. Both men and women participate in a range of these kinds of domestic *vrats*; however, many *vrats* are female-specific and are an important means of expression of female religiosity and agency. Most women's *vrats* are oriented toward the well-being of their families; they may be performed to obtain a good husband, then performed to keep him alive, and to bring general prosperity and auspiciousness (health, wealth, happiness) to the family; later, women may perform *vrats* for the birth of a child, specifically a son.

Vrats may be performed on a weekly basis (for example, on Fridays in devotion to the goddess or on Tuesdays in devotion to Hanuman), monthly according to the cycle of the moon (Satyanarayan Vrat, performed to Vishnu, is performed at the Hindu Temple of Atlanta and many other temples in the United States every full moon), or annually according to the Hindu lunar calendar. A woman may perform a particular *vrat* weekly for a specified period of time, such as for 13 Fridays to gain a good husband, or annually for the first five years of her marriage to assure its strong foundation. The tradition of maintaining weekly or annual *vrats* (as distinguished from one-time *vrats*) is often limited to families of some economic means because of the time and expense (in ritual foods, new clothing, and sometimes engaging a Brahmin priest) required to fulfill many of the vows.

A Telugu middle-aged woman who carried a voice of ritual authority in her extended family explained to me the difference between *vrats* and festivals as follows:

> *Nomulu* [Telugu word for *vrats*] have to do with women's *saubhagya* [auspiciousness] and festivals have to do with remembering things [historic events] like Dashera, Rama and Sita, for example Rama's victory over Ravana. We celebrate that in happiness. Or Divali, when Satyabhama killed Naraka, and we celebrate that in happiness. At Sakranti, the sun enters into a new phase; it's harvest, and we celebrate. Eating all these grains gives good health. If you eat *ber* [jungle fruit], then you get rid of coughs. If you eat sesame, you get good health. [These are all foods eaten during Sakranti celebration.] Then there's Ugadi, our New Year. It's about eating sweet, sour, and salt together.
>
> For *nomulu*, we celebrate these *pujas* for everyone in the family, for the well-being of everyone in the family.

Another woman performing Varalakshmi Vratam (an annual vow to the goddess Lakshmi) explained further the more socially restrictive nature of *vrats*, as compared to festivals in which everyone can celebrate in some small way:

Not many people do this [*nomulu*] Varalakshmi Vratam. It's limited to only a few. [JBF: Why?] There's Dipavali [Divali] Vratam [here, she uses the term *vratam* even for a festival] for everyone; Varalakshmi Vratam is only for a few. Mostly it's Brahmins and us [Velama caste] who perform this *nomu*. We also used to perform Dipavali Nomu, I was told. But since everyone does that – all other castes – that's why we stopped doing it for Dipavali. It's less work. Varalakshmi is more, that's why *we* do it. ... Dipavali Nomu is for Shiva, that's why you can complete it so quickly [the implication being that the goddess requires more service, her worship requiring more ingredients, and hence more expense].

Domestic *vrats* are generally celebrated by more restrictive social groups than are festivals; that is, many *vrats* are circumscribed by family, caste, village, and/or region (although there are a few pan-India *vrats*, such as Satyanarayan Vrat). When brides move out of their natal households, they usually take up the *vrat* traditions of their conjugal family, so that they may not celebrate the same *vrats* as do their mothers (even if marrying within the same region and caste). However, if particular *vrats* with which married women grew up are not performed in their conjugal homes, they sometimes return to their mothers' homes to perform them.

Women whose conjugal or maternal families do not perform *vrats* often participate in the *vrat* rituals of others by being invited as a *sumangali* (auspicious married woman) to the home of a ritual participant in their conjugal village or neighborhood. Some *vrats* require that the female householder performing the ritual offer *pasupu-kumkum* (turmeric-vermilion) and certain foods to a specified number of *sumangalis*; many urban families, in particular, may not have the requisite number of married women in the household, and so will invite neighbors. I was present at the Hindu Temple of Atlanta while one such *vrat* was being performed during Navaratri

(Nine Nights of the Goddess) and was asked by the sponsor of the *vrat* if I was married. When I answered affirmatively, she asked if I would be willing to sit in the line of nine *sumangalis* to accept the *pasupu-kumkum* (in this case accompanied by a sari-blouse piece, comb, and mirror – "women's things") that should be distributed to nine married women. The householder performing the ritual said that this is why she had chosen to perform what is traditionally a domestic ritual in the temple; there were few Indian families living in her immediate Atlanta suburban neighborhood, and she knew she would find at least nine married women at the temple during that particular festival week.

Vrat Kathas: **Ritual Narratives**

A distinctive element of many *vrat* rituals are the stories, *vrat kathas*, orally performed as part of the ritual itself. These *kathas* are reflexive, didactic narratives about the power of the ritual, a power that can explicitly change the destiny (fate or *karma*) of a participant and/or her family members. The stories describe the ritual work of the participants, and often take the form of etymological narratives about when a deity first told a devotee to perform a particular *vrat* in order to obtain the results promised from the ritual. Depending on the identities and ages of the participants in the *vrat* and when and where it is being performed, the story may be recited rather mechanically, read directly from a pamphlet, or it may be performed without a script, often with great drama and humor; some families hire a Brahmin male priest to recite the *katha* for some *vrats* (the *ritual* effects of the narration being equal in all cases). Audience members may be given grains of rice to hold for the duration of the *katha* recitation to ensure their concentration (presumably they drop the rice grains if they fall asleep). At the end of the recitation they sprinkle the grains over the image of the deity.

Vrat *kathas* directly and/or indirectly address the relationship between the vow, *karma*, and *bhakti*. That is, the *vrat* is successful because of both the power of ritual action and its fruits (*karma*), as well as the power of devotion (*bhakti*) to a particular deity, who may intervene on the devotee's behalf. The deity's actions can be interpreted as both cross-cutting the causal plane of the devotee's *karma* (superseding the negative *karma* of the devotee) and working within the cycle of *karma* (that is, the devotee's devotion and ritual act of performing the *vrat* create new, positive *karma*, which produces positive results) (Wadley 1983). Often these *vrat kathas* present alternative interpretations to those found in Sanskritic textual sources of caste, gender, *karma,* and ritual (Narayan 1997). However, practitioners themselves rarely think consciously or talk about *vrats* in these terms. They are most concerned with the immediate matter at hand: pleasing the deity and ensuring the well-being of their families through ritual action.

Two South Indian *Vrat* Traditions

Varalakshmi Vratam: On the Friday following the full moon of the month of Sravan (July-August), married women from a range of castes across South India and the South Indian diaspora perform Varalakshmi Vratam (*vratam* is the term used in Tamil and Telugu). If unable to perform the *vrat* on that day, women may perform it on any other Friday in Sravan, Fridays being special days to the goddess. *Varam* literally means gift or boon, and Lakshmi is the goddess of wealth and all things auspicious; thus Varalakshmi Vratam is that *vrat* performed to the goddess who bestows and *is* wealth and well-being. The *vrat* is a ritual performance that, quite literally, both exhibits and creates – through the wide array of required ritual items, including varieties of vegetables and sweets, flowers, new cloth, and turmeric and vermilion – abundance, wealth, and auspiciousness. Relatives and neighbors take time to visit each other's homes and take *darshan* of the Varalakshmi displays and partake of the *prasad* of *puja* to the goddess.

South Indian women who are acquainted with North Indian traditions often distinguish the broader aims of Varalakshmi Vratam (the well-being of the household) from the aims of the Karva Cauth

Figure 6.2   Varalakshmi temporary domestic altar, Hyderabad.

vrat tradition of the North that is explicitly performed for the long lives of husbands.[2] However, implicitly, the wealth and well-being of the household, for which the Varalakshmi Vratam is performed, is also associated with the well-being and long life of a husband.

The *vrat katha* performed at Varalakshmi Vratam, attributed by several participants to the Skanda Purana, is narrated by the god Shiva, from whom his wife Parvati has asked for a *vrat* that would benefit women on earth and bring prosperity to their homes. Shiva recounts for her the story of Charumati. Charumati was faithfully dedicated to her husband and thus rewarded by the goddess Lakshmi, who gave her instructions to perform Varalakshmi Vratam, which brought prosperity and wealth to the household. One can observe here the reflexivity typical of *vrat kathas*.

[2]   Karva Cauth is performed on the fourth day of the dark half of the month of Kartik. Married women abstain from all food and drink from sunrise to moonrise, at which time they perform *puja* and break the fast (see Pintchman 2003 and Pearson 1996).

An elderly Telugu woman summarized the story briefly:

There used to be a woman called Charumati. She used to serve her mother-in-law and her father-in-law well, and used to offer food to poor people. She spoke only truth and never lied. She was a pativrata [married woman faithful to her husband]. One day Vishnu came to her in a dream and said, "In Sravan, on the second Friday, if you do this puja, you'll get health, wealth, and everything."

Our family Brahmin priest told us this. He tells us to make nine varieties of vegetables, nine coconut-filled pastries, nine of all those things, to clean the house and do puja, and all this will bring good things [to the household]. This is what he says. So from then on, we do that here.

I participated in Varalakshmi Vratam in the month of Sravan 2007 in a village near Hyderabad. Participants were daughters and daughters-in-law of three households (about 20 women in total) who were from an extended, traditionally landowning, Velama-caste family. Some women lived in the village itself and others lived in Hyderabad and had come to the village to celebrate this ritual occasion.

Before the friend who had invited me (herself a daughter-in-law to the family) and I left for the village, we stopped at a large vegetable market in Hyderabad to purchase various *puja* items and the nine varieties of flowers and vegetables that we would contribute to the ritual (including a fragile, wild bitter gourd – *karela* – specifically associated with the season and this particular ritual). As soon as we arrived in the village, greeted the family, and were served tea, talk quickly shifted to the demanding schedule of the next day of the *vrat* itself – specifically, what time the women would need to get up to bathe and then start cooking (they estimated 5 a.m.), and who would cook what, what were the varieties of vegetables and sweets that would need to be prepared, and whether they had all the ingredients, and so on.

Figure 6.3 Preparing abundance (of food) for Varalakshmi Vratam in a traditional kitchen.

The center of activity early on the day of the *vrat* was the traditional kitchen of the main house; it was the only kitchen of the three households that still retained earthen floors and walls, natural sky-lights providing the only light, and earthen, wood-burning stoves (although even this kitchen had a two-burner gas stove). One elderly woman told us that this kitchen was 200 years old, an exclusively women's space, where women had traditionally gathered to relax and "play parcheesi." This kitchen still maintained the goddess who takes form in two clay pots filled with water poured off cooked rice (called *taravani* in Telugu) – a tradition becoming less common as kitchens modernize and rice cookers become more popular.

By the time I arrived at the kitchen at 8 a.m., it was filled with women rolling out pastries to fry, cutting vegetables, and cooking. There were no men in sight, nor did I see any the entire day, except for the officiating Brahmin priest, who showed up only for the formal ritual itself. In shifting social and geographic contexts of American diasporic communities, the performance of this *vrat* is becoming less gender-segregated; men often drive their wives to the home where the *vrat* is being performed and may gather in a room other than that where the ritual is performed. However, I attended one Varalakshmi Vratam in suburban Atlanta where the husband sat with and actively participated with his wife throughout the ritual as a co-sponsor of the *vrat* ritual.[3] In August 2010, a three-month ritual recitation of the names of the goddess (Koti Kumkum Archana), sponsored at the Hindu Temple of Atlanta, culminated with the Varalakshmi Vratam ritual in which several hundred married couples participated.

Back in the Andhra village, while the 11 (two more than the required nine) varieties of vegetables and sweets were cooking and being fried, the eldest two daughters-in-law of the family coordinated preparation of the *puja* ingredients in the large hall and *puja* room adjacent to the kitchen. The younger daughter-in-law was responsible for decorating with mango leaves, red flowers, vermilion and turmeric, a simple wooden "chariot" or cart that would hold the goddess for the duration of the ritual. The oldest daughter-in-law decorated nine clay pots, tying pieces of turmeric root around the mouths of the pots and drawing with lampblack, on their exteriors, eyes and a nose. Nine fried sweet pastries were placed in each pot and remained there for the duration of the ritual, after which they were distributed as *prasad*. In this case, the pots themselves were not worshipped as the goddess, as they often are in other rituals, but sat alongside the chariot that held the goddess in the form of a small turmeric ball. Another woman prepared nine dough oil lamps, made of the flour of a particular kind of lentil mixed with sugar, to be lit at the

---

[3] Similarly, some pre-wedding henna (*mehendi*) all-women's rituals are becoming less gender-segregated in diasporic contexts.

Figure 6.4 Decorated Varalakshmi Vratam clay pots and a platter of dried coconut halves to be offered to goddess.

end of the ritual and also distributed as *prasad*. While these preparations were underway, an elderly servant woman went from woman to woman to apply turmeric paste to their feet; turmeric both marks the auspiciousness of a woman (a quality shared with the goddess) and creates that auspiciousness.

Another daughter-in-law of the household stacked new sari-blouse cloth pieces on a brass plate, two cloth pieces given by each *vrat* participant, on top of which were placed pieces of dried coconut and betel nuts. The householder then formed two mounds of wet turmeric paste representing deities whom she identified as Gauri and Swamy, and placed them on top of the blouse pieces. Gauri is another name for the goddess Parvati, and Swamy is a term for deity/master/husband, or in relationship to Parvati, Shiva. I was struck by this appellation, since the *vrat* is explicitly performed to

156

Lakshmi. This may be a case of "all goddesses are one," with the participants conflating goddess names; or they may be conflating two discrete *vrats* to Lakshmi and Parvati, respectively, since these women, when asked about Varalakshmi Vratam, often interspersed commentary and description of Mangala Gauri Nomu (lit., Auspicious Gauri Vow). Gauri Nomu (described later in this chapter) is also performed during the month of Sravan by newly married women for the first five years after marriage.

The formal ritual began in the outer hall of the home with a *puja* to Ganesha, Remover of Obstacles, and then to the couple Gauri-Swamy, before the latter were taken into the inner *puja* room and seated atop the blouse pieces inside the chariot. The eldest daughter-in-law applied vermilion and turmeric on the wedding pendant (*tali*) of each participant before we moved into the *puja* room, the first of many such auspicious applications on the participants' *talis* throughout the day.

Beginning at about 11:30 a.m., for close to two hours, seven women sat in a semicircle in front of the chariot holding the deities, with the Brahmin male priest chanting and giving direction from behind them. The chief ritual participant was the youngest bride, dressed in a new sequin-sparkling sari and adorned in her wedding gold. This was her first year performing this *vrat* as a *saubhagya* (lit., she of good fortune, i.e., a married woman). Each woman went to the priest and extended her wrist, around which he tied several rounds of red and yellow thread, variously interpreted as marking the intention of the ritual participants, binding them to their vows, and/or protecting them for the duration of the vow. These threads are worn by the participants until they fall off naturally, sometimes several weeks, even months, later.

The priest chanted to the goddess in Sanskrit, as the female participants offered, at his instruction, water, *pasupu-kumkum*, coins, fruit, rice kernels, oil-lamp flames, and incense to the goddess. Quite soon, the cement flooring in front of the chariot was filled with color, texture, and fragrance, now all intermixing. The priest told the *vrat katha* in an abbreviated form, for about ten minutes, since, he said, he still had several other homes to visit this day. At the end, the

Figure 6.5 Abundance of offerings (including dough oil lamps) made to the goddess, creating auspiciousness.

Figure 6.6 Final flame offering (*arati*).

women left the room and closed the door, to give the goddess privacy as she ate the offered food, and then returned for the final *arati* (flame offering to the deity).

At the completion of the ritual, the priest sat at the *puja* room doorway as each woman set in front of him a platter of uncooked (rice) grain, banana, and packets of lentils and spices, and then covered the platter with the end of her sari as the priest blessed her. The contents of the food platters were consolidated, put in plastic bags and given to the Brahmin, who was by this time impatient to get to several more homes to conduct the same ritual again and again.

After the priest left, the women returned to the *puja* room to worship their permanent family deities. *Prasad* was distributed in the form of the dough oil lamps and spoonfuls of the nine vegetable curries; the stack of sari blouse pieces and pastries that earlier had been placed in the clay pots were distributed to the participating women. Finally, garlands of flattened cotton balls that had been

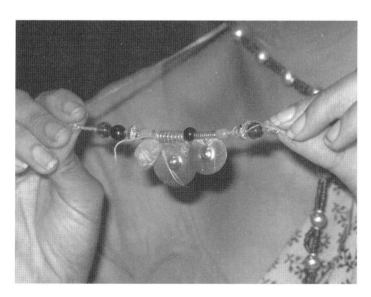

Figure 6.7   Varalakshmi "threads" tied to participant's wedding pendant (*tali*).

offered to the turmeric-formed goddess (representing offerings of clothing) were cut into pieces and tied to each woman's wedding pendant (*tali*); these threads, like those tied to the participants' wrists, are left on until the cotton thread naturally breaks and falls off.[4]

The long ritual sequence ended with the group of participants going outside to the courtyard and circumambulating the *tulsi* (basil) plant, another form of the goddess, pouring water on her and decorating her with colorful flowers. The turmeric forms of Gauri and Swamy were put on the family *puja* shelf until such time as a female family member would go to one of the two big rivers in the region, the Godavari and Krishna Rivers, at which time they would be immersed. It was close to 3 p.m. when all the women of the household sat down to eat a full meal together for the first time that day, amidst high-energy conversations and laughter.

At dusk, the women of our household went to visit the homes of two neighbor families who had also celebrated the *vrat*, to honor their goddesses and receive *prasad* from their rituals. In the growing darkness, we sat out on the back porch of one of the houses with a group of about six women, giving me an opportunity to ask more about the *vrat* they had just performed. I first asked them to list the eight Lakshmis, each embodying an attribute of "wealth," associated with the *vrat*. The women laughed as they could come up with four or five names, but never the full list of eight. Finally, putting the different listings together, the list included the following eight names: *dhairya*/courage Lakshmi; *dhana*/wealth Lakshmi; *vijay*/victory Lakshmi; *adi*/primordial Lakshmi; *saubhagya*/auspicious Lakshmi; *santana*/child-giving Lakshmi; *vidya*/knowledge Lakshmi; and *dhanya*/grain Lakshmi. One of the elders commented, "No matter how many Lakshmis we have, what we need, what is 'compulsory,' [using the English word] is *dhairyam* [courage]. If we lose *dhairya* Lakshmi, we lose all Lakshmis."

[4] See Gold 2011 for discussion of a Rajasthani *vrat katha* that narrates the dire consequences of a king breaking off his wife's Dasa Mata *vrat* threads, which he thought to be particularly ugly when he could afford buy his wife gold instead.

While women who work outside the home these days may find it difficult to take the time necessary to perform the rituals in the ways in which their mothers or mother-in-laws had done, with the full array of ritual foods and ingredients, time-consuming preparations, and long *pujas*, the tradition has taken on a new life in different ways in urban contexts – as a festival of consumerism and consumption. Many of the large jewelry stores in Hyderabad advertise heavily in newspapers and with large banners outside of their storefronts, offering special sales and free gifts on the occasion of Varalakshmi Vratam. And many middle-class women wear small Lakshmi-imprinted gold pendants on their *tali* chains that have been given to them by mothers or mother-in-laws on the occasion of this *vrat*.

Mangala Gauri Nomu is a South Indian *vrat* closely associated with Varalakshmi Vratam, this one performed exclusively by newly married women for the first five years after marriage on Tuesdays during the month of Sravan. It follows the same general ritual grammar as Varalakshmi Vratam, except that the ritual ingredients offered to the goddess come in fives rather than nines: five saris and blouse pieces, five *kumkum* boxes, five combs, five mirrors, five vegetables, five forms of sweets, and so on. Some newly married women perform both *vrats* and others only one, depending on the custom of their in-laws' household. One woman related the following experience of what happens if a woman doesn't perform the *vrat* correctly, or fully, for five consecutive years:

> You know [she began with a sad voice], my oldest sister didn't do the final fifth year *puja*. She did four years, but not the fifth … she was transferred to [the town of] Anantapur. I asked her to come home to complete the fifth year, but she didn't. Because my sister didn't perform all five years, my mother got scared and she didn't teach the tradition to the rest of us sisters. [I learned from another woman in the group that the oldest sister's marriage is troubled and that that is why her younger sister, the narrator, made these comments.]

> Mangala Gauri means [the goddess] Parvati. Gauri is Parvati. And we do Gauri Puja on the wedding day, right? It's very important. It takes up to two hours, before entering the wedding pavilion, the bride is left alone to do it; the room is silent; no Brahmin; just the bride and her own *puja*.[5]

The mother of the speaker above then related the story of Mangala Gauri Nomu, which is a more complete version than the one I heard for Varalakshmi Vratam, and serves as a good example of the genre of *vrat katha*:

It so happens that there was once a man who had no children and he had lots of troubles. Akashvani [a voice from heaven] announced to him, "Don't worry; you'll get peace of mind." Then someone came in disguise and asked for alms. The man offered him alms and the other man accepted them. The first man said, "I have no children." The visitor said, "You'll have a son, but he'll die in his sixteenth year. He'll have a life span of only 16 years." And he disappeared. He was Bhagvan [God] himself.

The man had a son. The boy turned 16 and then his mother started worrying. She had only one son. She was in pain. Then she thought of a plan, and asked her brother for help. She dressed her son in different clothes [those of an ascetic], hung a bag on his shoulder, and sent him with his maternal uncle to Kashi [Varanasi].[6] When they were leaving, she gave a ring to her son. On their way, they reached a village, the uncle and nephew. They stayed there in a garden. It was a Tuesday in the month of Sravan, and a king's daughter came to the garden to pick flowers [to use in ritual]. And all the girls who came with her

---

[5] In some South Indian families, the mother of the bride ties a *tali* around the clay pot who is the goddess that the bride will worship. That *tali* is tied around the neck of the bride and she must wear it for a specified number of days, after which she may remove it or tie it to the *tali* given to her by her husband.

[6] For someone living in South India, this would be a very long pilgrimage, indeed.

[her attendants] started arguing about the flowers. And in the quarrel they threw the flowers down, and the flowers all went back to their own trees. The girls asked, "How did the flowers go back to their own trees?" The princess answered, "Maybe it's because my mother performed Gauri Nomu when I was born." The nephew overheard this. And he and his uncle thought, "Only through this girl can we escape our curse."

The girl saw the boy and liked him. She wanted to get married to him, but her father didn't agree, saying, "How can I give you to a wandering ascetic?" But the girl wouldn't accept this and said, "I'll marry only him." So they got married. That night, they both lay down and slept. They had put a glass of milk next to the cot. After they went to sleep, a snake came to bite him.

[Another woman says, "You know, his 16 years were finished, that's why the snake came to bite him."]

[Back to narrator]: Yes, that's why. The snake came in and started drinking the milk. The girl saw this, and she got up and bowed to the snake and circumambulated around it. She brought a big silver pot and put it there. She put the pot there and, without fear, the snake went into the pot. Then the girl tied it closed with a cloth. The snake became a golden ornament on the pot.

Then the husband told her about his curse. He said "Now I have to complete my pilgrimage to Kashi. My mother asked me to go. I can't stay here." The girl protested; she told her father and he also protested. But the boy left.

This girl gave a ring to him and he gave a ring to her. He had a birthmark on his thigh, like a snake. She asked her father to feed the poor for one year. She said her husband would return in one year. She told him, "Offer food to everyone for one year. No matter how many people come, you must feed them. He said he'll return in one year. Offer food to the poor. He'll surely come back, and I'll recognize him."

For one year, the girl made her father offer food to everyone who came. He did this for one year. After a year, the boy returned. She took his hand, but the father didn't accept him. He asked, "How can you recognize him as your husband?" [She answered] "That ring and the birth mark on his thigh." Her father performed their wedding again, gave her appropriate ritual bride gifts, and sent her off.

[Scene changes] Someone told his parents, "Your son is going to come and he's gotten married."

Her mother had made the girl perform Mangala Gauri Vratam. Because she performed the *vratam* well, he escaped the curse. And that's why at Mangala Gauri Vratam, we make snakes out of dough.

[Younger woman, "This means, if a husband has some defect or curse and his wife performs Mangala Gauri Vratam, then he'll escape that curse. That's it. That's why newly married women do this *puja*. It's 'compulsory' [using the English word]."]

By the end of the narrative, it becomes clear that the curse under which the son was living is *naga dosham* (lit., snake blemish; see Chapter 8), caused by particular astrological alignments, and that the curse was lifted through his wife's performance of Mangala Gauri Vratam. But the narrator ends her narration by generalizing beyond *naga dosham*, saying that any defect or curse (*dosham*) can be lifted through a wife's *vrat* rituals. When I suggested that the *vrat* could, then, be understood as a ritual for a husband's long life, the narrator answered, "Husband's prosperity, wealth, long life, all those things. [laughing] It's the only day I wait for my husband for lunch. I bow to him [lit., go to his feet] only once a year."

Gender and *Vrats*

Women's *vrat* traditions such as Varalakshmi Vratam have often been analytically interpreted as a visible indication of women's secondary status in Hindu traditions; because while women fast for the long lives of their brothers and husbands, men do not fast for women's long lives. However, such an interpretation does not fully account for indigenous interpretations of female ritual power, which is not perceived to be simply symbolic, but quite literal. *Vrats* have performative power to shift *karma*, to strengthen devotional relationships with deities, to change the course of family life, and to bring prosperity at numerous levels.

For many women, *vrat* performances for the long lives of their male kin have less to do with men than with their own agency in creating a context in which their auspiciousness can come to full fruition. In many Hindu contexts, women's auspiciousness is equated with that of the goddess – that is, she shares in the very nature of the goddess. In Northwest India, for example, prepubescent girls may be honored at the end of some festival rituals as "goddesses." In South India, women's application of turmeric on their faces on Fridays, days special to the goddess, or on certain festival and *vrat* days may be seen as, quite literally, sharing the substance of the goddess and revealing the nature that they share with the goddess (Flueckiger 2006). However, traditionally, for such auspiciousness to be fully enacted, marriage (or the potential for marriage for prepubescent girls) is necessary. Marriage does not *give* women auspiciousness, but it does give the context for its fulfillment (a subtle but important difference). Thus when women implicitly or explicitly fast for the long lives of their husbands, or to obtain a husband, they are active agents ritually performing and shaping their own auspiciousness.

At least one Varalakshmi Vratam participant, a highly educated woman in her forties, thought that the gender imbalance of *vrat* performances may shift as more and more women begin to work outside the home. When I asked her (at the 2007 *vrat* performance described above) about the perceived gender discrepancy in the directionality of some *vrats* – that is, women performing for the well-being of the family much more often than men – she laughed and, speaking in Telugu, said:

> You're right. In India, 90% of women are dependent on 'gents' [using the English word]. But not now, not in our generation. Look

at this, men have to bring money home, only then we can eat. We have to do our *dharma* and they do their *dharma*. You say they're not performing *pujas* for us. That's true. But that's only one thing; but they do many other things for us. If they're happy in the house, they don't bother us.

I'm telling you, this is how it was – not now – 20 years ago. One person used to earn for everyone. Not like your America, where everyone earns for him/herself. For example, this woman's father [pointing to a friend sitting next to her], he earned and everyone ate and studied. What do you think? Is her father good or not? He didn't do *puja* for her mother, but he did his duty. That itself is a *puja*. For that reason we have to do *puja* for them, right?

[JBF: So do you think that in 20 years your daughters may not perform Varalakshmi Vratam?]

No, they won't do it. In the next generation, women won't perform all these *pujas*. They'll say [to their husbands], "I studied, you studied. I work, you work. I do *puja*, you do *puja*." [Other women listening laugh] But this will happen 20 years from now, not now. … [however,] men actually *do* perform some *pujas*, you know, like Satyanarayan Vratam. …

In 2012, the Jaipur edition of *The Times of India* included two Karva Chauth *vrat* advertisements that reflect the mutuality between husband and wife to which the woman above was referring. One was for the jewelry store named Nayaab, which shows a pair of diamond earrings accompanied by the text:

"AND THEY LIVED HAPPILY (aside from a few normal disagreements and re-agreements, misunderstandings and reconciles, pouts and kisses, and unexpected calamities) EVER AFTER. Happy Karwa Chauth! Let bygones be bygones. Open your heart to the new happiness."

The second Karva Chauth advertisement in the same paper pictures a very traditionally dressed husband holding a platter filled with fruit, a coconut, and a ritual oil lamp; he holds a mirror up to his similarly traditionally dressed wife, with a full moon behind her.

The fast of Karva Chauth ends when a woman first spots the moon. The accompanying text headline is:

THIS KARVA CHAUTH, GIVE HISTORY A NEW STORY. Once upon a time, a woman fasted all day to pray for the safety and longevity of her husband. Today, we know this festival as Karva Chauth. Here's your chance to show your wife that she means as much to you, as you do to her. The Times of India invites its male readers to follow their wives' example and observe the fast with them this year. Take the pledge. And watch tradition take a turn. Will you keep the Karva Chauth fast for your wife? SMS KC<space>YES or NO<space>Your Name<space>YourCity to 48888.

*****

Performatively, *vrats* such as Varalakshmi Vratam and Mangala Gauri Vratam are female-centered ritual occasions that bring together female relatives and neighbors, who cook and eat together, listen to each other's stories, and provide counsel. But, most importantly, *vrats* are believed to give their participants agency in shaping or reshaping their lives, bringing to them, their families, and their homes auspiciousness and – in the case of the two Telugu *vrats above* – the goddess Lakshmi herself.

References

Flueckiger, Joyce Burkhalter. 2006. Guises, Turmeric, and Recognition in the Gangamma Tradition of Tirupati. In *Incompatible Visions: South Asian Religions in History and Culture, Essays in Honor of David M. Knipe*, ed. James Blumenthal, 35–49. Madison, WI: Center for South Asia, University of Wisconsin.

Gold, Ann Grodzins. 2011. Damayanti's String: Epic Threads in Women's Ritual Stories. In *Damayanti and Nala: The Many Lives of a Story*, ed. Susan S. Wadley, 109–129. New Delhi: Chronicle Books.

Narayan, Kirin, in collaboration with Urmila Devi Sood. 1997. *Mondays on the Dark Night of the Moon: Himalayan Foothill Folktales,* Part I: Women's Ritual Tales. New York: Oxford University Press.

Vrats: *Ritual Vows and Women's Auspiciousness*

Pearson, Anne MacKenzie. 1996. *"Because It Gives Me Peace of Mind": Ritual Fasts in the Religious Lives of Hindu Women.* Albany: State University of New York Press.

Pintchman, Tracy. 2003. The Month of Kartik and Women's Ritual Devotions to Krishna in Benares. In *The Blackwell Companion to Hinduism*, ed. Gavin Flood, 327–342. Oxford, UK: Blackwell Publishing Ltd.

Raj, Selva J., and William P. Harman. 2006. *Dealing with Deities: The Ritual Vow in South Asia.* Albany: State University of New York.

Wadley, Susan. 1983. *Vrats:* Transformers of Destiny. In *Karma: An Anthropological Inquiry*, eds. Charles Keyes and E. V. Daniel, 147–162. Berkeley: University of California Press.

Recommended Readings

Harlan, Lindsey. 2007. Words That Breach Walls: Women's Rituals in Rajasthan. In *Women's Lives, Women's Rituals in the Hindu Tradition*, ed. Tracy Pintchman, 65–84. New York: Oxford University Press.

Lutgendorf, Philip. 2003. *Jai Santoshi Maa* Revisited: On Seeing a Hindu "Mythological" Film. In *Representing Religion in World Cinema: Mythmaking, Culture Making, Filmmaking*, ed. S. Brent Plate, 19–42. New York: Palgrave/St Martins.

McDaniel, June. 2003. *Making Virtuous Daughters and Wives: An Introduction to Women's Brata Rituals in Bengali Folk Religion.* Albany: State University of New York Press.

McGee, Mary. 1991. Desired Fruits: Motive and Intention in the Votive Rites of Hindu Women. In *Roles and Rituals for Hindu Women*, ed. Julia Leslie, 71–88. Madison, NJ: Fairleigh Dickinson Press.

7

Samskaras: Transformative Rites of Passage

Samskaras are a series of life-cycle rituals that mark the passage of a person from one stage of life to another and effect transformation of that person. The number of *samskaras* that a family celebrates depends on its caste, class, and region. The standard number in Sanskrit texts such as the Gryhasutras is between 12 and 18, but most Hindus celebrate far fewer, including birth rituals, tonsure of a baby or toddler, marriage, and death. The term *samskara* literally means "refinement, perfection." Hindus assume that these rituals themselves *refine* and purify the body, thereby morally and socially transforming the human body and self that undergo the *samskara*. Mary McGee observes, "The *samskara* process orients individuals towards that which is considered right, good, pure, true, auspicious, moral, and responsible within Hindu culture, and each subsequent *samskara* reinforces these cultural values … *Samskaras* help to situate human life within the larger cycle of the cosmos" (2007, 337–338). While the term *samskara* itself is not used by many Hindu families

Everyday Hinduism, First Edition. Joyce Burkhalter Flueckiger.
© 2015 Joyce Burkhalter Flueckiger. Published 2015 by John Wiley & Sons, Ltd.

who observe these life-cycle rituals (different regional languages have different terms for most of the individual rituals), the term gives us an analytic framework within which to think about these rituals as *effecting* change, not just reflecting it.

Pregnancy and Birth

Among higher castes, a common pre-birth *samskara*, usually performed in the fifth or seventh month of pregnancy, is the *simantam* (lit., parting the hair; often called a "baby shower" in American Indian English). The term *simantam* refers to the act of a husband parting his pregnant wife's hair (traditionally with a porcupine quill), an act that is said to ensure the well-being of both baby and mother and clear the way for safe delivery. However, this male participation with the quill is often dropped in contemporary *simantams*, and the female-centered ritual emphasizes gifting of bangles, fruits, special sweets, new clothes, and flowers to the pregnant mother by other auspicious women. Women say the purpose of the ritual is to bless the pregnancy and the new mother and to "make the baby happy" by hearing the clinking together of the bangles put on the pregnant woman.

After giving birth, a woman and her baby are traditionally sequestered indoors and do not go out in public for a given number of days (seven, nine, 11), which vary by region, caste, and community. During this time, the new mother is often pampered and fed particularly nutritious foods, although she does not directly touch anyone but her baby. Thereafter, a purifying and protective bath is performed for both mother and baby, which facilitates and marks the new baby's entry into the community and the mother's social reintegration. After the bath of mother and baby (traditionally, by a woman of the washermen or barber service-caste), in some upper-caste families, the baby is placed in a vessel filled with unhusked rice and presented to the family deity. For a few minutes the baby is left alone with god, during which time the god Brahma is believed to write the baby's fate on his/her forehead. This ritual also protects the baby from the evil eye as it enters the social world. Several Indian friends have asked me what American women "do" to mark and effect this transition from a new mother's post-partum confinement. When I have replied that "we" don't have any similar ritual, they have responded with astonishment: "You mean you don't *do* anything? You just go out like that?" They are aghast that a new mother would re-enter the public world without purification and ritual protection. Traditionally, a baby is not named until 12 or 21 days, or even three months, after the birth – a timing that developed when infant mortality was extremely high; however, these days many babies are named at birth.

First-Year *Samskaras*

There are several important rituals during the first year of a child, when she/he is rapidly developing, and the rituals help to effect this development. The feeding of first solid food at five or six months (*anna prasanna*) is one important ritual transition. Another is, for many families, the ritual piercing of a baby's or toddler's ears during the first year or after the age of three. One Brahmin family told me that they looked forward to this ritual for their little toddler boy who was "so naughty," and hoped it would calm his high energies (the Hindi word they used for the ear-piercing is *nathna*, the same word used to put a ring in a bull's nose to control his behavior).

Before the age of one or after three, most babies or toddlers undergo a *mundan* (tonsure) that rids the child of all remaining traces of birth pollution that may be held in the hair (hair being particularly absorbent of such pollution). Many women say the *mundan* has no specific "religious" meaning, but that it is simply "custom," which assures that the child will grow thick black hair. Nevertheless, it is a ritual that is *dharmic* according to their families' specific traditions and is often performed at pilgrimage sites or family temples, where professional barbers are employed for the tonsure. Since there are no barbers associated with American temples, many families perform the ritual with the assistance of a temple priest, who simply clips a lock of hair; the parents then complete the full tonsure either at home or have the baby's head shaved at a barbershop. The hair is carefully gathered and ritually disposed of (burying it, for example) so that it is not left to the vagaries of the evil eye. Babies and young children, who are particularly vulnerable to the jealous evil eye cast by humans or supernatural forces, are also often protected with a black dot of kohl on one side of their foreheads, on a cheek, and/or at the bottom of their feet; they may also be protected by evil eye–deflective black glass bangles.

Upanayana and Rituals of Transition to Adulthood

The next significant *samskara* for upper-caste boys (the twice-born *varnas*, Brahmin, Kshatriya, and Vaishya; although today primarily Brahmin) is the *upanayana* (lit., the act of bringing near), traditionally performed between the ages of eight and 11. During this ritual, a boy's father or another senior male relative transmits to him the powerful and sacred Gayatri Mantra (found in Rig Veda 3.62.10): *"May we reach that Savitr [sun god], who moves our mind, who is the supreme light,"*[1] thereby initiating the boy ("drawing him near") to religious learning and ritual responsibilities. A multi-stranded cotton thread (*janeu*) is put on over the left shoulder of the initiate, crossing his torso to the right (some Brahmins wear the thread all the time, but many take it off and wear it only for ritual occasions). From that day onward, the boy is (at least theoretically) considered an adult and is eligible to conduct family rituals. Today, however, the *upanayana* is often performed immediately prior to a young man's wedding ritual itself – that is, a male must be "made" a full adult before entering marriage.

Among some American Brahmin families, the *upanayana* has recently been given higher public visibility as a ritual for young or pubescent boys (rather than its performance being delayed until right before their weddings). In 2011, I attended two Telugu Brahmin

---

[1] Translation by V. Narayana Rao.

upanayana rituals in Atlanta within a month of each other, along with over 100 other guests at each occasion. Both hosting families explicitly equated the *upanayana* to the Jewish *bar mitzvah* or Christian confirmation, as a coming-of-age ritual. Public celebration of this ritual may be one way through which these Hindu-American young boys find a recognizable "place," equivalent to their non-Hindu peers, in the American social landscape.

The two *upanayanas* were held in the garages of suburban homes, which were transformed into ritual spaces with *rangolis* (rice-flour geometric or floral drawings) on the floor and a temporary altar. Women attendees wore fancy silk saris and gold ornaments much like they would to a wedding; tents were set up outside the house under which a meal was served; and cash gifts were given to the young boys. One of the boys was an eight-year-old grandson of a prominent member of the Indian community and flew down to Atlanta from the Northeast for this ritual; the other was an 11-year-old son of a local professional family. Both boys were dressed (for the first time) in a white silk *dhoti* and shawl. They enacted the initiate's traditional journey to Kashi (Varanasi) to begin religious learning, equipped with a walking stick and holding out their shawls to accept "alms" from those they met on the road (the on-looking guests). Upon return from his "journey," each boy sat next to his elder male relative (grandfather in one case and father in the other), who whispered the Gayatri Mantra to him, a shawl hiding both of their heads. Although traditionally the *mantra* should be transmitted secretly, in these cases, the boys repeated the *mantra* through a microphone, for all present at the occasion to hear, displaying their new knowledge. A fire-offering (*homam*) and *pujas* were subsequently performed, before the guests partook of a meal together.

Some non-Brahmin castes celebrate a boy's transition to adulthood with a ritual in which he puts on a *dhoti* (traditional male garment wrapped around the lower body) for the first time, rather than the *upanayana*. These same castes perform a similar ritual for girls when they first wear a sari, traditionally a sign of adulthood. However, since in contemporary society these young boys and girls are still going to school, they do not continue to wear saris or *dhotis*

Figure 7.1 Grandfather whispering the Gayatri Mantra to his grandson, Atlanta.

on a regular basis. These rituals involve gift giving, often a small piece of gold or gold chain, by close relatives.

Women were traditionally excluded from learning the Vedas and, hence, traditionally not taught the Gayatri Mantra or initiated into textual, Sanskritic learning. However, in South India, many girls undergo their own coming-of-age rituals when their families publicly celebrate a girl's first menstruation.[2] The pubescent girl is anointed with female-associated auspicious turmeric paste for the first time, dressed in silks (often wearing a sari for the first time, if she hasn't performed the sari-wearing ritual earlier) and new ornaments – a display of her newly auspicious status as a

---

[2] In Telugu, the ritual is called *peddamanishi avadam* (lit., becoming a big person) or *cira kattadam* (lit., wearing a sari); in Tamil, the ritual is sometimes called *mancal nir* (lit., yellow [turmeric] water, with which the girl is bathed). In all Indian languages, menstruation is spoken about euphemistically, such as "becoming untouchable," or "going out of the house," or a woman "in her month."

Figure 7.2 The initiate beginning his trip to Kashi, Atlanta.

potentially fertile woman – and relatives and friends are invited to a celebratory feast.[3]

Although some middle- and upper-class families (who consider it "backward" – i.e., not "modern") no longer celebrate their daughters' first menstruation, other rising middle-class families in South India and diasporic communities have begun to celebrate girls' puberty rituals in more ostentatious and public ways than their families traditionally did. A social hall or restaurant may be rented for the occasion and guests may number in the hundreds; more

---

[3] Traditionally, one reason for this public puberty ritual was to announce a girl's marriageability, and sometimes the ritual was delayed until a family had saved the resources to pay for a wedding according to their class status or aspired status. However, in contemporary India, most girls have reached puberty several years before they get married (the legal age of marriage for girls is 16 and for boys is 18).

expensive gifts are given the girl; and a videographer or photographer is often hired to document the occasion. Some South Indian families in the Unites States (highly variant depending on local community) have also introduced the ritual to the American landscape or return to India to celebrate the ritual.

I attended one such ritual for the14-year-old daughter of a Tamil Brahmin professional couple living in Atlanta. The mother wanted to celebrate her daughter's "coming of age" to affirm her equality to her brother, who had undergone his *upanayana* a few years earlier. She was particularly disconcerted by the fact that girls were traditionally denied the Gayatri Mantra and given no equivalent sacred verse; and so she taught the *mantra* to her daughter, who recited it for all present to hear. The family invited six of the girl's best friends and their mothers (none of whom were Hindu), as well as several India-associated friends of her mother. Each adult woman wrote something for the girl – a blessing or a memory of the girl's childhood – in a scrapbook, which was subsequently read aloud to the girl; and each guest brought a small gift. The girl's maternal uncle (who traditionally has special obligations to his sister's children) had flown in to Atlanta from Houston to be present for the occasion and had presented the girl with her first sari. A computer was set up with Skype so that the girl's grandparents in India could witness the occasion and give their blessings. Another American Brahmin teenage girl told me, on the occasion of her younger brother's *upanayana*, that her parents had offered to perform a coming-of-age ritual for her, but that at the time, she said, she had been "too embarrassed" and declined; now, several years later, she thought she'd made a mistake, as she saw the attention and (primarily cash) gifts her younger brother was receiving at his *upanayana*.

In Northwest India, a ritual known as Kumari Puja (lit., worship of a virgin) is celebrated during Navaratri, during which nine prepubescent girls are honored as embodiments of the goddess. But North Indian families do not celebrate a coming-of-age ritual for girls; rather, onset of menstruation is usually highly secretive, even within the girl's family itself. The mapping of regions in India where girls' puberty rituals are celebrated correlates in interesting ways with the sex ratios of girls to boys under the age of six in those regions, with the ratio being higher in regions where girls' puberty is publicly and ritually marked. Sex ratios are often used by international agencies such as the World Bank as an indication of the relative status of women/girls in a particular region or country. While there is no direct cause and effect between girls' publicly marked coming-of-age rituals and sex ratios, and many other economic and social factors come into play (such as whether the region is rice- or wheat-growing – the former requiring female labor – literacy rates, etc.), their correlation raises interesting questions about the relationship between this *samskara* and women's status.

Ranga Pravesham: Ascending the (Dance) Stage

Girls – and proportionally many fewer boys – who have trained in Indian classical dance forms celebrate what has come to be another kind of "coming of age" ritual, usually performed several years after reaching puberty: the *ranga pravesham* or *arangetram* (lit., entering or ascending the stage). This occasion marks a dancer's readiness to "ascend the stage" and give a full-length (often up to two hours) solo dance performance – a graduation, of sorts. While the dance concert is not called a *samskara* by its participants or audiences, analytically it "works" as such, ritually and performatively transforming the young dancer and marking the fulfillment of learning a particular body of knowledge.

Traditionally in India, this ritual was low-key and private, marking the readiness of a young dancer to perform publicly, either in a private salon or in a temple; the primary ritual was the blessing of her ankle bells. However, today *ranga praveshams* in both India and the United States are often elaborate, expensive affairs for daughters of middle- and upper-class Indian families – with fancy invitations (these days, often online e-vites) and glossy programs with a professional photograph of the dancer, large audiences, a chief guest, speeches, and a catered meal. That is, the ritual performance is often a context in which not only to show the expertise of a dancer, but also to display her family's wealth and status. In the United States, like the *upanayana*, *ranga praveshams* have been compared by their participants to a *bar* or *bat mizvah*, which similarly mark the culmination of training in a tradition. While traditionally the *ranga pravesham* was the beginning of one's public dance career, today it often marks the end of a dancer's training and performance, and she goes on into another profession.

In the American diaspora, proportionally many more girls than in India study classical Indian dance. Girls, in particular, are encouraged by their parents to learn dance as a way to learn Hindu mythologies, Indian gendered body language (grace, modesty), minimal Indian language skills, and other cultural values such as respect for elders and gurus – that is, as a means through which to *embody* particular Hindu and/or Indian values and identity. Arthi Devarajan has analyzed the "cultural capital" Indian classical dance instruction and the *ranga pravesham*, in particular, create for the dancer and her family in American contexts (including its benefits on college applications) (2012).

Marriage

Hindu weddings are elaborate affairs consisting of many rituals, often performed over several hours to several days. It's difficult to generalize Hindu wedding rituals, as in this *samskara* there is perhaps the greatest variation between regions, castes, sub-sects, and families.

Traditionally, Hindu weddings are *family* affairs, beginning with the negotiations between families in arranging their children's weddings (and the great majority of marriages are still arranged, although what are called "love marriages" and cross-caste marriages are increasing). This is one of the occasions where caste most matters in contemporary India; parents look for a match with someone from the same *jati* or *kulam*, which means, in practicality, someone whose family speaks the same regional language, performs the same rituals and festivals, eats the same kinds of foods, and so on. An Indian American student, who said she had been raised with no explicit mention of caste growing up in the American South, told me she was dismayed when, upon graduation from college, her parents began to talk about caste in terms of her marriage. She exclaimed that she had learned, "Not only do I have to marry an Indian, a South Indian – I have to marry a Reddy [Telugu caste]!" Many Indian American young people choose their own spouses; others find partners through a "semi-arranged" process, through which their parents identify potential partners, the couple meets, and then determines whether they want to follow through with exploring the relationship further.

For both North and South Indian arranged marriages, the bride and groom should belong to different *gotras* (patrilines). In North Indian rural families and communities, traditionally a marriage match would be made *outside* the village or circle of relatives (those in the village are considered kin; of course this is changing in urban India); whereas among many South Indian communities, a desirable match is traditionally a cross-cousin (mother's brother's child, father's sister's child, or a cousin who fits in this category – a match that is *outside* of a shared *gotra*, since a woman joins her husband's *gotra*). These differences in marriage-arrangement practices impact the experience of the new bride, whether she is marrying into a "foreign land" (as some North Indian folksongs call the home of marriage) or into a known family (at least theoretically, if not in fact).

To aid in their search for brides and bridegrooms, families may employ the services of a matchmaker, rely on friends and family to suggest appropriate matches, or place matrimonial ads in the newspaper and/or on the internet (on sites such as shaadi.com). When a desirable match is found, traditionally the horoscopes of the couple are taken to an astrologer to determine if the astrological charts of the couple are compatible and then to determine an auspicious month, day, and time for the wedding. The specific timing for the ritual that actually "makes" a couple married is performed at a select *sumuhurtam* (auspicious time), which may occur very early in the morning or late at night. What this ritual is varies between castes and regions: in some communities, the ritual of stepping seven times around or in front of the sacred fire is performed at the *sumuhurtam*, and in other communities the ritual that makes a couple married is tying the *mangalsutra* (wedding pendant); in Telugu Brahmin communities, the ritual that should be performed at the *sumuhurtam* is when the bride and groom place a jaggery-cumin paste on each other's heads.[4]

In India, family negotiations often include discussions of dowry or bride-price. While demanding or taking dowry (the payment made by a bride's family to that of a bridegroom) is illegal (punishable by a prison term and/or fines) according to the Dowry Prohibition Act of 1961, it remains a common, even growing, practice among many families.[5] Bride-price is payment by the groom's family to the bride's family to compensate for the female labor that the bride's family is losing. Some lower castes among which female labor, in particular, is valued (such as working in agriculture, where women are highly involved in transplanting and harvesting rice paddy) practice bride-price rather than dowry. In contemporary India, many families from these castes are shifting from the practice of bride-price to that of dowry, emulating middle- and upper-class and caste customs that they may have observed in movies, on television, or (for village-to-urban immigrants) among their urban neighbors.

---

[4] One Telugu Hindu-American wedding program explained this ritual as follows: "The *Sumuhurtam* is the auspicious time calculated for the marriage at exactly 11:40 a.m. The bride and groom place a paste made up of cumin seeds (*jilakarra*) and brown sugar (*bellam*) on each other's head, symbolizing the union of their two souls."

[5] Prosecution under this act is difficult, since it is often difficult to distinguish what consumer goods and cash are given by a bride's family as gifts and what have been demanded by the groom's family as dowry, and the distinction may depend on oral testimony of each side. In 1983 an amendment was added to the Indian Penal Code to protect women from "cruelty" by her husband and/or in-laws. While the amendment does not specifically refer to dowry, it has been used to prosecute what is colloquially called "dowry harassment" – continuing demands for more dowry by a groom's family to a bride's family *after* the wedding.

Yamini Atmavilas has observed this shift among female garment workers in the South Indian city of Bangalore, where young women from castes that have traditionally practiced bride-price have begun to save up for their own dowries out of their own earnings; they consider this ability to be a sign of their independence and agency (2008).

Pre-wedding ceremonies include what (in Telugu) is literally called "making the bride," during which the bride is blessed by married women, who give her new bangles and apply vermilion and turmeric powders to her forehead and cheeks. In North India, the groom may appear at this all-female ritual to apply vermilion powder for the first time in the hair parting of the bride (a sign and creation of her married status), after which married women transfer vermilion from their own hair partings to that of the bride. The transfer or application of vermilion and turmeric is a material means through which married women share with the new bride their own auspiciousness, help to *create* her auspiciousness, and give her their blessings. Both groom and bride are given a "turmeric bath" (*mangala snanam*; lit., auspicious bath) the day of the wedding, which is said to make the skin glow and further aids the ritual transformation of the couple.

Most Hindu weddings include some form of "gifting the bride" by her father to the bridegroom (called *kanyadan,* lit. gift of the virgin). In some South Indian upper-caste weddings, the bride sits in a basket that is carried by the maternal uncle, and she is, quite literally, handed over to the groom. Other brides may stand in large brass platters that their fathers ritually give to her in-laws; or families may hand over a coconut in place of the bride herself to enact this *kanyadan*. For most Hindu weddings, the union is solemnized in the presence of the sacred fire (Agni), which may burn in a ritual fire pit or charcoal brazier. With the end of the bride's sari and the end of the groom's shoulder scarf or *dhoti* tied together, the couple takes seven steps (*saptapadi*) around or in front of the fire. In most upper-caste weddings that employ the services of a Brahmin priest, the following verse is recited in Sanskrit as the couple rounds the fire:

One step for vigor; two steps for vitality;
Three steps for prosperity; four steps for happiness.
Five steps for cattle (or progeny); six steps for seasons.
Seven steps for friendship.
With this seventh step may we become friends,
Devoted to each other.

(McGee 2007, 350)

In the United States, where the couple and many guests may not understand the Sanskrit recited during the wedding rituals and do not know what the various ritual steps are, the families of the couple often provide a printed program that explains each step and gives English translations of some of the Sanskrit recitations, such as the verse above. It should be noted that in India, too, many (even most) participants do not understand Sanskrit, but they are typically less concerned about understanding the discursive meaning of what is being recited than they are that the correct ritual is being performed to effect the appropriate end.[6]

While a bride may wear "generic" saris and glass and/or gold bangles in her everyday life before and after the wedding – or, if she is an upper-class professional woman, she may wear neither sari nor bangles on a daily basis – during these rituals she often wears traditional hand-woven saris (in some families, changing multiple times for different rituals) and gold or silver ornaments that perform her regional, caste, and family identities. Of particular significance is the wedding pendant – called a *tali* in South India and a *mangalsutra* (lit., thread of auspiciousness) in the North – whose shape and symbolic significance vary by family and caste. During the wedding rituals, the groom ties a woman's *tali* around her neck, and some scholars and Indian women have interpreted this act as both male protection and "binding" of a woman's mobility. In *The Powers of Tamil Women*,

---

[6] At weddings in India, guests often mingle and talk with one another as these rituals are being performed; rituals are effective whether or not guests are watching or listening. In American Hindu weddings, however, guests are usually seated in chairs in rows, watching the ritual with (relative) silence.

Holly Reynolds goes further in concluding that a husband *gives* his wife her auspicious status when he ties the *tali*:

> When a man ties a *tali* around the neck of a woman, he binds her to him with a symbol of all his culturally and socially derived identities, *makes* [my emphasis] that woman a *cumankali* [auspicious; *sumangali*], and entrusts to her the well-being of himself and his lineage, an act that paradoxically makes the wife the protector of the husband. … In owning the *tali*, the husband controls the auspiciousness of his wife: he confers *cumankali* [*sumangali*] status upon her at marriage and deprives her of it at his death (1991:45–46).

However, South Indian puberty rituals, during which a girl may be given a small *tali* and when her potential fertility is celebrated (see above), suggest that a pubescent girl is already auspicious before marriage. According to dominant cultural norms, husbands and marriage are needed to act upon this fertility and auspiciousness, but these puberty rituals suggest that it does not *give* auspiciousness to a woman. (See Chapter 1 for discussion of *gramadevata* goddesses who wear the *tali*, but have no husbands.)

Most women I have spoken with about their *talis* and the rituals they perform around them rarely mention their husbands or attribute to him the kind of agency McGee talks about above. One elderly Tamil woman talked about the agency of the *tali* itself (seemingly independent of the husband), showing me how the strength of the *tali*, and hence the strength of the marriage, is maintained by rubbing the *tali* thread or chain with turmeric once a week; other women continue to wear their *talis* even if they are separated from their husbands and may not even know where he is. They remain, regardless of the "health" of their marriage, auspicious women until they become divorced or widowed, when most women remove the *tali*. *Talis* are a center of female power (*shakti*) that, in South India, are significantly not displayed openly, but are tucked inside a woman's sari. The *tali* thread or chain often holds a house key, an amulet, the ubiquitous Indian woman's safety pins, and perhaps small gold pieces given to a woman by her mother on festival days. When South Indian women visit each other in their homes, at leave-taking, the hostess traditionally

Figure 7.3   Telugu Cakali-caste *tali.*

Figure 7.4   Tamil Brahmin Iyer-caste *tali.*

Figure 7.5   Tamil Mudaliar-caste *tali*.

Figure 7.6   Chhattisgarhi Kolta-caste *mangalsutra*.

185

marks the visitor's *tali* with vermilion powder, and the visitor does the same to her hostess – an act of sharing auspiciousness.

While many of the wedding-associated rituals and customs described above (such as ornamentation, clothing, or the transfer of vermilion and turmeric between married women and the new bride) may not be considered "religious" in the English connotations of the word, they are *dharmic* – that is, they help to order the world and, like other *samskara*s, effect transformation.

Death Rituals

The transition of a body and soul at death is fraught with the danger of pollution and the potential dissatisfaction of the deceased's soul. The purpose of the death-ritual *samskara,* called *antyesti* in Sanskrit (lit., last rite), is to help the soul transition to the realm of ancestors or the next life (depending on the context in which a Hindu may talk about it); the souls of those who die an untimely death, in particular, may not want to move on, away from their families, and must be ritually encouraged to do so.

Most Hindu corpses are cremated (traditionally within 24 hours), although some castes and sects (such as Virashaivas) practice burial; and persons who die of poxes (indicative of the presence of the goddess) or snake bites, and infants and renouncers are also traditionally buried. In India, the corpse is carried on a bier in a procession, often led by professional drummers, through the streets to the cremation ground or crematorium. The oldest adult son has the responsibility to light the funeral pyre or, in the case of electric crematoriums, lower the switch to start the fire. This responsibility is one explanation for the need for sons, although nephews and brothers may also light the cremation fire; more recently some daughters (when there are no sons), too, have begun to take up this responsibility.

The mourning period is designated for a variously prescribed number of days (up to 13 days), depending on the identity of the deceased. During this time, close relatives of the deceased are considered to be ritually polluted – so, for example, they would not traditionally attend weddings, celebrate festivals, and so on – and immediate male family members shave their heads (an example of the Hindu concept of the permeability of human hair, in this case absorbing the pollution of death). Numerous rituals are performed during this period, until, on the final day, *pindas* (rice balls) are offered by the family, amidst long rituals, to provide a body with which the deceased can transition to the world of the ancestors (*pitr loka*, realm of the fathers) and *become* an ancestor (Knipe 1977). The family of the deceased then sponsors a feast for relatives and community, which reintegrates the family into its social worlds. In the same way that brides are ritually "made," so, too, are widows "made" when, on the day ending the period of mourning, they break their glass bangles and take off their wedding pendants that have performed their auspiciousness.[7] Many castes perform a series of rituals on behalf of the deceased during the first year after the death and thereafter annually, giving families time and an active role through which to process the deep losses of death.

The cremains (ashes) of the deceased are immersed in a sacred body of water, ideally the Ganga River or its regional equivalent. Families may keep the ashes for weeks or months until they can make pilgrimage to a site along the Ganga such as Varanasi, Gaya, or Haridwar. The ashes of most Hindus who die in the United States are taken by relatives back to India for immersion in a sacred body of water, although some Hindus are beginning to immerse the ashes of their loved ones in American rivers, thereby acknowledging the sacred potential of the American landscape.

As mentioned in the Introduction, the question of what happens to the soul after death is complex and a good example of the context-specificity that characterizes Hindu traditions; the answer depends on when the question is asked – in relationship to a particular recent death, or more generically outside the context of such a death. The rituals around death take place in the context of

---

[7] I have been chastised for wearing only silver bangles when I've done so in rural Chhattisgarh, as an arm with no glass bangles is that of a widow and invites inauspiciousness.

the worlds of ancestors. But were one to ask the question of what happens to a soul after death outside the context of a specific death, one may hear the answer that the soul transmigrates or reincarnates into a new body. Many Hindus believe that the god of death, Yama, or one of his attendants comes to fetch a person at his/her fated time of death (the time of which is written on a person's forehead by Brahma at birth). Yama "weighs" the good and bad acts of a person (*karma*) to determine whether the soul goes to heaven or hell or the form into which the soul is reincarnated.

While one's death may be considered to be fated, there are ways to divert fate, primarily through devotion. The commonly known story of Savitri (which appears in the Mahabharata, but circulates independently in oral tradition and is pictured in lithographs and paintings) narrates this dynamic; it opens with the power of ritual to counteract what would seem to be fated – in this case, a king's infertility:

Once there was childless king who performed many ascetic and devotional rituals that resulted in the birth of his daughter, Savitri. She grew into a beautiful and devoted young woman whose sterling reputation seemingly intimidated potential suitors, and no man asked for her in marriage. Finally, her father told her to find a husband on her own. She set out on a pilgrimage for this purpose and, in the jungle, came upon a young man, Satyavan, who was serving his blind father (a former king) who had lost everything, including his sight and his kingdom. Savitri decided that she wanted Satyavan to be her husband. When she returned home to announce her choice, she found her father speaking with Sage Narada, who told the king that Savitri had made a terrible mistake: although Satyavan was perfect in every way, he was destined to die one year from that day. Savitri insisted that she had already made her decision and would not change it.[8]

[8] Note the similarities, to this point, with the Mangala Gauri Vratam story in Chapter 6.

Savitri and Satyavan got married and lived in the forest hermitage with Savitri's in-laws, whom she served as a "perfect" daughter-in-law. Three days before the predicted death of her husband, Savitri began to fast; and on that fateful morning, she asked her in-laws' for permission to accompany her husband into the forest, where he went every day to collect firewood.

While Satyavan was splitting the wood, he suddenly became weak and lay down. And then Yama, the god of death, came to claim his life, as had been predicted. As Savitri followed him, Yama told her that while she could follow her husband as a faithful wife in life, she could not follow him in death. But Yama told her that, because of her loyalty, he would give her a boon; only she could not request that the life of her husband be given back. Savitri asked for restoration of her father-in-law's eyesight. And she kept following Yama, who offered her another boon; this time Savitri requested restoration of her father-in-law's kingdom. She kept following Yama, who granted her a third boon; this time she asked for one hundred sons for her father. Finally, undeterred by Yama's insistence that she turn back, Savitri was offered a fourth boon, which like the others, excluded Satyavan's life; she asked for a hundred sons for herself. Yama then realized the dilemma he had created: to fulfill the boon of sons, Savitri needed a living husband. Because of the power of his word, Yama was compelled to fulfill her request and restore Satyavan to life.

This story is frequently told as a model for a faithful wife; but it raises other dynamics: the power of ritual to counter fate and the independent agency of boons (and in other narratives, curses) that, once offered, must be fulfilled.

As mentioned in Chapter 2, Hindu traditions also incorporate a concept of heavens and hells, to which the soul migrates until the good or bad *karma* of its life is "burned off," at which time it returns to a life form in this world. The game of snakes and ladders, which originated in India, is another visualization of the *karma* of particular good and bad deeds; a player who lands on a square with a good deed climbs a short or long ladder towards *moksha* (liberation), whereas if she/he lands on a square with a bad deed, she/he slides down the board on a snake to a lower level, the lowest level being hell.

While many Muslim families celebrate some *samskaras* in ways similar to their Hindu neighbors – first solid food feeding, first menstruation (in South India, where many Hindus and Muslims publicly celebrate this transition; called *aqiqa* in Urdu), the turmeric "bath" of bride and groom before marriage, and henna rituals for the bride – other rites of passage rituals perform the distinction of Muslim and Hindu identities, including male circumcision in Muslim families and the means of disposal of the corpse (burial or cremation). While some Hindu castes practice burial, no Muslims (or Indian Christians) practice cremation. Many stories circulate of saints, in particular, who in life identified as neither Hindu nor Muslim, but whose religious affiliation became an issue upon death, when a decision needed to be made whether to bury or cremate their bodies. A story is told of the fifteenth-century poet-saint Kabir: in life, it was difficult to categorize him as either Muslim or Hindu; he critiqued the hypocrisy and external rituals of both communities. However, after his death, each community vied for his body; Muslims wanted to bury it and Hindus wanted to cremate it. As the debate was still ongoing, someone lifted the shroud over the body and found that it had turned into a heap of flowers, which could be equally divided, one portion for burial and one for cremation (Hess and Singh 1983, 4).

A more recent example from the 1980s is the story of a *baba* (ascetic, saint) who mysteriously appeared on the stairs of a sari store in the central bazaar of Raipur (Chhattisgarh); he spoke no language any one could understand – some thought he may be from Afghanistan – and he was naked except for a wool blanket with which he covered himself. Gradually, passersby noticed that he didn't eat (although he did smoke cigarettes), nor did he defecate or urinate – miraculous signs that were interpreted as indications of his spiritual power. People started to light cigarettes in his presence and considered it his blessing if he accepted them – and other miracles began to occur: infertility was healed, failing businesses began to thrive, and students gained admission to competitive schools. His photograph could be found in nearly every rickshaw and tea stall in Raipur. After ten years, the *baba* died; and, like Kabir, a decision had to be made whether he was Hindu or Muslim and thus whether his corpse would be cremated or buried. The case was decided by a court, which ruled in favor of the Muslim community, and the body was buried. In life, Hindus, Muslims, and Christians all came to the *baba* for healing and he was not identified with any single religious community; in death, he became a Muslim and a large Muslim shrine grew up around his grave – an example of the transformative nature of *samskaras*, in this case the *samskara* of burial.

*****

Samskara rituals make explicit the transformative, active power of ritual in Hinduism more generally. In a Hindu worldview, rituals are not performed as simply a symbolic reflection of a pre-existing theology or condition, but are explicitly acknowledged as agentive in effecting human transformation, in creating new identities, and as identifying and sustaining social communities.

References

Atmavilas, Yamini. 2008. Of Love and Labor: Women Workers, Modernity and Changing Gender Relations in Bangalore, India. Ph.D. Thesis, Emory University.

Devarajan, Arthi. 2012. Dancing Krishna in the Suburbs: Kinaesthetics in the South Asian Diaspora. *Studies in South Asian Film and Media* 4, 2: 167–177.

Hess, Linda, and Shukdev Singh. 1983. *The Bijak of Kabir*. San Francisco: North Point Press.

Knipe, David M. 1977. *Sapindikarana*: The Hindu Rite of Entry into Heaven. In *Religious Encounters with Death: Insights from the History and Anthropology of Religion*, eds. Frank E. Reynolds and Earle H. Waugh, 111–124. University Park: Pennsylvania State University Press.

McGee, Mary. 2007. *Samskara*. In *The Hindu World*, eds. Sushil Mittal and Gene Thursby, 332–356. New York: Routledge.

Reynolds, Holly. 1991 [1980]. The Auspicious Married Woman. In *Powers of Tamil Women*, ed. Susan S. Wadley, 35–60. Syracuse: Maxwell School of Citizenship and Public Affairs, Syracuse University.

Recommended Readings

Anantha Murthy, U. R. (transl. A. K. Ramanujan). 1978 [1989]. *Samskara: A Rite for a Dead Man*. New York: Oxford University Press.

Elmore, Mark. 2006. Contemporary Hindu Approaches to Death: Living With the Dead. In *Death and Religion in a Changing World*, ed. Kathleen Garces-Foley, 23–44. Armonk, NY: M. E. Sharpe.

Hopkins, Thomas J. 1992. Hindu Views of Death and Afterlife. In *Death and Afterlife: Perspectives of World Religions*, ed. Hiroshi Obayashi, 143–155. Westport Connecticut: Praeger.

Perry, Jonathan P. 1994. *Death in Banaras*. New York: Cambridge University Press.

Wilson, Elizabeth, ed. 2003. *The Living and the Dead: Social Dimensions of Death in South Asian Religions*. Albany, NY: State University of New York Press.

8

Ritual Healing, Possession, and Astrology

Ritual healing is a dominant religious idiom that crosses boundaries of different religious traditions in India. Hindus seek the expertise of ritual healers for a range of illnesses that some biomedical practitioners may distinguish as psychological or physical (or not as illnesses at all), including: infertility, restlessness, chronic pain, financial difficulties, failing businesses, runaway children, difficulties in marital relationships, failure-to-thrive or colicky babies, and childhood fevers and illnesses. Generally, they come for what in Hindi is called *pareshani* – general trouble. The implication is that the physical, social, and spiritual worlds are somehow out of order (*adharmic*) and need righting. And so, the term "healing" in this chapter is used in its broadest implications, as an indigenous response to suffering.

Everyday Hinduism, First Edition. Joyce Burkhalter Flueckiger.
© 2015 Joyce Burkhalter Flueckiger. Published 2015 by John Wiley & Sons, Ltd.

Accessing Multiple Healing Sites

If a problem has been diagnosed through ritual means, possession, or astrology as being caused by a spiritual force, its cure is assumed to be found in spiritual healing; if its cause is biological, then biomedical medicine may be the answer. Some problems are readily identified as being caused by a spiritual force (possession outside a ritual context, for example); others are not so easily distinguished by patients, which is why they may simultaneously seek the advice and prescriptions of both a biomedical practitioner and a ritual healer.

Patients and their families often go to ritual healers who belong to religious communities outside of their own; further, they often access several different healing systems, or different practitioners within a single "system," at the same time. For example, a Hindu patient may visit both a Hindu temple and Muslim grave-shrine (*dargah*) known for particular kinds of healing at the same time that she/he is being treated by a biomedical doctor and consulting with an astrologer, without experiencing any conflict between them. Indeed, such religious and ritual healing options are numerous, and may be combined in different permutations by those who seek relief.

One example, drawn from the city of Hyderabad, demonstrates the density of religious healing sites in one neighborhood, as well as the tendency that Hindus, Muslims, and Christians have to seek solutions to their problems at sites from multiple religious traditions. Within a mile radius of the healing room of a female Muslim healer, there are numerous spiritual healing sites that are visited by Muslims, Hindus, and Christians: a Hindu village goddess (*gramadevata*) shrine where Hindu petitioners tie coconuts in the limbs of surrounding trees and Muslims offer bamboo representations of the tomb of the Prophet's martyred grandson Hussein in hopes of becoming fertile; a *dargah* of a Muslim saint where an elderly Muslim man sits on the sidewalk selling rings of precious stones associated with the planets that are said to protect the body and restore the balance of its elements; St Anthony's Church where Christian and Hindu petitioners line up every Thursday to receive healing blessings from the resident saint; and a Christian charismatic church that self-identifies as a "healing church" where prayers for healing are offered on behalf of worshippers.

Another vignette illustrates the access to different religious healing traditions by one individual. Several years ago, I was invited to dinner at the home of a Hindu high school teacher in Hyderabad. When I arrived at her home, she asked me if I would mind postponing dinner until she had visited a particular Hindu goddess temple in fulfillment of a vow she had made to visit the temple for 11 consecutive Thursdays. My friend explained that she had made this vow on behalf of her young servant girl who had been diagnosed with leukemia. Biomedical treatments, which the girl's family had first sought out and involved a bone marrow transplant, were beyond the means of the girl's family or even of my hostess. And so they were trying ritual alternatives. On the way to the Hindu temple, we stopped at a small roadside Christian Marion shrine, where my hostess lit an oil lamp; and later in the evening when she heard about the female Muslim healer with whom I had worked, she asked if I would take her and the young girl to her.

Accessing multiple healing systems at the same time is an example of the polytheistic imagination that has traditionally characterized Indian culture[1] and of a shared worldview and ritual grammar that crosses many religious boundaries in India. This worldview accepts the permeable boundaries between human bodies and supernatural forces (whose agency is assumed) and the possibilities of non-human forces entering and affecting the physical and social worlds of humans. Many of these supernatural forces are not inherently destructive, but simply restless, jealous, or unhappy, whether

---

[1] Many Americans also access multiple healing systems at the same time, but it is not always as readily accepted and often patients are reluctant to tell allopathic doctors of the other systems they are trying.

because they have not been acknowledged or served appropriately, or because they are "out of place."

Hindus may treat what they perceive to be a spiritual problem, or a problem for which they think a deity can intervene on their behalf, without going to a healing specialist. For example, a woman and her female kin may perform specific vow-rituals (*vrats*; see Chapter 6) in order to find a "good husband," even before the search has begun, or if they think that pregnancy is not being achieved as soon as they think "normal." Some rituals and pilgrimages may be performed either as a kind of preventative medicine or to fulfill a vow, while others fulfill a prescription pronounced by a specialist. Ritual specialists are chosen according to their reputation for success, their specialties in dealing with particular kinds of problems, and/or their charisma and long-term relationships that the patient's family has formed with them.

Distinction between different kinds of ritual healers comes primarily in their methods of diagnosis and the ritual prescriptions they offer. Diagnoses include the spiritual cause of the illness: demon or ghost affliction, spirits of the dead who do not want to "move on," astrological forces, sorcery, evil eye (*drishti, nazar*), curses, or failure to recognize the presence of a deity or to serve him/her appropriately, among others. Diagnostic rituals may include "reading" or interpreting the patterns in rice grains, lemons, or other ingredients brought from the patient's home; the healer becoming possessed by a deity who will interrogate the patient and pronounce the problem; consultation with astrological texts and charts; or mathematical calculations. Sometimes the diagnosis is made only after a ritual has been performed and the problem solved (such as infertility).

Ritual prescriptions depend, of course, on the diagnosis. If a deity has not been appropriately served or the spirit of an ancestor is restless or wants to continue to live in the human world rather than moving on to the next birth or afterlife, the prescription may be to establish a worship place for that deity or spirit and to start serving him/her (Sax 2008; Gold 2000, Chapter 2). Other prescriptions may include rituals that quite literally "lift off" the evil eye

Figure 8.1 Cradles holding images of baby Krishna tied to a tree, Mundakkanni Amman Temple, Chennai. Courtesy of Amy L. Allocco.

Figure 8.2 Close-up of cradle holding image of baby Krishna (2–3 inches tall).

(a glance by a human or supernatural being upon someone or something that she/he is attracted to or envious of that causes harm to the evil eye's recipient), rituals that make specific kinds of offerings to the appropriate deity, or going on a particular pilgrimage.

Infertility is one illness that has numerous potential physical and spiritual causes for which Hindus often seek spiritual healing. A common ritual performed without intervention of a ritual specialist is the offering of a "cradle" that is tied to a tree at a temple whose deity is well known for curing infertility; or simpler red threads may be tied around the limbs of such trees. Along the footpath to the top of the mountain where the famous temple of Venkateshvara is located, particular trees are filled with cloth cradles wrapped around a stone that stands in for the desired baby.

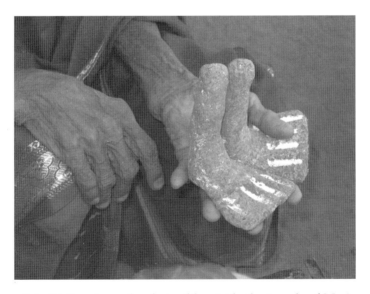

Figure 8.3 Votive straw-clay feet sold outside the temple of Mariamma, Kumbakonam, Tamil Nadu, to be offered to goddess for relief of feet problems.

Similarly, ailing worshippers at some temples may offer white metal or clay votive offerings in the shape of the body part that is causing them pain or other problems: arms, torsos, legs, feet.

Healing across Religious Boundaries

As mentioned at the opening of the chapter, many Indians access ritual healing across religious boundaries. One such example is the practice of a female Muslim healer whom her patients call "Amma," whose healing room is in the South Indian city of Hyderabad.[2] At the height of her practice in the late 1990s, Amma saw between 30 and 50 patients a day – Hindus, Christians, and Muslims. The majority of Amma's patients were women (who are generally responsible for the health of their family members) and who were mostly (but not exclusively) from lower- to middle-class families. Patients came to her with many of the troubles mentioned earlier in the chapter; and many said they chose to come to her for her reputation of unusual patience, love, and healing success. Significantly, very few patients came to Amma's healing room by themselves; they were usually accompanied by one or more family members, who often also asked for diagnoses from Amma for their own problems.

The primary diagnostic method in this healing system is a mathematical calculation based on numbers associated with the Urdu/ Arabic letters of the patient's name, his/her mother's name, and the astrological date. The resulting number gives the diagnosis of a particular kind of evil eye – one cast by humans or non-human beings (ghosts, jinn, or spirits), knowingly or unknowingly. If the mathematical

---

[2] Amma died in 2001; however, her practice has been continued by her primary disciple (himself a Hindu convert to Islam) and her son and grandson. The field-work upon which this description is made was conducted between 1995 and 2001 (see Flueckiger 2006). The religious diversity of patients continues in the practice of her son and grandson; most of the disciple's patients are Hindu, since he lives in a Hindu-majority neighborhood.

Figure 8.4 Amma blowing benedictory prayers on a Hindu patient at the end of a consult.

end result was zero, Amma declared that the problem had not been caused by a spiritual force and that the patient should go to a biomedical practitioner (the names of which she often suggested).[3]

While the specific ways in which it is diagnosed or recognized may vary, belief in the evil eye is a phenomenon shared across religious boundaries in India. Mothers of young babies and toddlers often apply a black dot of kohl on the foreheads and the bottoms of the feet of their babies to deflect the evil eye; brides and grooms across religious traditions are considered to be similarly vulnerable to evil eye because of their beauty, and cash is often circled around their heads by their female kin to deflect or absorb the evil eye (the cash is subsequently given to the poor).

Amma's ritual prescriptions externalized and manipulated the negative forces that had caused illness. Most prescriptions were

[3] Most patients were not satisfied with a diagnosis of zero and asked Amma to "give them *something*." She complied by giving them amulets of protection and listening to their illness narratives, assuring them that a doctor would be able to help them.

different kinds of paper amulets (*taviz*) on which Amma wrote verses from the Quran, the names of Allah and/or his agents (including angels), the name of the patient, and sometimes the name of the person or spirit who had cast the evil eye. Amma continually reminded me that the diagnostic calculations she carried out were simple and could be done by "even a parrot;" her spiritual wisdom and authority and her relationship with god were needed for any of her prescriptions to be effective.

Depending on the diagnosis, the amulets Amma wrote were worn on a string tied around the neck or waist of the patient, burned, buried, hung from a doorway (for missing children), or (for high fevers) smashed with a sandal. While this focus on the *written* word of god can be identified as an Islamic practice, the power of the word and the authority of a trained, charismatic religious specialist are assumed by Hindu patients to be potentially efficacious. Amma often gave patients a handful of different kinds of amulets that should be used at different times of day and in different ways (distinguished for the patients by the ways in which they were folded); and new patients of both Hindu and Muslim backgrounds were often confused about what should be done with which amulet. But it was rare that a patient questioned the efficacy of the prescriptions themselves or Amma's healing authority.[4]

Another often-prescribed prescriptive ritual in this healing system is one that literally lifts the evil eye off a patient (called *utara*, from the verb "to lift"). Amma prescribed that a clay pot be filled with ingredients attractive to the forces that had cast the evil eye: cooked rice, 100 grams of uncut, uncooked liver, an uneven number of white or yellow flowers, and an iron nail on which is impaled a lemon.

---

[4] I met a Muslim woman at a *dargah* that she visited daily at sundown to perform rituals that she hoped would alleviate her mental "distress." When she heard I was conducting research on Amma's healing practice, she said she had visited her, too, but that her prescriptions had not been effective. When I asked if she had returned to Amma to report the failure, she said no: "It isn't her problem [or that of the prescription per se]; it is only that one needs to visit different healers until one finds the right one [implying that the right relationship between healer and patient is needed for given prescriptions to be effective]."

The ingredient of liver sometimes caused difficulties for high-caste vegetarian Hindus. One Hindu female college student in her early twenties, who had come to Amma for help with what had been diagnosed by a psychiatrist as obsessive compulsive disorder, said that although meat had never entered her grandmother's home, her grandmother had sent a servant girl out to the market to buy the liver and permitted the ritual to be performed in her home – which everyone in the family concluded had made some positive difference in the young woman's condition.

Amma prescribed that the filled *utara* pot should be circled three times around the head of the patient, and three times up and down his/her body, thus attracting and absorbing the evil eye. Then, without turning around, someone in the family should carry the pot to a crossroads, where the evil eye is dissipated or carried away by another person. While the ingredients in this ritual may be specific to Amma's prescriptions, the "grammar" of the ritual of circling attractive objects (including cash) around an afflicted person, and absorbing and carrying away the evil eye, is well understood by her Hindu patients. This shared ritual grammar is one way in which religious healing is able to work across religious boundaries.

Patients themselves, Hindu, Christian, or Muslim, paid little attention to the specifics of Amma's mathematical calculations or what she was writing on the amulets. Rather, they focused on what Amma said – her narratives of successful healing, her recommendations for family and neighbor dynamics, and her pronouncement of a resolution to their illness. An important ingredient of the love and charisma that patients identified with Amma is demonstrated through how she took time to listen to their illness narratives. And an unnamed prescription was the way in which Amma reformulated and performed these illness narratives – she named the problem and its cause, and declared that the problem *would* be resolved through her ritual prescriptions: you *will* get pregnant, your runaway son *will* return home, your property disputes *will* be resolved, your baby *will* thrive. These narrative performances can be analytically understood to be religious acts that restructure relationships with spiritual or human forces – that is, *dharmic* acts that structure the world.

Amma's healing room was a ritual space in which differences of religious identities were minimized. As Amma often reminded me when she asked what I was writing in my little notebook and learned that I was identifying a patient by his/her religious identity: "There is no Muslim or Hindu here." What she meant was that *at this place*, in this context, specific religious identities were less important than the shared human condition of her patients, their shared acceptance of the possibilities of powerful spiritual forces impinging on human physical and social bodies, and their confidence in ritual resolutions to their problems.

Although, in the healing room, Amma performed and articulated a ritual grammar and narrative motifs that were shared among her Hindu, Muslim, and Christian patients, this does not mean that there were no differences. Outside of the healing room, these differences became important in contexts of marriage, death, daily rituals such as Hindu *puja* and Muslim *namaz* (daily prayers), or acceptance or not of image worship. Hindu, Muslim, and Christian distinct identities are also often performed in the ways in which a corpse is handled: burial for Christians and Muslims or cremation (most commonly) for Hindus (see Chapter 7).

Possession

Possession is an English term that covers a wide range of practices in Hindu traditions, many of which are, as mentioned above, associated with healing. Individuals may be possessed by a deity (usually a goddess) or a ghost, spirit of a deceased relative, or malevolent spirit (*bhut-pret*). Possession may be a desired state that indicates the presence of a deity, or a negative phenomenon for which the person afflicted seeks healing or relief. Finally, possession may be spontaneous or ritually and performatively elicited through drumming and singing. Some individuals who become possessed by deities or spirits of ancestors outside of ritual contexts may seek treatment by religious specialists that will "regularize" this kind of possession, so that it takes place only in ritual contexts in which the deity or spirit is called or invited and in which it can be more easily managed.

One working definition of possession is: the experience by an individual of an altered state of consciousness and behavior attributed to the presence in or on a human body by a spirit, deity, or other supernatural being. In Indian languages, the deity is variously said to "ride," "dance," or "play" on the human whom she/he is possessing. Further, there is a particular kind of deity who possesses, most often unmarried goddesses and *gramadevatas*, and rarely, if ever, *puranic* deities such as Rama, Shiva, or Lakshmi.

Ethnographic studies of possession have most often focused on the human actors of possession, analyzing the presence of the possessing entity within frameworks of human psychological and social concerns, of agency and power, and of subjectivity, memory, and the human body.[5] However, those who commonly experience and witness possession emphasize its supernatural origins. Possession is a gendered and caste-associated phenomenon; that is, many more women than men become possessed, and possession is more common among lower castes and classes than upper castes and classes; possession is very rare in Hindu communities in the United States in part because of the caste identities and class status of those who immigrate. Its demographics are one reason possession is often psychologized by scholars, who emphasize the low-status identity of possessed individuals (women and low-caste persons) and speculate that possession is one way through which disempowered individuals may express agency.

Possession in festival celebrations: In some festivals celebrated (primarily) by lower castes, deities are called by particular drumming rhythms and regularly make their presence known through possession of a human body. An example is the Chhattisgarhi festival of Gaura that celebrates the wedding of Shiva and Parvati

---

[5] For example, Kalpana Ram, in her 2013 book *Fertile Disorders: Spirit Possession and Its Provocation of the Modern*, asks: "What is a human subject under such conditions? What kind of human subjectivity must already be in place to allow possession to occur? … What is a 'human' body, if it can be claimed by a whole array of entities? What is agency if people can be 'claimed' in this manner? What is gender, if there can be periods when the woman is a woman no longer?" (238).

(here called Gaura and Gauri), sponsored by Gond communities in Chhattisgarh. Gonds are a group that has been labeled by the state as *adivasi* (tribal); however, in the central plains of Chhattisgarh, they have been integrated into the caste system as a distinct caste. Here, they worship Hindu deities and celebrate Hindu festivals while retaining many of their Gond-specific deities, rituals, and customs.

As the first rice paddy is harvested, women of Gond communities (particularly those who work in the fields of higher-caste land-owners) dance the *sua nac* (lit., parrot dance; dancers dance around small images of parrots) in the courtyards of landowners. The dance is believed to transform the rice paddy into the goddess of wealth Lakshmi herself. At this time of year, landowners are dependent on their laborers *and* their transformative ritual dance performance; they reciprocate by paying their laborers and dancers in both grain and cash. Gonds often say they perform the *sua nac* in order to col-lect monies to sponsor their own festival of Gaura, which coincides with the pan-Indian festival of Divali.

Gaura celebrants begin their preparations by digging up clay from riverbanks or water tanks, with which they make their own creative images of Gaura and Gauri, sometimes accompanied by images of other *puranic* deities.[6] The divine wedding couple and its entourage are placed in an open space in the middle of a rural or urban Gond neighborhood. Professional drummers begin beating their drums and women gather together to sing Gaura wedding songs, both of which are said to call the deities to be present at their own wedding and to manifest themselves through possession on the bodies of festival celebrants. Celebrants sing and drum throughout the night; then, in the morning, they all go in proces-sion, carrying the Gaura images on their heads, to a body of water

---

[6] In one village the line of deities included Durga and Shiva sitting on his white bull Nandi; in another urban neighborhood, Gaura and Gauri were accompanied by a flying Hanuman holding up the mountaintop he brought down from the Himalayas to Lanka to deliver healing herbs to the mortally wounded Lakshmana. More recently, many of these images are being made by professional potters, rather than by lay members of the Gond community.

Figure 8.5 Gond women carrying Gaura festival *murtis* of Shiva and Parvati (Gaura, Gauri); coconuts tied in their saris, Chhattisgarh.

where they immerse the clay images. This procession is another time during which possession is common.

I once asked some Gond women if they could sing for me Gaura songs outside the festival context, as the voice recordings I had made during the festival itself were almost unintelligible due to the loud drumming. They looked at one another, wondering if they really should do this, as the songs themselves could call the goddess even though there were no ritual boundaries to contain her. But, after some discussion, they finally concurred they could sing for my voice recorder. However, soon, a young woman began to sway back and forth, then stood up and "danced" (in possession) until the appropriate offerings were brought to send the goddess on her way. During the festival itself, if a drummer sees a celebrant begin to sway back and forth, he often approaches that person, loudly drumming in his/her ears, so as to accelerate or complete the possession that has showed signs of beginning with the swaying.

Possession is an auspicious sign of the success of the festival, but not all celebrants become possessed, nor do all want to. As one woman told me, the deities come to particular individuals who are open or susceptible to their presence, and she was one of these. She recalled first becoming possessed as a young post-pubescent girl; since then, she said, she becomes possessed every Gaura festival. She had some ambivalence toward being so chosen: "You never know what you're going to do," she explained; because of this unknown, her ambivalence is also shared by other women. This Gond woman said she used to sometimes stay home when the drumming began; but even then, the goddess would come on her in her own home, so she concluded it was better to go to the communal space where there would be other people to perform the appropriate rituals to the possessing goddess. Non-Gond, upper-caste women of this same village were surprised I would go to witness the Gaura celebrations known for possession; they asked if I wasn't afraid of becoming possessed. They had no skepticism of the possibilities of possession, only they did not themselves want to become inadvertently possessed, even from the sidelines.

Most people who experience possession say they have no memory of the actual possession, and they rely on other spectators to report to them what happened. To keep women modest in their possession movements during Gaura celebrations, they always have companions with them who adjust their saris, but who also loosen their hair to give the deity full access into the possessed women's bodies.[7] After several minutes of possession, other women, or the male Gond shaman (*baiga*) directing the Gaura celebration, bring a lit oil lamp and incense on a brass tray, which also holds a coconut and a few flowers, and wave this in front of the possessed person. This ritual acknowledges the presence of the deity, but also invites her to leave

---

[7] Hair is a particularly permeable boundary of the body, and the deity can enter more easily if it is loose. Hindu women also loosen their hair in times of mourning, but otherwise, because it leaves a woman vulnerable to entry by outside forces, traditionally Hindu women have bound their hair in buns (a custom that is shifting rapidly among some upper-class, educated, urban women).

Figure 8.6   Gaura possession.

the human body.[8] The possessed person often then collapses in exhaustion on the ground, as the drumming and singing continues, to invite the deity to come in/on other celebrants.

Possession as presence: While there may be some ambivalence among individual festival celebrants about becoming possessed (possession *itself* is crucial for the success of the festival, just not always "in my body"), in other contexts, individuals actively seek possession. Most of these persons are healers of some kind, whose religious authority is validated by and whose livelihood

[8] At one Gaura celebration, I witnessed a young man becoming possessed, which was not entirely unusual. However, when the appropriate offerings were brought in front of him to "dismiss" the deity, he continued his possession movements. The celebrants I was standing with began to complain that he was not really possessed (i.e., was "faking it"), because if he were, the goddess would leave when she was ritually acknowledged with offerings.

Figure 8.7 Gaura ritual to end possession.

depends on the active possession-presence of the deity. One such healer, Pujaramma,[9] is an elderly Mudaliar-caste widow living in Tirupati, whose experience typifies possession of this kind on several levels.

Petitioners come to Pujaramma with a wide range of problems typical of patients of ritual healers; they bring with them the essential ingredients that Pujaramma uses in her possession rituals: camphor, vermilion and turmeric powders, a coconut and a clay pot that itself becomes the goddess. She first draws a geometric design (Telugu, *muggu*) on the stone floor of her small home, on whose intersecting lines she places nuggets of camphor, which the patients are responsible to keep lit and replace throughout the possession. Sitting cross-legged in front of the *muggu*, Pujaramma closes her eyes, and begins

---

[9] Pujaramma literally means "mother of *puja*," and was the name she was called by most who knew her, but was not her given birth name.

to chant a litany of the names of various deities (not only the goddess, although she is the one who comes to her) and to sway back and forth. She circles her head around, making the hissing sound of a snake. Soon the goddess comes to her and speaks to the patient, asking some questions and making pronouncements about the cause of the patient's difficulty or commenting on his/her life (see Flueckiger 2013, Chapter 9).

While Pujaramma goes in and out of possession during particular rituals, she implies that she is always, at some level, possessed by, or in direct communication with, the goddess. (She calls the goddess simply "Amma," or mother; referring, in this context, to one of the *gramadevata* Seven Sisters). For example, she identifies her matted hair as the presence of the goddess. She tells the story of having tried to cut off her matted locks numerous times when she got lice and actively arguing with the goddess about this – the goddess telling her that she will cause them to grow again, and Pujaramma saying that she'll keep cutting them. Ultimately, though, she said the goddess won and Pujaramma has kept her matted hair. It embodies an intimacy with the goddess and also gives Pujaramma authority to call on her. To be able to bear this intimate, intense relationship with the goddess requires a personal strength; it is not easy to be in this relationship, which may cause some social ostracism (that is, while Pujaramma is ritually powerful, she remains socially marginal due both to her status as a widow and to her intense relationship with the goddess). Pujaramma explains: "You must be born for this in order to bear her." Pujaramma told many stories of the goddess coming to her, speaking to her, protecting and guiding her; and it was often unclear in these personal narratives whether the goddess came to her in a state of possession, dreams, visions, or simply through her continual presence.

Possession is commonly experienced in ritual healing contexts – both by patients and by healers – but it is also a significant means of intimate communication between human and divine or spirit worlds, through which the deity makes him/herself and his/her desires known.

Astrology

Most Hindus, whether or not they actively consult with an astrologer, live in a world impacted by what we might loosely call astrology: horoscopes, the influence of the planets, stars, the sun and the moon, eclipses, and certain auspicious and inauspicious times of day. While there is great variation in astrological practices across regions and castes – some being textually based and others transmitted only orally – these practices imply a relationship between human fortune/misfortune and the movement and placement of the planets. David Knipe observes:

> Astrology appealed to the simple, fundamental human desire to know how one corresponds to the great scheme of things, to the movements of planets and stars in which Time is reckoned and personal fortune, destiny and death are named and formed (1995, 221).

Many Hindus consult daily, or before they embark on an important activity, with a *panchangam* (lit., five limbs, referring to five attributes of the moon's movements) almanac-calendar that specifies the times of day that are inauspicious and during which one should not perform certain rituals, embark on a journey, or begin a new important task. These times of day are place-specific (dependent on local timings of sunrise, sunset, etc.), and calendars are printed or available on the internet for specific geographic locations, including major cities in the United States. For example, the online *panchangam* for Atlanta, Georgia, for July 14, 2014 identified the *durmuhurtam* (lit., bad time; inauspicious time) to be from 2:09 until 3:04 p.m. and again from 5:02 until 6:58 p.m.; *rahu kalam* (lit., time of the mythical planet Rahu, also inauspicious) was from 7:30 until 9:00 a.m. The *panchangam* also notes the phases of the moon (new, half, full), eclipses, the alignment of planets (if unusual), and many other astrological details. In a Hindu worldview, time has its own agency or power to affect human activity and is a good example of the context-specificity that characterizes Hindu practices.

211

Before marriages are arranged, the horoscopes of the bride and groom are exchanged to be sure they are compatible, and the season, lunar month (certain months are considered inauspicious for weddings), and time of day (however inconvenient in the modern world some of these early morning or late night timings may be) of the wedding itself are traditionally set by astrological criteria. Politicians often consult astrologers to find out the exact auspicious time they should take office, and travelers may rely on astrology to determine the best time to begin a trip or pilgrimage. During solar and lunar eclipses, many Hindus stay inside to protect themselves against their possible negative impact, and temples are often closed. During an eclipse, in front of many homes and businesses, pumpkins are smashed against the ground, then sprinkled with vermilion powder (sometimes interpreted as a vegetarian substitute for animal sacrifice) to divert the inauspicious gaze of the eclipse and its associated potentially negative forces.

And finally, many Hindu and non-Hindu Indians wear gemstone rings associated with particular planetary bodies to maximize their positive influences or protect themselves against their potential negative impact. The *navaratna* (nine gem) ring has all nine planetary *grahas* (lit., seizers)[10] represented; other rings are single gems representing a particularly feared or protective *graha* or one that is weak or strong in one's horoscope, such as sapphire for Shani (Saturn) and pearl for the moon. Some astrological forces are time-limited, such as Shani's cycle of seven-and-a-half years; others are permanent in one's astrological chart.

Navagrahas: Many *puranic* temples (and some *gramadevata* temples that are being transformed according to upper-caste and middle-class aesthetics and values) house a shrine to the *navagrahas* (lit., the nine seizers),[11] which include the sun, moon, five visible planets (Mars, Mercury, Jupiter, Venus, and Saturn), and the two shadow or

---

[10] The term *graha* is related to the same verbal root as the word for image of a deity, *vigraham* (see Chapter 3).

[11] *Grahas* may also refer to spirits, demons, and deities, but in the astrological text of the Jyotishastra, they are limited to planets.

mythical planets Rahu and Ketu.[12] In these shrines, the small anthro-pomorphic stone images of the nine *grahas* stand together in a square, facing away from each other. Worshippers at these shrines circumambulate the *navagrahas* nine times and leave at the feet of individual *grahas* particular offerings that are said to please them: for example, sesame oil for Shani, red or black lentils for Rahu and Ketu, respectively, and particular colors of cloth for each *graha*. The circumambulation and offerings to the *navagrahas* as a group are performed both for general protection and to deflect the potential negative forces of the *grahas* that may inflict illness or troubles on individuals in whose horoscopes they have certain positions.

The *grahas* most commonly identified for their potential negative impact on human lives are Rahu, Ketu, and Shani, whose influence is called *kalasarpa dosham* or *naga dosham* (for Rahu and Ketu, whose impact is considered together) and *shani dosham*; and their rituals are performed independently of the rest of the *navagrahas*. The diagnoses of *naga* and *shani doshams* seem to be growing in modern India and its diaspora, as Hindus are confronted with new "modern" problems, anxieties, and illnesses. Many articles in popular magazines and websites alert readers to the possibilities of these astrological *doshams* (blemishes, negative influences) and describe the appropriate rituals individuals can perform in order to alleviate them.

Naga Dosham: *Naga dosham* (lit., snake blemish) is one common diagnosis for infertility and late marriage, particularly in South India. This *dosham* is caused by the malefic influences of the "shadow" planets Rahu and Ketu, a condition that is believed to be growing in this Kaliyuga (the last of the four *yugas*, in which people do not and are ultimately unable to fully follow their appropriate *dharma*). *Naga dosham* is believed to be caused by the killing of a snake, in this or a previous lifetime, by oneself or one's ancestors, which then manifests as a defect in a person's horoscope. Those who suffer late marriage and infertility (and other problems) – primarily, but not only, women – go to an astrologer to have their

---

[12] The Indian medical system of Ayurveda identifies specific body parts that may be affected by particular *grahas*.

Figure 8.8 Woman making offerings to group of *naga* (snake) stones at Mundakkanni Amman Temple, Chennai. Courtesy of Amy L. Allocco.

charts read. If he diagnoses *naga dosham*, he prescribes particular rituals to be offered to the snake goddess – including offerings of milk and eggs to anthills where snakes often take up residence, offerings of stone snake images to be installed behind particular temples (most commonly those of *gramadevata* goddesses), or making pilgrimage to temples known for ameliorating or mitigating *naga dosham* (Allocco 2014).

Hindus living in the diaspora may also suffer from *naga dosham* (planets don't recognize geographic boundaries), which may be diagnosed in India on return trips, via call-in astrological consultations, or through information about various kinds of *dosham* in internet discussion forums. However, diagnoses are also made in the diasporic communities where the patients are living. For example, priests at the Hindu Temple of Atlanta serve as the diagnosticians of *naga dosham* for Hindus living in the region. Initially, the priests performed the appropriate remedial rituals at the homes of those so diagnosed (or on an individual, on-demand basis at the *navagraha* temple shrine), but as the numbers grew and the priests no longer had time to go to so many homes, the temple began sponsoring *naga dosham* rituals in the temple itself once every three months (and *navagraha puja* once a month). Symptoms of *naga dosham* among American Hindus are similar to those manifest in India, including infertility, perceived psychological problems, and general non-well-being. For example, the parents of an Indian-American female college student thought she had "no direction," and took her back to India to see if her "problem" could be *naga dosham*; it was so diagnosed and the family conducted a series of rituals at several South Indian temples known for *naga dosham* rituals. Another family brought their 12-year-old son to the Hindu Temple of Atlanta's *naga dosham* ritual not because the condition had been diagnosed, but "just in case," as a preventative measure.

Shani Dosham: The most fearful of all the *grahas* is Shani, the powerful and potentially destructive deity associated with the planet Saturn. On Saturdays (in Hindi, Shanivar), the day over which he "rules," one often finds small portable Shani shrines on Delhi sidewalks in commercial areas. His iron image, roughly hewn, is attached to a small bowl of black sesame or mustard oil, into which passersby toss coins, to prevent Shani's potential negative impact on their lives; the dark oil is believed to absorb and deflect his force. Increasingly, more permanent shrines and temples have been built to Shani, to which those afflicted with his *dosham* (diagnosed by astrologers or intuited by lay persons) and others who perform preventative rituals go on Saturdays (Bellamy 2014).

Many Hindus believe that the deleterious impact of Shani in one's life is unavoidable, but that the misfortunes his influence creates can be somewhat mitigated through performance of particular rituals, such as offering sesame oil and other dark-colored offerings and/or reciting Shani's *mantra*, or performing rituals that transfer the *dosham* of Shani to a variety of objects (such as an iron nail, an iron image of Shani, or a Shiva *linga*). The *dosham* may also be ritually transferred to certain classes of Brahmins who are understood to be capable of absorbing it without negative consequence to themselves (Knipe 1995, 229).

Figure 8.9   Shani shrine on New Delhi sidewalk (10–12 inches high).

Vastu: Another phenomenon loosely associated with astrology that may impact the fortunes of a temple, family, or business is *vastu* (lit., dwelling), the principle that both human and divine well-being is affected by the spaces in which they live and worship (similar to the East Asian concept of Feng Shui). Correct *vastu* is determined by the balance and flow of the five elements that make up the created world: earth, water, air, fire, and space. A great deal of emphasis in contemporary *vastu* practices is placed on the appropriate directionality of dwellings – such as the direction of their entrances, the placement of kitchens and bathrooms, the direction a bed or desk is facing, and so on – to enable the correct flow of these elements. There is no single authoritative *vastu* text; rather, this knowledge has been traditionally transmitted orally between generations of traditional architects (*sthapatis*). Today, many popular magazines and websites make this knowledge readily available to lay persons, who may experiment with *vastu* layouts in their homes or businesses without consulting a specialist.

The entrances, walls, and interiors of many family homes, businesses, and government offices are periodically adapted to *vastu* requirements, particularly when the inhabitants of a dwelling are experiencing difficulties. For example, a Mudaliar-caste family living in Chennai had experienced a long series of misfortunes: a maternal uncle had been in a bad car accident, family investments were not doing well and they had had to shift to a cheaper-rent apartment, the family was having difficulty arranging the daughter's wedding, and family illnesses seemed to be compounding. The family consulted with an astrologer and a *vastu* expert who both suggested that they change the direction of the entrance to their apartment and change the level of the floor in which a particular family member was convalescing, so that it was not a step down from the main level of the apartment, but was raised to be level to it. The family was assured by the experts they had consulted with that these changes would mitigate their difficulties.

Other examples of *vastu* include changes in public buildings. In the 1990s, when I was staying at the American Studies Research Center on the campus of Osmania University (Hyderabad) and the center was experiencing severe financial difficulties that threatened to close it, the library entrance was changed according to *vastu* prescriptions three times in one year. More recently, in March 2014, when the governments of the newly formed states of Telangana and Andhra Pradesh were dividing the Secretariat building to be used by both governments, an *Indian Express* newspaper article reported:

> While doing so, officials are also looking into the Vastu aspect. "The old gate of the Secretariat was closed for Vastu reasons. The CMO is located in the corner of C-Block only for Vastu reasons. We cannot reopen the old gate. The existing entry to the Secretariat will be used for Telangana chief minister. We will erect a new gate for Andhra chief minister, considering all Vastu rules," an officer explained. …

217

"We cannot hire Vastu experts for the purpose. The architects in the R&B department are well versed with basic Vastu principles. So, they apply the same rules while creating a new office for Andhra CM and finding new entry and exit points," an officer said (Balakrishna 2014).

*****

Like the practice of *vrats*, the healing systems described in this chapter interact with the concept of *karma* or fate (Hindi, *bhagya*) in complex ways. An individual may attribute the negative forces on his/her life – such as evil eye, possession by an unwanted spirit, or a "bad" horoscope – to his/her *karma* accrued in this or a previous lifetime, to fate (often said to be written on one's forehead at birth), or to living in this degenerate age of the Kaliyuga. These explanatory models for suffering take away some individual responsibility for its origins. At the same time, healing rituals give individuals some agency in the face of these seemingly over-determinate forces when they perform rituals that can cross-cut or minimize their effects; and ultimately, this successful healing itself may also be attributed to *karma*.

References

Allocco, Amy L. 2014. The Blemish of "Modern Times": Snakes, Planets, and the Kaliyugam. *Nidān: An International Journal for the Study of Hinduism* 26, 1: 1–21.

Balakrishna, V. V. 2014 (March 21). Two CMs to Function From the Same Secretariat. *Indian Express*. Accessed online July 10, 2014.

Bellamy, Carla. 2014. The Age of Śani in Modern Delhi. *Nidān: An International Journal for the Study of Hinduism* 26, 1: 22–41.

Flueckiger, Joyce Burkhalter. 2006. *In Amma's Healing Room: Gender and Vernacular Islam in South India*. Bloomington: Indiana University Press.

Flueckiger, Joyce Burkhalter. 2013. *When the World Becomes Female: Guises of a South Indian Goddess*. Bloomington: Indiana University Press.

Gold, Ann Grodzins. 2000 [1988]. *Fruitful Journeys: The Ways of Rajasthani Pilgrims*. Prospect Heights, IL: Waveland Press.

Knipe, David. 1995. Softening the Cruelty of God: Folklore, Ritual and the Planet Sani (Saturn) in Southeast India. In *Syllables of Sky: Studies in South Indian Civilization in Honour of Velcheru Narayana Rao*, ed. David Shulman, 206–248. New Delhi: Oxford University Press.

Ram, Kalpana. 2013. *Fertile Disorders: Spirit Possession and Its Provocation of the Modern*. Honolulu: University of Hawaii Press.

Sax, William. 2008. *God of Justice: Ritual Healing and Social Justice in the Central Himalaya*. New York: Oxford University Press.

Recommended Readings

Ferrari, Fabrizio M., ed. 2011. *Health and Religious Rituals in South Asia: Disease, Possession and Healing*. New York: Routledge.

Ferrari, Fabrizio M. 2014. *Religion, Devotion and Medicine in North India: The Healing Power of Sitala*. London: Bloomsbury Academic.

Nabokov, Isabelle. 2000. *Religion against the Self: An Ethnography of Tamil Rituals*. New York: Oxford University Press.

http://shanidham.in/ (website of Delhi Shani temple).

Afterword

One of the central themes of this book has been the ways in which everyday Hindu practices are shaped by and also shape their environments of space, time, caste, class, and gender. I have drawn most of my examples from ethnographic research, which places these traditions in particular communities and families. However, it is not easy to make generalizations about Hindu practices even in specific contexts – exceptions can always be found. Although not all Hindus practice certain rituals or tell and hear the same narratives – and the ways certain festivals are celebrated or the means through which Hindus may come to know a narrative may change – a recognizable "grammar" of Hindu practices and narratives is shared across different contexts of contemporary Hindu communities. For example, the *puranic* deities Shiva, Vishnu, and Devi – and their narratives and festivals – are recognizable as "Hindu," as are the means of worshipping god or the goddess through the presence of *murtis* and rituals of *puja*. And a Hindu temple is recognizable as such, even if,

Everyday Hinduism, First Edition. Joyce Burkhalter Flueckiger.
© 2015 Joyce Burkhalter Flueckiger. Published 2015 by John Wiley & Sons, Ltd.

in the United States, it may simply be a room in a community center, or its interior is carpeted (unlike India), or it houses a different (and wider) configuration of deities than do temples in India.

One important context affecting everyday Hindu practices in contemporary India is the emergence of a rapidly growing, increasingly literate, middle class, fostered, in part, by the initiation of economic liberalization and opening of Indian markets in 1991. This shifting context has shaped a growing consumer culture, an increasingly dominant middle-class aesthetics and morality, and a particular "sensibility" (way of being in the world) in contemporary India. Some traditions are being lost as families take up new practices shaped, in part, by images and advertisements popularized in newspapers, television serials, and Bollywood movies. These changes are *reshaping* how Hindus practice Hinduism.

Modern education and increasing literacy have led to many changes in gender roles, including new opportunities for women to work outside the home and enter new professions. However, modern education has also affected women in other ways; many women from lower castes and classes who used to feel comfortable in public spaces and traditionally *did* work outside the home (working in the fields or constructing and repairing roads, for example), have begun to curtail their movements as they become modern-educated and enter, or aspire to enter, the middle class. For example, several years ago, I joined a group of Gond-caste female friends as they went out to dance the *sua nac* harvest dance in the streets of Dhamtari (Chhattisgarh). We passed a home in whose doorway stood a young woman who had just graduated from high school. When the women called out to her to join them, she responded that she wasn't able to; her brothers had forbidden her to "go out like that" now that she was a "graduate."

Increasing literacy has also affected male gender roles. For example, as many traditional performers are becoming educated in government and private schools and leave their families' arts to pursue other occupations, some oral regional and caste performance traditions are being lost. Similarly, with modern education, some Brahmin males whose families used to perform rituals for other families have left these traditional ritual roles to enter other occupations; the same situation is occurring in families of other caste-specific ritual specialists.

An example of the impact of middle-class aesthetics and sensibilities can be found in the personnel, architectural, and ritual shifts in a Tirupati *gramadevata* Gangamma temple over the last 25 years. While *gramadevatas* have been traditionally served by lower-caste women and men, when Gangamma's largest Tirupati temple began to accrue financial resources and grew from a small shrine to a sizeable temple, the government Temple Endowments Department took control of the daily administration of the temple, evicting the female attendants of the goddess and replacing them with Brahmin male priests – and the temple introduced ritual practices of *puranic*-deity temples. The male priests recite Sanskrit *mantras* and perform *brahminic* rituals (such as the periodic fire ritual of *homam*) to a goddess to whom these rituals would have initially felt "foreign." As the temple has continued to expand in size, its architecture and aesthetics now resemble other middle-class, *puranic*-deity temples, with brightly colored sculptures of *puranic* deities atop the outer roof, lights strung above its temple gates and walls, and *bhajans* broadcast on festival days from large speakers. With the introduction of Navaratri and other "new" festivals and rituals at her temple, Gangamma is becoming increasingly identified as one of many manifestations of the *puranic* goddess Devi.

Another influential change impacting Hindu traditions is the continuing expansion of media such as television and the internet, which have already changed, and continue to change, the ways in which many Hindus come to know the stories of the deities and even how they worship them. As we saw in discussion of the television serialization of the Ramayana (first broadcast in 1987–1988), new media are having a significant impact on the ways Hindus know some narratives, and in the process some narratives and rituals (including some *vrat kathas*, or ritual vow stories, now available in print) are becoming more standardized. On the other hand, these same media may bring increased or new knowledge to Hindus of traditions practiced in different communities, regions, and countries other than their own. The annual Gangamma Jatara, the Jagannath procession in Puri (Odisha), and Gujarati Navaratri *garba* dancing, for example, are broadcast on television, bringing them increased visibility beyond the communities that traditionally participated in these festivals.

As Hindu traditions are entering wider transnational contexts, particularly for Hindu diasporic communities living as minorities, there is a growing awareness (and concern) among some Hindus about the ways in which Hinduism is represented and may be interpreted by "outsiders." The Hindu American Foundation (HAF) is one organization that monitors these representations and advocates for Hindus living in the United States and worldwide. The HAF has posted on its website various position statements on a wide range of issues including: international and US domestic policies that affect Hindus (including prayer and yoga in public schools); scholarly publications about Hinduism; and broader issues such as "Hinduism and the Ethical Treatment of Animals" (http://hafsite.org).

Initially, I thought I would write a separate chapter on Hindu traditions as they are practiced by diasporic (specifically, Hindu American) communities and families. However, I decided not to do so, since these traditions do not exist in isolation from those practiced in India, and the flow of ideas and persons across the oceans impacts traditions on both sides. For example, most Hindu temples in the United States bring sculptors from India to create the finishing touches on the temples and all *murtis* are brought from India; most diasporic Hindu families make frequent trips back to India to visit relatives or to perform specific rituals, and their family members visit them in the United States and other countries and often Skype-in across the oceans for weddings and other family rituals; and women who learn certain *bhajans* here in the United States from women of other communities and regions may share them with their relatives on visits back to India. But there are also significant differences, many of which have been identified in earlier chapters, between living as a Hindu in India and living as a member of a Hindu minority in diasporic contexts.

Most Hindus in the second and following generations in the diaspora, unlike most first-generation immigrants and their Indian relatives, have grown up speaking English (or another non-Indian language) as their first language; and the English that they learn is not Indian English. While many Hindus living in India speak English fluently, it takes on the color and nuances of the Indian languages that surround it – such that, for example, the word "idol" in Indian English means a *murti* in which the deity is present, without the negative connotations implied by the word in American English; and the English phrase "god is one" does not mean a singular theistic being, but rather encompasses myriads of deities who are manifestations of an unknown ultimate reality (*brahman*). As more Hindus grow up with American English (or other languages in non-English-speaking diasporic communities) as their first language, the ways they imagine and experience the worlds conveyed through that language and its dominant cultures will shift.

*****

We end this book on everyday Hinduism with the story of a Kummari-caste (potter) family in Hyderabad that is experiencing many of the generational and class changes in practices and worldview mentioned above. In the fall of 2014 I returned to Hyderabad to investigate the changes *gramadevata* shrines (and their goddesses) are undergoing as an expanding urban landscape has encompassed them. One such shrine to the goddess Pochamma is within walking distance of the family with whom I live in Hyderabad.

I stopped by the shrine one morning and met a man who was offering incense and flowers to the goddess; I learned that his family had established Pochamma at this site and was responsible for serving her. He gave me a phone number that I could call to arrange a meeting with his wife, who is the shrine's primary caretaker. A week later while visiting the shrine again, I made the phone call and the woman answering the phone (speaking Hindi) said she would come over to meet me right away. Arriving on a scooter, she turned out not to be the matriarch of the family, but her daughter – a 32-year-old woman wearing leggings, a long shirt, and long loose hair, speaking English fluently. She works at an IT call center for a Canadian phone company.

Subsequently, I met her Telugu- and Hindi-speaking mother at the shrine and visited the family home. The matriarch, in her mid-fifties, wore a large vermilion *bottu* (forehead marking) indicating a high level of religiosity and intimate relationship with the goddess.[1] She told me the story of the shrine. Pochamma had come to her in a dream shortly after she had gotten married and days after her husband had been in a traumatic accident, during which he had suffered a severe brain injury. The goddess told the matriarch that she should light a *dipam* (oil lamp) to her – that is, establish a shrine – on the banks of a particular water tank. She assured the then-young bride that if she did so, "everything will go well for you."

The young couple followed the directions of the goddess, setting up a tiny, roughly carved Pochamma *murti* under a tree on the banks of the water tank. Shortly thereafter, the husband was hired by the state insurance commission and later as an aide to a government minister, employment that, for 35 years, had adequately sustained their family of four children. All of the children have completed college degrees; two of the four have married outside of their caste; and the young IT professional remains unmarried, saying that she still has "too much to learn and too many places to travel" to be tied down by marriage. The patriarch of the family has recently retired and gone back to his "family business" of selling clay pots on the side of the main road around the corner from the shrine.

The water tank on whose bank the shrine was built was filled in with earth many years ago, and a college was built on the site – the once open, uninhabited space traditionally preferred by *gramadevatas* now transformed into an urban neighborhood. To protect Pochamma's shrine from further encroachment, about 15 years ago the family had built a small cement enclosure around her (on whose walls are painted images of the goddesses Kali and Durga); boundary walls enclose the shrine's small courtyard. The daughter first identified the goddess in the shrine's interior as Durga, as did another young male worshipper who said he stopped at the shrine

---

[1] A friend to whom I showed the matriarch's picture immediately asked, "Does she get possessed?" – something that the large *bottu* suggested to her.

every Tuesday and Friday – suggesting that the *gramadevata* herself may be undergoing transformation from village goddess to *puranic* deity, in part aided by the paintings on the outside of her shrine and her permanent cement enclosure. Over the course of a long conversation, the IT-employed daughter of the non-literate matriarch asserted that she had spent very little time at the shrine, since she was busy with her education and work, and really didn't "believe" (using the English word) in the goddess her mother served.

This Kummari family and their goddess Pochamma have experienced rather astounding transformations over the period of a single generation. The college-educated, English-speaking children have entered the middle class; their experience of caste identity, expectations of marriage and gender roles, and the possibilities for a life of travel and learning that the young IT professional imagines are dramatically different than those of their less-educated, non-English-speaking parents. The second generation of this Kummari family no longer lives intimately with Pochamma, and the goddess herself is gradually entering what we might identify as a middle-class worldview and ethos and a broader class- rather than strictly caste-based devotional community. She no longer lives under the open sky, but is now enclosed by a shrine whose paintings identify her with *puranic* goddesses. Changes in the urban physical and social landscape surrounding Pochamma may potentially change who she is and who serves her. Even in this brief example, we can see how the deities, devotees, and practices that make up everyday Hinduism are dynamic and shifting and how this religious tradition continues to shape, and be shaped by, the changing world around it.

Glossary

abhishekam: a ritual during which a *murti* is anointed with a series of liquid substances

adharma: that which is not in accordance with *dharma* and threatens the world order

alamkara: adornment

arati (harati):   lit camphor or oil lamp offering to image of deity (*murti*)

ashrama: stage of life; in the *brahminic* model for male stages of life, they are: *brahmacharya* (student stage), *grihastha* (householder stage), *vanaprastha* (forest stage, withdrawing or retiring from householder responsibilities), and *sannyasa* (stage of renunciation of the world)

asura: anti-god; demon

avatara: lit., descent; incarnation; specifically, the *dasa avataras* (10 incarnations) of Vishnu

Everyday Hinduism, First Edition. Joyce Burkhalter Flueckiger.
© 2015 Joyce Burkhalter Flueckiger. Published 2015 by John Wiley & Sons, Ltd.

Glossary

bhagvan:	god
bhagya:	fate
bhajan:	devotional song or chant
bhakti:	devotion
brahman:	ultimate reality without form or qualities
dargah:	grave-shrine of Muslim saint
darshan:	sight; auspicious sight of a deity
dharma:	correct action, ethics; what keeps order in the world
dosham:	blemish, negative influence; specifically, the result of the negative force of astrological configurations
garbagriha:	lit. womb-room; innermost sanctum of temple, where primary *murti* of the god or goddess resides
gopuram:	South Indian temple gate-tower
graha:	lit., seizer; certain planets such as Saturn (Shani); eclipse
gramadevata:	village god or goddess
jati:	lit., species, birth; caste identification according to birth
karma:	action; fruits of action; fate
kirtan:	devotional song or chant
kolam:	South Indian term for rice-flour design drawn outside homes or in front of ritual spaces (called *rangoli* in North India)
kulam:	caste; lineage
kumkum:	vermilion powder
linga:	aniconic (phallic) stone form of Shiva
mandali:	singing group
mandir:	temple
moksha:	release from the cycle of transmigration (*samsara*)
muggu:	(Telugu) geometric design drawn with rice flour at entrances of South Indian homes or at a site of ritual
mula murti:	primary, permanent image in a temple
murti:	physical image of a deity
namaste:	verbal or physical gesture of greeting
navagrahas:	nine planets
nirguna:	without qualities

228

panchangam:	astrological calendar/almanac, synced with Gregorian calendar
pranapratishta:	ritual establishment of the "life breath" in a physical image of a deity
prasad:	food, flowers, or other offerings to a deity in *puja* and returned to worshippers as blessed by the deity
puja:	worship of a deity (image of a deity) through offerings such as fruits, flowers, etc
purana:	lit., old story; classification of narrative texts that are the basis of much Hindu mythology; 18 Sanskrit *puranas* and numerous regional-language *puranas*
rangoli:	North Indian term for rice-flour design drawn outside homes or in front of ritual spaces (called *kolam* in South India)
saguna:	lit., with qualities; deity with physical and narrative qualities
samaj:	society; also used to refer to caste (*jati*)
samsara:	cycle of birth and rebirth based on *karma* (actions and their consequences)
samskara:	life-cycle ritual
shastra:	authoritative textual traditions; teaching
sthala puranas:	"old" stories about a specific place (temple and/or pilgrimage site)
suprabhatam:	morning song, sung to wake up deity in *puranic* temple
tirtha:	crossing-place or ford at a riverbank; pilgrimage site on bank of river
Trimurti:	lit. three forms; traditionally identifying Brahma, Vishnu, and Shiva as creator, sustainer, and destroyer/transformer of the universe, respectively
vahana:	animal mount with which a deity is associated; for example, Shiva and his *vahana* Nandi (a bull), Ganesha and his *vahana* the mouse, and Durga and her *vahana* the tiger or lion
varna:	lit., color; caste-level

vigraham: physical image of a deity

vrat: vow; vow ritual

yugas: the four eons of the universe that devolve in observance of *dharma* until the end of the last *yuga* (Kaliyuga), when the universe is dissolved and recreated and begins again with the first *yuga*; the four are: Satyayuga (golden age), Tretayuga, Dwaparayuga, Kaliyuga

Index

Everyday Hinduism, First Edition. Joyce Burkhalter Flueckiger.
© 2015 Joyce Burkhalter Flueckiger. Published 2015 by John Wiley & Sons, Ltd.

Index

Index

Index

Index

Index

Index

Index